MW00737022

Education Policy

Series Editors

Lance Fusarelli, North Carolina State University
Frederick M. Hess, American Enterprise Institute
Martin West, Harvard University

This series addresses a variety of topics in the area of education policy. Volumes are solicited primarily from social scientists with expertise on education, in addition to policymakers or practitioners with hands-on experience in the field. Topics of particular focus include state and national policy, teacher recruitment, retention, and compensation, urban school reform, test-based accountability, choice-based reform, school finance, higher education costs and access, the quality instruction in higher education, leadership and administration in K-12 and higher education, teacher colleges, the role of the courts in education policymaking, and the relationship between education research and practice. The series serves as a venue for presenting stimulating new research findings, serious contributions to ongoing policy debates, and accessible volumes that illuminate important questions or synthesize existing research.

Series Editors

LANCE FUSARELLI is a Professor and Director of Graduate Programs in the Department of Leadership, Policy and Adult and Higher Education at North Carolina State University. He is co-author of *Better Policies, Better Schools* and co-editor of the *Handbook of Education Politics and Policy*.

FREDERICK M. HESS is Resident Scholar and Director of Education Policy Studies at the American Enterprise Institute. An author, teacher, and political scientist, his books include *The Same Thing Over and Over: How School Reformers Get Stuck in Yesterday's Ideas* and *Common Sense School Reform*.

MARTIN WEST is an Assistant Professor of Education in the Graduate School of Education at Harvard University. He is an Executive Editor of *Education Next* and Deputy Director of Harvard's Program on Education Policy and Governance.

Ohio's Education Reform Challenges: Lessons from the Frontlines
Chester E. Finn, Jr., Terry Ryan, and Michael B. Lafferty

Accountability in American Higher Education
Edited by Kevin Carey and Mark Schneider

Freedom and School Choice in American Education
Edited by Greg Forster and C. Bradley Thompson

Gentrification and Schools: The Process of Integration When Whites Reverse Flight
Jennifer Burns Stillman

Intersections of Children's Health, Education, and Welfare
Bruce S. Cooper and Janet D. Mulvey

President Obama and Education Reform: The Personal and the Political
    Robert Maranto and Michael Q. McShane

Educational Policy in an International Context: Political Culture and its Effects
    Edited by Karen Seashore Louis and Boudewijn van Velzen

The Politics of Parent Choice in Public Education: The Choice Movement in North Carolina and the United States
    Wayne D. Lewis

The School Choice Journey: School Vouchers and the Empowerment of Urban Families
    Thomas Stewart and Patrick J. Wolf

The School Choice Journey

School Vouchers and the Empowerment of Urban Families

Thomas Stewart and Patrick J. Wolf

Foreword by
Joe Lieberman

THE SCHOOL CHOICE JOURNEY
Copyright © Thomas Stewart and Patrick J. Wolf, 2014.

All rights reserved.

First published in 2014 by
PALGRAVE MACMILLAN®
in the United States—a division of St. Martin's Press LLC,
175 Fifth Avenue, New York, NY 10010.

Where this book is distributed in the UK, Europe and the rest of the world,
this is by Palgrave Macmillan, a division of Macmillan Publishers Limited,
registered in England, company number 785998, of Houndmills,
Basingstoke, Hampshire RG21 6XS.

Palgrave Macmillan is the global academic imprint of the above companies
and has companies and representatives throughout the world.

Palgrave® and Macmillan® are registered trademarks in the United States,
the United Kingdom, Europe and other countries.

ISBN: 978–1–137–44265–9

Library of Congress Cataloging-in-Publication Data

Stewart, Thomas (College president)
    The school choice journey : school vouchers and the empowerment
of urban families / by Thomas Stewart and Patrick J. Wolf.
        pages cm — (Education policy)
    Includes bibliographical references and index.
    ISBN 978–1–137–44265–9 (hardcover : alk. paper)
        1. Educational vouchers—United States. 2. School choice—
United States. 3. Education, Urban—United States. 4. Educational
change—United States. 5. DC Opportunity Scholarship Program—
Evaluation. 6. Scholarships—Washington (D.C.) 7. Educational
vouchers—Washington (D.C.) 8. School choice—Washington (D.C.)
9. Education, Urban—Washington (D.C.) I. Wolf, Patrick J. II. Title.

LB2828.8.S84 2014
379.111—dc23   2014006013

A catalogue record of the book is available from the British Library.

Design by Newgen Knowledge Works (P) Ltd., Chennai, India.

First edition: August 2014

10 9 8 7 6 5 4 3 2 1

Thomas Stewart dedicates this book to his wife, Nicole Stewart, for her patience and steadfastness particularly when this project required his undivided attention, and to his son, Nicolas, and daughter, Tommie, for their playful inspiration.

Patrick J. Wolf dedicates this book to his wife, Kathleen Wolf, his soul mate in the journey of life.

Contents

Figures and Tables

Figures

Tables

Foreword to
The School Choice Journey

By the Honorable Joseph Lieberman
February 10, 2014

School choice is good for America's school children. In my 24 years of serving in the US Senate, I enthusiastically supported parental school choice initiatives like the District of Columbia Opportunity Scholarship Program (OSP), which this book is about, because parents know best the educational needs of their children, and they should be empowered to decide where their children attend school.

Those who can afford to send their children to private schools, when they are dissatisfied with the public schools their children would otherwise go to, do so for obvious reasons: to provide their children with the best education available. They do so as good parents who care about their children's future. Why should we deny that opportunity to lower-income parents who also want the best future for their children?

In America it should not be a privilege for any of our children to get a first-rate education. In my opinion it is a right, although often a right that is not honored. Without equal education for all, there cannot be equality for all, the kind of equality that our founding documents promise.

The DC Opportunity Scholarship Program has become the proverbial mouse that roared. It is a $20-million-a-year pilot program in the multitrillion dollar federal budget. It arouses large interest, in part because it raises big hopes in the hearts and minds of the parents and the children who are involved in it and stirs strong opposition from politicians and interest groups that oppose school choice, especially if the options available to low-income families include private and faith-based schools.

The DC Opportunity Scholarship Program was authorized by the District of Columbia School Choice Incentive Act of 2003, which I cosponsored. The act provided new funding, in equal parts, for DC traditional public schools, public charter schools, and private school vouchers that are officially called Opportunity Scholarships. The "findings" section of the law states that "available educational alternatives to the public schools are insufficient, and more educational options are needed. In particular, funds are needed to assist low-income parents to exercise choice among enhanced public opportunities and private education environments."

The purpose of the OSP program is to provide low-income parents residing in the district, particularly parents of students who attend public elementary or secondary schools identified for improvement, corrective action, or restructuring, with expanded opportunities for enrolling their children in private schools if the parents themselves decide that such schools are better for their children. The act directed the then secretary of Education, Rod Paige, to award a grant for up to five years to an eligible entity to operate the program. The Washington Scholarship Fund (WSF) was chosen as the first grantee of the program. Under the OSP, annual scholarships were awarded to children from low-income families to attend private schools in the district. Initially, the maximum scholarship amount was $7,500 but the reauthorization language that I authored in 2011 increased that ceiling to $8,000 for elementary school students and $12,000 for high school students, both more realistic numbers.

This book, by Drs. Thomas Stewart and Patrick J. Wolf, is not just about the implementation of an education policy. It is about a journey, as the authors aptly say, toward a destination of student success and parental empowerment. When the OSP was initially enacted in 2004, we legislative supporters thought that we had created a new and better path for DC parents to exercise greater school choice, one that would not be controversial because for every dollar that went to a voucher another dollar went to the public schools and a third dollar to public charter schools. Nevertheless, the program provoked enormous controversy and opposition, and the parents themselves had to battle to save the OSP.

As Chapter 6 of the book discusses in great detail, the biggest difficulties began when the Omnibus Appropriations Act of 2009, which became Public Law 111–8, was passed on March 11, 2009. It included funds for the OSP program for the 2009–2010 school year but also imposed new requirements on the OSP program and included a harsh proviso that no funds after that school year would be available for the program unless a reauthorization bill was passed by Congress and the District of Columbia City Council approved the reauthorization. The Department of Education then decided that no new applicants could be accepted for the 2009–2010 school year, and on April 9, education secretary Arne Duncan sent letters to the 630 students who had applied for scholarships for September of 2009, including the 216 children who had already been informed that they would receive a scholarship, that the program was going to end. On May 6, 2009, President Obama announced that he would support a proposal to allow current students to remain in the program through graduation, but would not allow any new students to enter the OSP.

Although I was relieved that the administration decided not to force students out of their chosen private schools, I still was deeply disappointed that the program had been capped so that it would wither on the vine. If the OSP was not working, it should have been terminated for all children. If it was working well enough for the children who were continuing in the program until they graduated from high school, then it should also be continued for new generations of students. The question of whether or not any particular school program improves the educational performance of the students involved is not a Democratic or Republican question, or even the question of a political Independent like me. Nor is it a liberal or conservative question. It is a practical question based on factual information including professional evaluations, test scores, and customer satisfaction.

To me it is clear, based on the facts, that the OSP works. It certainly works well enough to keep it going for new students. I based that conclusion on the official reports of the independent evaluator of the program, Dr. Patrick J. Wolf, who is a coauthor of this book. His annual reports showed that students improved their reading achievement by statistically significant amounts during many years of the pilot program, and that the OSP boosted the high school graduation rate of students by 21 percentage points, from 70 percent to 91 percent. Dr. Wolf's findings were based on rigorous statistical methods and convinced me that the OSP was really making a difference for the students involved.

This book is essentially a follow-up study, by Stewart and Wolf, using qualitative research methods that bring to life the actual experiences of OSP families. It shows how the DC Opportunity Scholarship Program benefited parents as well as their children. Most of the parents who enrolled their children in the OSP had little or no experience choosing schools. They brought a passive client mentality to the situation. School choice, however, demands that parents be more than just submissive recipients of a school assignment; it requires that they more actively direct the educational experience of their child. They need to gather information about multiple schooling options, conduct school visits, decide which school is best for their child, complete forms, interact with the school staff, and actively participate in making their school choice a success for their children. As the authors observed from focus groups and interviews, many OSP parents changed from passive clients to empowered school consumers.

Equally impressive was how the OSP parents responded to the threat to end the program in 2009. I chaired a lot of committee hearings during my 24 years in the Senate but few were as charged as the two Senate hearings I chaired in 2009 and 2010 on the reauthorization of the OSP program. The hearing room was packed with parents and students clamoring for a continuation of the program that had brought them so much hope and opportunity. We heard passionate testimony from OSP parents such as Latasha Bennett, whose son was thriving in the second grade of private school in the OSP but whose younger daughter was one of the children whose Opportunity Scholarship awards were revoked after the program was capped. And I will always remember Ronald Holassie, a high school junior in the OSP, who skillfully argued one of my fellow senators who opposed the program into silence. That is a rare occurrence.

The parents and students who filled the room cheered the many statements of support for the OSP. Six leaders of interest groups that opposed the OSP were invited to testify at the 2009 hearing. They all declined but their silence spoke loudly.

This story of the school choice journey of the OSP families and the legislators who supported them disproves several myths. First, it is both false and demeaning to say that low-income parents are not capable of selecting quality schools for their children.

Second, politicians cannot and should not take urban parents for granted. The predominately low-income minority parents in DC became a political force to be reckoned with when the Congress and the Obama Administration acted to wind up this program. It was the grit and determination of OSP parents and their supporters that ultimately won the day and created the political conditions whereby the program could be continued and improved.

Finally, it is not true that politicians cannot work in a bipartisan manner to get things done. I began my political career as a Democrat and concluded it as a political Independent. To reauthorize the OSP, I worked very closely with Senator Susan Collins (R, ME) and Senator Diane Feinstein (D, CA). But it was speaker John Boehner (R, OH) who was truly the indispensable champion of the cause of OSP reauthorization in Congress. Ultimately, President Obama reversed his initial course and accepted a budget agreement that included the reauthorization of the OSP. Our job was also made easier because of a diverse group of local leaders representing the traditional public and public charter schools who supported our cause, including Anthony Williams, former mayor of the District of Columbia; Kevin Chavous, chairman of the City Council Education Committee and board member of the Black Alliance for Educational Options; Joe Roberts and Kaleem Caire from Fight for Children; Peggy

Copper Cafritz, president of District of Columbia Board of Education; Virginia Walden-Ford, founder of DC Parents for School Choice; and many others. These local leaders united to form a "three sector strategy" that focused on ensuring that the needs of children of low-income parents in traditional public and public charter schools, as well as private schools, were adequately addressed. The goal was not an easy one, as is well described in this book, but political agreements are possible when children's futures are at stake.

More than anything else, the story of the OSP is one that depicts what is possible when parents are allowed to choose schools and when policy makers are persuaded, sometimes reluctantly, to support their right to do so. It is a story about the empowerment of urban families and a better education for their children. It is a choice that must be preserved and a journey that must be continued.

Acknowledgments

Many people contributed to the success of this ten-year project. We owe a great debt to Bruno Manno, previously at the Annie E. Casey Foundation and now at the Walton Family Foundation, for his unflagging support of this work. We are grateful for a series of grants from the Annie E. Casey Foundation that supported our qualitative data collection efforts, though we acknowledge that the findings and opinions presented here are those of the authors alone and do not necessarily reflect any official position of the foundation.

Stephen Q. Cornman made outstanding contributions to the work in the early stages. We are grateful for the assistance with qualitative data collection provided by Darnita Akers, David Banks, Jessica Boccardo, Donald Brown, Jonathan Butcher, Ashley Campbell, Elizabeth Cohen, Sara Garcia, Rachel Greszler, V. E. Grobes, Daniel Hoople, Colleen Morrison, Margaret Price, Kenann McKenzie-Thompson, Gerard Robinson, Yoslyn Rodriguez, and Benjamin Traster.

Paul T. Hill provided extensive and constructive comments on an earlier draft of the manuscript. We also received helpful suggestions at various points in the project from John Bishop, Anna Egalite, Howard Fuller, Laura Hamilton, Jeffrey Henig, Frederick Hess, Jelani Mandara, Jonathan Mills, Macke Raymond, Mark Schneider, Paul Teske, and Robert Yin.

We received excellent support from the entire team at Palgrave Macmillan, including Sarah Nathan, Mara Berkoff, Deepa John and Kristy Lilas. We are grateful to Prairey Walkling for her outstanding help in finalizing the manuscript and to Albert Cheng for putting together some excellent graphics.

Finally, we owe a great debt to the more than 100 parents and students of the Opportunity Scholarship Program who openly shared the details of their school choice journey with us.

Introduction

The School Choice Journey: School Vouchers and the Empowerment of Urban Families

History was made on January 29, 2004, when President George W. Bush signed the *District of Columbia School Choice Incentive Act of 2003.*[1] The law established the first federally funded private school choice program in the United States. A total of 2,454 students in over 1,500 families received what came to be called Opportunity Scholarships through the program in 2004 and 2005, which allowed them to enroll in the participating private school of their choosing. Through a series of focus groups, in-depth interviews, and real-time opinion polling, we followed 110 of the families in the program, documenting their joys, struggles, setbacks, and triumphs as participants in a pioneering parental school choice program. This is their story.

We quickly learned that parental school choice is not so much a destination; it is a journey. Like any journey, school choice requires careful preparation and sometimes assistance. That is the essence of what we learned after five years of shadowing families participating in the District of Columbia's Opportunity Scholarship Program (OSP). The OSP is best conceptualized as a vessel that carried over a thousand low-income District of Columbia families on their school choice journey starting in the spring of 2004.

The journey entails both adventures and challenges and can conclude at a variety of endpoints. Sometimes along the voyage, the passengers even have to help steer the ship. Most of those travelers feel that their lives have been enriched by the journey, regardless of whether or not they reached their desired destination.

The General Motivation for the Study

Why should we be concerned about the school choice experiences of a relatively small number of low-income families in Washington, DC? What can we learn from their participation in a politically controversial government pilot program that can help us address larger issues associated with poverty and education reform generally, and with student achievement and attainment specifically? On the surface, families participating in the OSP might appear to have relatively little in common with other families across the United States and around the world. Upon closer examination, however, it becomes evident that the issues faced by OSP families reflect educational and social challenges confronting low-income families worldwide, which in turn represent a microcosm of the challenges that the United States and other countries must overcome in order to participate effectively in the twenty-first-century global economy. The journey of this very particular group of people in one of the world's least typical cities still yields lessons that are, in many respects, universal.

Globalization has brought two important realities home to families and educators in the United States. First, the economy of the twenty-first century is information-based, with brains and service valued in place of the brawn and geographic location so important to the economy of the twentieth century. The change to an information-based economy means that effective K–12 education is both more important and also very difficult, with a greater reliance on instruction in the thinking and problem-solving skills required of the modern-day worker.[2]

Second, globalization has metaphorically made the world "flat."[3] The economic activity of today faces few geographic barriers and experiences low transaction costs. As a result, capital and industry can "vote with its feet," moving to places around the world that possess a desirable mix of stable institutions, low costs of doing business, and, most importantly, a well-educated workforce. The US educational system needs to get moving before the jobs of the twenty-first century do.

The US educational system, however, appears to be weak overall and riddled with inequalities in spite of decades of reform focused on racial integration and adding more money and accountability to the existing public school system.[4] Recent statistics on student outcomes from both elementary and secondary education in the United States are alarming. The United States spends either the most or the second-most per student in the world, depending upon the measure used. In spite of this largesse, the performance of 15-year-old students in science ranks 17th among 22 member countries of the Organization for Economic Cooperation and Development (OECD) whose students took the Program for International

Student Assessment (PISA) exams in 2006.[5] American students do even worse, compared to their international peers, in math literacy, scoring just 24th out of 28 OECD countries on that essential subject test.[6] Thirty-three percent of US students fail to demonstrate basic reading literacy by the end of fourth grade.[7] Only about 70 percent of students obtain a high school diploma four years after starting ninth grade.[8]

At the same time, developments in the global economy have placed new pressures specifically on low-income families. Such pressures that did not exist in more traditional societies now have significant implications for the academic performance of the children of these families. As a report by the Project on Global Working Families points out: "There has been a dramatic transformation in the workforce worldwide, with hundreds of millions of people leaving the home or farm to join the formal labor force;...more than 930 million children under fifteen are being raised in households in which all of the adults work."[9] While there is growing evidence that parental involvement in children's education has beneficial impacts on academic performance,[10] the economic pressures on families make it increasingly difficult for parents, especially in low-income households, to participate effectively in their children's schooling and to provide a home environment that is conducive to maximizing the academic attainment that is so important in the contemporary economy. Under these dire circumstances many families seem to be left waiting for Superman.

Waiting for Superman *Arrives and* Won't Back Down

Filmmaker Davis Guggenheim effectively captures the educational pressures and challenges facing US families in his Oscar-nominated 2010 documentary *Waiting for Superman*. The film draws its title from a story told by education reformer Geoffrey Canada about his childhood dream that a superhero would mysteriously appear and save his low-income urban family from the many trials that they faced. Access to quality schools is the metaphorical Superman in the film, as Guggenheim poignantly documents the efforts of a handful of disadvantaged families to "rescue" their children from a bleak educational future through exercising parental school choice.

What, exactly, is parental school choice? *Parental school choice* is a term commonly used to describe the opportunity for families to pursue educational options that they judge to be in the best interests of their children. Parental school choice, specifically, begins when families have access to multiple school options.[11]

Parental school choice has always existed for families who have the financial wherewithal to move to a neighborhood with good schools or self-finance private schooling. The majority of American families who lack such resources face a much different reality. In far too many situations across this country, children attend schools that lack the quality and fit that any reasonable parent would want for their children. With few exceptions, most traditional urban school systems with sizable percentages of low-income families have been unable to provide more than a small minority of these families with quality school options.

Each year, for the past two decades, more states have considered targeted programs to improve educational options and outcomes for disadvantaged students. These approaches include charter schools, which are public schools outside of the traditional school system that operate under an explicit charter that grants them much freedom of operation in exchange for a commitment to deliver high levels of student performance. The overwhelming majority of public charter schools are located in the urban core of major US cities. Most of them have fewer openings in the school than they have students who want to attend. As a result, most applicants to charter schools face a random lottery to determine if they can enroll in the school. The families that Guggenheim follows in *Waiting for Superman* all seek to enroll their children in high-performing public charter schools.

Another instrument used by an increasing number of states and localities to promote greater access to quality schools for disadvantaged students is school vouchers. School vouchers are "an arrangement whereby public funds are made available to qualified parents to cover some or all of the expenses associated with enrolling their child in a participating private school of their choosing."[12] Voucher programs are often distinguished by whether they are financed directly by government funds or indirectly through tax credit "scholarships." School vouchers are more politically controversial than public charter schools because they result in public funds flowing to private schools, albeit through the actions of parents, and therefore more directly challenge the public school system's monopoly over K–12 education.[13] In 2002 the US Supreme Court ruled that school vouchers, as typically designed, do not represent an establishment of religion and thus are constitutional.[14]

Recently, school vouchers have exploded onto the policy scene. The decade of the 1990s began with the establishment of the first school voucher program, a pilot program in Milwaukee limited to low-income students. That decade closed with just three more programs added: direct voucher initiatives in Cleveland and the state of Florida as well as the first ever tax-credit scholarship program in Arizona. The Cleveland and

Arizona programs, like the Milwaukee voucher initiative, were targeted at low-income students, while the Florida program was limited to students with disabilities. From 2000 through 2010, seven more government-financed voucher programs were established in Georgia, New Orleans, Ohio (two statewide programs), Oklahoma, Utah, and Washington, DC. During that decade, eight additional tax-credit-financed scholarship programs were launched in Arizona (two new ones), Florida, Georgia, Indiana, Iowa, Pennsylvania, and Rhode Island. By the fall of 2010, a total of 19 school voucher programs throughout the United States enrolled almost 200,000 students—each with a specific disadvantage that qualified them for the program.

Supporters of education reform dubbed 2011 "The Year of School Choice."[15] In a single legislative season, 11 states and the federal government enacted laws that either established new school voucher programs or dramatically expanded existing programs. New voucher programs were approved for Arizona, Colorado, Indiana (two new programs), North Carolina, Ohio, Oklahoma, and Wisconsin. Existing programs were expanded in Florida, Georgia, Indiana, Iowa, Ohio, Utah, Wisconsin, and Washington, DC. Momentum continued through 2012 and 2013, as Alabama, Mississippi, New Hampshire, Ohio, Virginia, and Wisconsin enacted new private school choice programs. From the East Coast to the mountainous West, from the Midwest to the southern tip of the United States, hundreds of thousands of children have enrolled in private school choice programs over the last half decade. What does school choice look like for these children and their families? How might vouchers change education in the United States? How might the school choice journey alter the course for parents and students who are on it?

The movie *Won't Back Down* is a story of empowerment. The main characters, a parent named Jamie Fitzpatrick (played by Maggie Gyllenhaal) and a teacher named Nona Alberts (played by Viola Davis), are frustrated with the dysfunction in an urban public school and feel powerless to stop it. They discover a policy mechanism, now commonly known as a "parent trigger," to take over the school from the district and run it according to their vision for education. Parent triggers are another form of parental school choice. Instead of parents seeking out a better quality school for their child as an alternative to their neighborhood public school, they seek to transform their neighborhood school into a better option for their child. The political challenges involved in pulling this parent trigger appear to be insurmountable in the film, a dramatic portrayal that is proving to be quite realistic.[16] However, after the parents and teachers in the film become politically active, they surprise everyone by succeeding in convincing the local school board to allow them to take over and run the school.

Is the story of political empowerment through school choice and reform depicted in *Won't Back Down* a fairy tale? Could expanded parental school choice through a school voucher program like the OSP produce the kind of citizenship activism portrayed in that movie? Could the school choice journey bring parents all the way from passive clients of government services to informed consumers of educational options and to empowered citizens willing and able to shape public policy in their own interests? The movie *Won't Back Down* suggests that can happen in Hollywood. Can it happen in Washington, DC?

The Unique Research Opportunity

The District of Columbia is an excellent city to examine these school choice questions for two very important reasons. First, it is the home of the OSP—an initiative to provide low-income students with "expanded opportunities to attend higher performing schools in the District of Columbia."[17] The second good reason to study school choice in Washington, DC is completely fortuitous. If one had to choose a city with a unique contrast of poverty and wealth in the United States, of the powerful and the dispossessed, the District of Columbia would almost certainly be at the top of the list. According to 2008 US Census Bureau estimates, 591,833 individuals reside in the nation's capital. Fifty-three percent of the district's population is African American, 33 percent is white, 9 percent is Hispanic, and 3 percent is Asian. In 2008, the population included an estimated 75,755 children between the ages of 5 and 18.[18] That same year, 60,638 children enrolled in 223 District of Columbia traditional public and public charter schools in kindergarten through twelfth grade. Another estimated 20,000 students attended the city's 108 private schools, many of which enroll students from outside of the city limits.

The District of Columbia is a city with a rich cultural heritage defined equally by its history of power and influence in the nation and the world as well as the significant disparities in education, income, quality of life, and political influence of its white, black, and rapidly emerging immigrant residents. The city is divided into eight wards, with Ward 3 composed of one of the most affluent and well-educated populations in the world. Ward 8, on the other hand, is composed of one of the poorest and most undereducated urban populations in the country. Based on census data from 2000, Ward 3 had a population of 73,718 compared to 70,914 residents in Ward 8. In Ward 3 only 8 percent of children lived in poverty while 47 percent of children in Ward 8 were poor. The median household income in Ward 3 was $71,875 compared to $25,017 in Ward 8, with 79 percent of Ward 3 residents possessing at least a bachelor's degree compared to 8 percent of residents in Ward 8.[19] Forty-nine percent of Ward 3 residences were owned by their occupants compared to just 21 percent of Ward 8 households. In the District of Columbia as a whole, less than one-third of white school children attend public schools compared to 90 percent of black and Hispanic children.[20] In 2000, 84 percent of Ward 3 residents were white and 6 percent were black, while 5 percent of Ward 8 residents were white and 92 percent of them were black.

At the time of the research that informs *The School Choice Journey*, 26 of the 108 private schools in the District of Columbia were members of the Association of Independent Schools of Greater Washington (AISGW), which has an overall membership of 84 schools from the District of Columbia, Northern Virginia, and Southern Maryland. In 2008–9, these 26 schools enrolled 11,304 students from across the greater Washington, DC metropolitan area. These schools had a total student body that included 36.6 percent students of color and charged an average annual tuition of $25,105 for middle school and $26,626 for high school. These schools also provided 18.2 percent of enrolled students with a total of $29,507,813 in needs-based financial aid. The median endowment of these schools was $3,478,417. The average teacher salary in AISGW schools ranged from $35,132 for first-year teachers to $75,159 for teachers with more than 31 years of teaching experience. This compared to a range of $42,370 for new teachers with a bachelor's degree to $87,583 for experienced teachers with a master's degree teaching in the District of Columbia Public Schools in 2008–9.

The remaining 82 private schools operating in Washington, DC at the time of our research included a wide assortment of Catholic, other religious, and secular schools. The Catholic Archdiocese of Washington, DC operated 22 elementary schools and one high school within the city limits of the district in 2004. Annual tuition levels at these Catholic schools were consistently below $6,000 even before discounts were applied for families that had low incomes or multiple children at the school. The remaining 60 private schools were about equally divided between non-Catholic faith-based schools, including those affiliated with the Baptist, Lutheran, and Seventh-Day Adventist faiths, and secular, independent private schools, including specialized schools that served only students with severe disabilities and music and ballet schools. The private schools of Washington, DC are a diverse lot that provide many contrasts to the traditional public schools of the district.

The Specific Impetus Behind *The Journey*

Discussions about expanding parental school choice to disadvantaged families have been led mainly by policy makers, scholars, and others interested in macro-level reform. These discussions have two noteworthy characteristics. First, much of the focus has been on the supply side of education reform, namely, what schools are and what they do in an attempt to improve deplorable outcomes for disadvantaged students. However, the demand, or family side, of the equation has been inadequately addressed in most of these discussions. What do families seek through parental school choice, and what do they need in order to obtain it? The research literature is often silent on these crucial questions. Second, when participating students and parents are discussed, quantitative estimations of the effects of school reform on test scores and other academic outcomes dominate the discussion. While these investigations are important, rarely heard or considered are the actual voices and experiences of the families who are involved with and are impacted by these school reforms, in this case low-income urban families.

Finally, no academic book has been published about the implementation of a specific private school choice program (or small number of programs) in the United States, in context, since 2002. In 2002 two such books[21] existed even though only six programs were in place. Since then, no new book that presents a private school choice case study has been published, even though six times as many programs now exist, with new ones being designed, passed, and implemented every year.

Our study was developed to address these glaring shortcomings in the policy debate over school choice. In doing so, the study has revealed crucial information about inner-city families and their experiences of participating in parental school choice, which has fundamental implications for the future design of school reform initiatives intended to help the United States to compete more effectively in the global economy.

We are uniquely positioned to examine the OSP from the demand side of program participants. Our background research into other contemporary school choice programs over the past decade has revealed a dearth of literature about the actual experiences of the families who participated in them. The fact that popular discussions about education reform initiatives like school choice have generally been ideologically driven dramatically limits our understanding of the ways in which these efforts influence the lives of participating families. Large-scale policy reforms often entail a process of change that is more obvious to students, parents, and others who are directly impacted by it than to policy makers and those who have a limited bird's-eye view of the issue. Many policy designers are not directly involved on a day-to-day basis with the families affected by government policy and do not see the reality faced by the low-income urban families that are typically targeted by parental school choice programs.

This study originated in 2004 when we submitted a request to the Annie E. Casey Foundation to underwrite the cost associated with chronicling the experiences of families participating in the OSP. In response, the foundation agreed to fund a qualitative study that would feature an annual set of discussions with participating families and the production of reports based on the experiences of the participating families and schools. In contrast with the formal government evaluation of the program led by Dr. Patrick Wolf,[22] coauthor of this book, our objective in this study was to document the lived experiences of the OSP families from their own perspectives and to gain insights into the personal and behavioral impacts on them as participants in the nation's first federal school voucher program. The annual focus groups, which were augmented by personal interviews and electronic polling, were used as the primary information-gathering techniques, and the data generated from these formed the basis for a four-part series of annual reports.[23]

The School Choice Journey takes up the story where *Waiting for Superman* and *Won't Back Down* leave off. *Superman* ends with some of the families featured in the documentary winning lotteries that will allow them to attend their school of choice, while other subjects are on the losing side of the lottery results. The school choice lottery winners walk away happy with the opportunity that chance has provided to them, but what, exactly, will that school choice opportunity entail? *Won't Back Down* ends shortly after the reformers achieved their surprising and perhaps short-term victory at the school board meeting. However, the long-term objective for these families remains in doubt.

As we began engaging OSP families in this study, we quickly recognized that they, like us as researchers, were embarking upon a journey with no clear destination. Once the project was underway, we further recognized that from a national and international standpoint, the United States, actually faces a similar journey, one in which it confronts the challenge of moving from an antiquated public education system designed to meet the standardized needs of an industrial economy to one focused on meeting the specialized needs of the information and knowledge-driven society of the twenty-first century. In addition to capturing the journey of the individual families, therefore, we realized that we were documenting a critical stage of contemporary urban school reform that has considerable significance for the future of the United States.

The Focus of *The School Choice Journey*

To understand the broader implications of this study and its findings, it is essential to consider how *The Journey* builds on the small but growing body of national and international literature that explores the impact of social policy programs on the empowerment and political participation of recipients, specifically low-income urban families. In this book, we define empowerment in terms of a continuum reflecting a relationship between families and schools that ranges from (1) clientism to (2) consumerism to (3) active citizenship.

The impact of social policies on the empowerment of low-income families was at the forefront of social policy research in the 1990s. At that time, a number of key studies demonstrated how the design and delivery of social policies resulted in "social constructions" of target populations and the internalization of these characterizations by recipients, with impacts on their self-image, orientation toward government, and likelihood of political participation.[24] Empirical research at this time showed how programs such as Head Start were successful in empowering low-income families by providing them with the experience, skills, and support needed to help improve their own lives.[25] In contrast, other social programs that were not designed to offer similar benefits were found to have disempowering impacts on program participants. This suggests that not only can well-designed social programs achieve their programmatic goals more effectively by equipping target groups with the tools and competencies to make the most of the services offered, but also that such interventions can produce broader antipoverty effects by empowering participants. The findings of this body of research are pertinent to the situation currently facing the United States in which high levels of poverty persist, and the crucial skills needed to compete effectively in the labor market are being denied to the children of many low-income families. Yet relatively few studies have been conducted on this issue in recent years, particularly in relation to the design and delivery of educational interventions in general and school choice programs in particular.

The Journey contributes to the literature on the empowerment of low-income families by examining how school choice, specifically parental school choice using vouchers, plays out in this area. The OSP, though designed as a local education reform initiative, was specifically intended for students from very low-income families who were attending poorly performing public schools. In many respects, this meant that the OSP was potentially as much an antipoverty program as it was an education reform initiative. In order to achieve its potential in either of these areas, however, there was a need to ensure that the participating families were adequately prepared and equipped to make effective use of the educational opportunity available to their children.

We found evidence from our research with OSP participants that the combination of service delivery, family structure, and family resources had a strong influence on the level of parent empowerment and effective participation in the program. In turn, this affected parents' thinking about student outcomes. Whether the empowerment of parents by the OSP actually improved the levels of educational achievement and educational attainment of participating students is a matter for quantitative research on the program to determine.[26] What we found in our qualitative research is that many parents reported becoming more actively involved in directing their child's education as a result of being given the opportunity and responsibility for selecting their child's school. When the program surprisingly was capped by policy makers and threatened with extinction, many parents rose up to defend it, contributing to a political compromise that reauthorized and expanded the OSP. Bumps came up along the way, to be sure, but the reports of parents in this study suggest that the OSP experience left them feeling that they were playing a more formative role in their child's development, and events revealed that these parents, like those in the movie *Won't Back Down*, indeed would not back down.

Implications of Our Findings

As the United States continues to adopt educational reform policies based on expanded educational options, we must question whether all Americans are easily able to assume the responsibilities associated with exercising parental school choice. Improving the overall quality of public and private schools through school choice will require that all parents (and to some extent the students, too) demonstrate at least a fundamental level of education-related consumer skills. There is currently an unspoken assumption among many proponents of school choice that such skills are innate in all parents. We beg to differ.

In *How to Change 5000 Schools*,[27] for example, the author notes that "the central challenge for public education in the coming years, at every level from school to nation, is to maintain and strengthen public confidence and support for public education so that people will want to send their children and provide their tax money." While we cannot argue with the need to improve public confidence and support for public education, this statement would be more precise by substituting "public" with "parents." Thus, parents would demonstrate "confidence," make a conscious decision to use the public education system for their children, and recognize their capacity to make a choice.

If, instead, the consumer skills needed to exercise choice tend to evolve over time as a result of parents' firsthand experiences with school choice, as we find in our research, families that are new to school choice will need support and assistance in order to reap the full benefits of participation in a school choice program. Limited resources stemming from poverty in many parts of the United States could hinder efforts to provide low-income families with quality school options that give their children a fighting chance of improving their future prospects. On the other hand, well-designed programs that provide the support and assistance needed to help families participate more effectively in their children's education, whether in the context of a school choice program or in the traditional public school system, can have empowering impacts on families and help maximize the potential for positive academic outcomes. Thus, strategies for the empowerment of low-income families must become an important aspect of education reform. An effective solution to this problem in the District of Columbia or any other part of the country has potential implications for millions of low-income families and for various types of school reform around the world.

The Journey challenges policy makers, philanthropists, and others interested in educational improvement to look beyond simply increasing the supply of new schools and expanding school choice programs, as so many lawmakers did in the past few years. To improve the impact of programs that target low-income families, we must increase our understanding of how family structure, family resources, and program design influence the process and outcomes of school choice. We must examine the reasons that families pursue school options, the challenges they face when engaging in the process, and how these factors influence the quality of the short-term and long-term outcomes for their children. One of the first questions that policy makers and education entrepreneurs should address when considering school choice initiatives is: "What forms and level of support will participating families need, based on their demographic and psychographic characteristics?" For example, given the large number of low-income families that are headed by single mothers, it is crucial to consider the unique challenges and transitional support needs of this group when designing programs.

An Overview of *The Journey*

We begin by placing publicly funded voucher programs, specifically the District of Columbia's OSP, into a larger social and historical context.

We explore the fundamental question: What is the nature of the parental school choice journey with regard to urban poverty, education reform, and student achievement? In chapter 1, we discuss the often-overlooked matter of how social programs are designed and the effects program design has on the attitudes and behaviors of program participants. In chapter 2, we discuss private school vouchers as a policy reform and introduce the reader to the OSP, the nation's first federally funded school voucher program. We review the disturbing history of K–12 education in the District of Columbia and the decade-long effort by congressional leaders and grassroots advocates to initiate a school voucher program in the nation's capital. We also discuss the results of the quantitative evaluation of the OSP, sponsored by the US Department of Education, to set the context for *The Journey*.

Chapters 3–5 illuminate many of the discrete aspects of parental school choice that the OSP families experienced on their journey. In these chapters, we explore what motivated families to participate in the OSP, what families looked for in schools, the importance of information, what challenges they faced in their new school environment, how they defined educational success for their child, and how satisfied they were with their school choice experiences. In each case, we explain how their experiences either reinforced previous thinking and behaviors or empowered parents in a way that their previous schools had not. These critical aspects of parental school choice are examined primarily through the actual statements of parents and students participating in the program. They were the travelers on this school choice journey, and we essentially present here a travelogue of their trip.

Chapter 6 describes an unexpected and traumatic event in the school choice journey: the effort by some Congressional leaders and President Barack Obama to eliminate the program eventually by closing it to new applicants and defunding it. Congress limited the OSP to continuing students starting in 2009, and both Congress and the president proposed major cuts in the appropriation supporting the program beginning that year. Senator Joe Lieberman (IndependentCT) and House Minority Leader John Boehner (Republican-OH) led the bipartisan political opposition to these attacks on the OSP at this time, with the editorial boards of the *Washington Post* and *Wall Street Journal* also joining the calls to save the program. Although the parents in the OSP tended to lack the resources and skills typically associated with active involvement in politics, a series of rallies in support of the program attracted hundreds of them to the battle to save the OSP. A dozen OSP parents and students became political activists, testifying before Congress, speaking to journalists, and contributing to political documentaries all geared toward affecting public policy. When the US House switched from Democratic to Republican control in the wake of the 2010 elections, John Boehner became Speaker of the House, and he got the leverage he needed to negotiate the reauthorization of the District of Columbia's OSP, for which the activated OSP parents were clamoring. Sometimes Hollywood fairy tales actually do come true.

Chapter 7 concludes by examining the features of the program that seemed to work most and least effectively, with the goal of highlighting the key lessons learned and how these lessons can raise our understanding of the role of parental school choice for this unique segment of education consumers. We also consider the ongoing political battles over ending, restricting, or expanding school voucher programs in the United States. Ultimately, will increasing numbers of families be invited to take *The School Choice Journey*?

1

What Is School Choice, and Why Did Some Parents Choose School Vouchers?

One of the potential by-products of poverty for urban families is a relationship with public agencies that deliver vital supports and services. Families that meet necessary financial eligibility requirements, which often means that household income for the prospective family is at or below the poverty level, can access public-support resources such as child-care assistance, supplemental nutrition programs, and medical services. For example, the US Department of Agriculture's Supplemental Nutrition Assistance Program (SNAP) provides food stamps that help more than 26 million eligible Americans (of which over 89,000 live in the District of Columbia) to put meals on their tables. Another example is the Temporary Assistance for Needy Families (TANF) program, which offers a variety of situational support services to help families facing financial distress navigate the obstacles associated with maintaining a family while working. At the beginning of 2009, TANF had 3,950,357 recipients nationally, including 12,510 within the District of Columbia.[1]

Although social programs of this type are intended to help reduce the impact of poverty on families, a growing body of research suggests that participation in these programs may have a disempowering effect on individuals who receive their services. Based on mounting evidence, the social programs themselves are not the problem. Instead, the way in which programs are designed and delivered determines whether they produce a positive or negative effect for participants and the upward social mobility of their families.

Some of our deepest insights about the nexus between poverty and school vouchers were sparked by comments made during personal interviews with the OSP participants in the very early stages of the programs.

For example, Paula explained the trade-offs low-income families must make as they explore new private school options. She is a native of Washington, DC who graduated from the public school system. She describes school as one of the best experiences of her life. She now has one child in the OSP. When asked how she would compare her parenting style to that of her parents, she explains that, like her parents, she stresses the importance and seriousness of education to her children.

In her second year in the OSP, Paula became increasingly concerned about the quality of the teachers at her child's school. She is most concerned about the fact that perhaps her child's private school is not equipped to handle the increased number of OSP students. Though she felt the school was not meeting her daughter's academic needs, she kept her in the private school primarily to ensure her safety. In addition to her disappointment with the quality of the teachers at the school, Paula was surprised that the class size was no different from the public school they had left. Furthermore, she was disgruntled because she felt she was paying for services that the school had advertised, such as tutoring, but which were not being offered.

While she is considering enrolling her child in a public charter school, Paula remains very concerned about safety. Her advice to parents who are attending or are considering attending private schools through the OSP: conduct surprise or unannounced visits to make sure that the schools are really offering what they advertised. She believes the program is most beneficial if students enroll in elementary school, as opposed to middle or high school. Her greatest concern could be best addressed by establishing a monitoring or accountability system to ensure that private schools that participate in the OSP have both the qualified teachers and the core program features that they advertise to parents.

When conducting focus groups with our sample of parent participants in the OSP, the levels of satisfaction with the program they reported also caught our attention. They seemed unusually high for a social program targeting low-income families. During the final stage of our research, we used interactive polling devices to ask parents how successful they thought the OSP had been, and then we compared their responses by year of entry to the program. The respondents were divided into two cohorts based on whether they entered the program in the first year (Cohort 1) or the second year (Cohort 2). Although levels of satisfaction with the OSP were high among both cohorts, satisfaction was somewhat higher among Cohort 2 parents compared to Cohort 1 (see Figure 1.1). It is possible that the truncated implementation schedule for the first year of the OSP prevented program personnel from performing due diligence on the participating schools, thus influencing levels of satisfaction for parents in

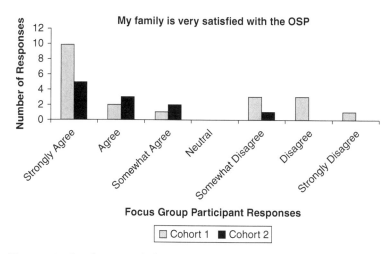

Figure 1.1 Satisfaction with the Opportunity Scholarship Program, 2009

Cohort 1 such as Paula. Cohort 2 families had more time to learn about the program, apply, and search for placements in schools. Moreover, with a year of implementation behind them, the parents reported that the Washington Scholarship Fund, the entity responsible for managing the day-to-day operation of the program, was more efficient in its administration of the program.

These numbers triggered our curiosity about which aspects of the program were contributing to these high satisfaction levels. We also began to wonder whether the participants' positive experiences with the OSP were influencing their consumer and citizenship behaviors in distinct ways. We began to examine other bodies of research that explore the nature of the relationship between low-income families and the public agencies that provide housing, health care, and other services, in an attempt to elucidate the relationships that may exist between social program participation and political attitudes and behavior.

The findings from this research challenged us to develop a framework for thinking about the OSP and public schools as social service delivery agents. It became clear from the literature that there are substantial knowledge gaps in our understanding of schools as service delivery organizations. Although previous researchers have identified the existence of links between social program participation and citizenship behavior, very few studies have explored this general topic, and virtually no previous research has examined the family effects of participation in school choice programs. We saw an opportunity, therefore, to use the data generated by our study to contribute to an understanding of how the interaction between program participants and the deliverer of social services can influence the consumer and political attitudes and behaviors of low-income families such as those in a school voucher program.

The framework that we developed is intended for use in exploring how well-designed parental school choice programs can help explain parental satisfaction with programs and can constitute powerful antipoverty tools over and beyond any immediate educational benefits they bestow upon low-income families. They do so by facilitating the development of the skills needed to become more astute consumers and active citizens. The framework can also be used to examine the impacts of other types of social programs on the recipients of their services.

The remainder of this chapter discusses our theoretical framework and uses it to present some of the main relevant findings from our own research and other studies of how social services can have transformative impacts on recipients.

Key Concepts

Three key concepts underpin our theoretical framework, all of which have been derived in large part from previous research: "clientism," "consumerism," and "citizenship" (see Figure 1.2). These concepts refer to different types of relationships that can exist between public agencies and social program participants. They are each associated with specific attitudes and behaviors on the part of program participants, and they reflect the nature of the relationship between service providers and end users. The arrow in the background represents the general continuum of participant empowerment that is lowest for clients and highest for citizens.

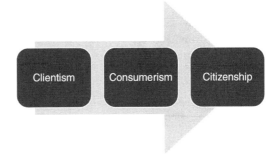

Figure 1.2   Transition from Clientism to Consumerism to Empowered Citizen

The term *clientism* is used to refer to a relationship where a recipient of a service is easily intimidated by the much larger amount of power, information, and expertise that a service provider appears to have. Public agencies demonstrate a client approach to engaging participants and delivering services when they place a low premium on soliciting input from program participants about their needs and preferences. These agencies often view participating individuals and families as little more than recipients of public services with no control over what they receive or how it is delivered to them. It is well documented in the literature that, for program recipients, the client relationship often involves having to endure demeaning and embarrassing comments and behaviors from service providers.[2] At one extreme, this is typified by the relationships between public agencies and the most marginalized or disadvantaged groups in society, such as prison inmates, the homeless, or people struggling with substance abuse. Client relationships also dominate many welfare programs targeting low-income individuals and families, such as food stamps, housing vouchers, and Aid to Families with Dependent Children (AFDC), which was a predecessor of TANF.[3]

We use the term *consumerism* to connote a more balanced relationship between public service recipients and the agencies charged with providing those services. The conceptualization of public service users as "consumers" has been one aspect of the "New Public Management" paradigm that has become increasingly dominant over the past few decades, as the defining feature of consumerism is choice.[4] The extent of choice available and the options for exercising a true consumer relationship in the context of receiving government services have often been limited. Real consumerism entails not just the provision of choices on the part of agencies or service providers but also, most importantly, the ability of the recipient to make well-informed choices. This capability generally assumes that program participants can draw upon relevant knowledge and skills, things which are often lacking among individuals who have had limited exposure to, or experience with, the services in question.[5]

The third key concept, and the one which is seen as most important in relation to social program participation as an antipoverty tool, is *citizenship*. This is the most difficult of our three concepts to define in succinct terms because the word has many different meanings.[6] For the purpose of the theoretical framework we develop here, citizenship is political participation, defined by Judith Shklar in the following terms:

> Good citizenship as political participation…applies to the people of a community who are consistently engaged in public affairs. The good democratic citizen is a political agent who takes part regularly in politics

locally and nationally, not just on primary and election day. Active citizens keep informed and speak out against public measures that they regard as unjust, unwise, or just too expensive. They also openly support policies that they regard as just and prudent.[7]

Like consumer behavior, citizenship involves knowledge and skills that often have to be learned or come from experience. We argue, however, that the acquisition of active citizenship-related attitudes and behaviors among low-income adults and families is potentially one of the most powerful ways in which parental school choice initiatives and other social programs can help to lift low-income families out of poverty.

Key Findings of Previous Research

In a democratic society, political participation is the means by which citizens further their own interests and those of the social group or the set of interests that are most important to them. The finite resources available for public spending often mean that this takes—or appears to take—the form of a zero-sum game. As Andrea Campbell observes, "Mass participation influences policy outcomes—the politically active are more likely to achieve their policy goals, often at the expense of the politically quiescent."[8] Within most participating countries in the international Income and Current Election Participation Study, voters were found to have had higher average incomes than non-voters.[9] This phenomenon has been attributed at least in part to factors such as the lack of time, money, information, and personal connections among people from low-income backgrounds compared with those of greater means. But there is growing evidence to suggest that the low levels of political participation also result from, and are reinforced by, the design of public policies and the attitudes toward recipients by service providers. As a result, rather than ameliorating poverty and social inequality, public policies and social programs often exacerbate them.

Anne Schneider and Helen Ingram explained this provider paternalism in terms of the ways that the design and delivery of social policies result in the formation of "social constructions" of target populations.[10] For example, the intended recipients of such policies are often seen by policy officials and the general public as either "deserving" or "non-deserving," and either able to take care of themselves or needing active intervention from government in order to do so. Programs such as Social Security and Medicare, which are universally available to all elderly Americans regardless of income, are targeted at people who are seen as deserving of them.[11] Most Americans view means-tested government programs, such as Aid to Families with Dependent Children (AFDC) and Medicaid, as being aimed primarily at the "non-deserving," that is, individuals who have been unable to support themselves and therefore require intervention in their lives.

A maxim popular in social policy circles states that programs limited to the poor end up being poor programs. In general, universal programs are associated with high levels of benefits and relatively few burdens on their participants, while means-tested programs bestow low levels of benefits and impose high demands on recipients. For example, participants in means-tested government programs are expected to divulge a great deal about their personal lives and make their homes available for random inspections from social workers or other service delivery agents. Such intrusive requirements are likely to discourage some qualified people from participating in these programs.[12]

Those who do receive services from means-tested programs often internalize the prevailing social constructions of the program's target population, with significant impacts on their self-image as well as their orientation toward government and likelihood of political participation.[13] The experience of participating in social programs influences both "internal political efficacy" or the extent to which individuals believe they have the skills and abilities to be politically active, and "external political efficacy" or the extent to which they believe they will be able to influence political outcomes.[14]

In reality, the experiences of participating in a social program and any subsequent impact on political attitudes can best be understood from the perspective of the participants themselves. A number of qualitative studies in this area have provided important insights into the ways in which experiences of social program participation can have an impact on participants' attitudes and beliefs about government and self-empowerment. For example, Joe Soss conducted a comparative study of the experiences of participating in a Social Security Disability Insurance (SSDI) program and the AFDC program, based on in-depth interviews.[15] In the case of the SSDI, which is available to clients regardless of their income, there was no requirement for mandatory reviews with service recipients, and contact with the agency was generally infrequent and mostly initiated by the participant. The SSDI recipients developed a relatively strong sense of their ability to play an active role in the program and a positive image of the responsiveness of the agency:

> Well, if there is any power, I guess they have more than I do. But I haven't come into a situation where I've seen it...I always feel like I have some say-so in the process.[16]

In contrast, participants in AFDC were means-tested and therefore subjected to regular case reviews and interactions with government supervisors. They rarely initiated contact with the agency themselves but simply complied with requests for attendance and information and often experienced disrespectful or condescending attitudes and behavior toward them. Participants were often summoned to the agency with the threat of termination of support if they did not attend. These AFDC recipients developed a set of beliefs in which the agency, in general, and the individual officials in it were powerful influences in their lives over which they had little or no control:

> I figure if I say something back, they know a way of getting me cut off AFDC. And then I wouldn't have anything for me and my kids, just because I said something. That's their power, right there. That's the power. That's why nobody complains. [17]

Soss also found evidence that his research subjects' experiences of the SSDI and AFDC programs were shaping their views about government as a whole and, most importantly, their beliefs about the effectiveness of taking political action. Most of the SSDI participants he interviewed indicated that they saw the government as being open and responsive to citizens, even if they perceived that the process involved was too slow.[18] In contrast, the AFDC recipients tended to expect that all government departments would operate in a similar negative way and that officials would not listen to their concerns due to the stereotypical perceptions the officials held of low-income program participants.[19] As this research reveals, means-tested initiatives may tend to be poorly implemented programs that fail to transform families in part because of paternalistic attitudes that society and government officials hold toward people with low incomes.

Other qualitative studies have provided evidence that it is not the characteristics of the client group that determines how the individuals are treated by program officials but, rather, the ways in which officials interpret and carry out their responsibilities in relation to delivering the program or services, and especially the nature of their interaction with participants. Two separate studies conducted in homeless shelters in New York illustrate this point. Aaron Skinner conducted a case study of a transitional living shelter for young homeless mothers.[20] He observed that the staff members at the center, many of whom had no previous experience working with homeless adolescents, were disempowering the mothers through the ways in which they exercised their power and control over them. Although the staff members were supposed to be helping the young women with their daily needs, Skinner found that they viewed their role primarily as wardens and were therefore primarily concerned with enforcing the shelter rules, with total disregard for the mothers' needs and concerns.[21] For example, food was regularly confiscated from women's rooms, despite the fact that the mothers reported getting hungry at nighttime. Skinner also observed many examples of what he called "non-engagement with the women," when the staff ignored their requests for help or brushed them off saying they were too busy.[22]

Marcia Cohen studied the relationship between participants and staff of a residential program for mentally ill, homeless women in New York.[23] In contrast to Skinner, she found that the women were empowered by the way in which they were involved in the planning of the program and were in other ways treated as competent adults by the staff. As a result, the participants developed a sense of efficacy and were able to take a high degree of control over their immediate environment, even forming a tenants association.

Within the public education sphere, Head Start is frequently cited as an example of a publicly funded program that empowers low-income families by providing them with the experience and skills needed to help improve their own lives. Head Start has mandatory requirements for parent participation in policy councils and program decision making. Some of the AFDC participants in Soss' study were also enrolled in Head Start, and commented on the positive impacts of that program on their confidence and self-esteem compared with AFDC:

> They not only give you the opportunity to help with little stuff in the classroom; they give you the opportunity to go to a meeting where you are making decisions. You are actually involved in the hiring. No one can get hired for this program unless they're interviewed by a group of parents. And that in itself is like, "Wow! Really? I can do that?" It gives you control over the education your child is getting, the kind of food your child is getting to eat, the kind of curriculum in the classroom, the people [who] are actually working with your child. That sense of empowerment starts there.[24]

Participants in Head Start were significantly more willing to voice grievances in AFDC than the AFDC-participants who had no other organizational involvement. Those AFDC participants with Head Start experience were also more likely to report seeing the political system as open and democratic and to believe that their participation would be effective. The research findings showed that most recipients of AFDC expressed a willingness to be more active; however they questioned "whether the government would not listen or respond to people like them."[25]

The Implications for School Choice

Given the lessons learned from previous studies of citizenship in general and the influence of government programs on civic efficacy in particular, we might expect to see crosscutting forces affecting the participants in school choice programs. School voucher programs in the United States, which enable parents to use government grants to select private schools for their children, tend to be targeted to disadvantaged students and families. The school voucher programs in major cities such as Milwaukee, Cleveland, New Orleans, and the District of Columbia are all means-tested and largely limited to those families with levels of income that would qualify their children for the federal lunch program. As initiatives targeted to the poor, we might expect these urban school voucher programs to foster the spirit-killing paternalism demonstrated in many of the means-tested programs discussed above.

On the other hand, school choice programs are designed to rely on the effective participation of parents to make them work. Parents are expected to seek out information about their child's newly available schooling options and determine whether it is a good fit for that child's needs. The whole point of school choice is to place educational decisions in the hands of parents, as free-acting and responsible agents of their child's educational future. As parental activist Virginia Walden Ford likes to say, parental school choice is about *Voices, Choices, and Second Chances.*[26]

Several prominent researchers, however, have argued that expanding school choice and thereby encouraging more parents to be active consumers of their child's education would reduce levels of active citizenship in our country.[27] In the context of our tripartite theory of clients, consumers, and citizens, these scholars claim that extending school choice to low-income parents who previously enrolled their children in residentially assigned public schools would have the likely effect of transforming them from community-minded citizens to self-centered individualist consumers. These authors argue that the commercialization of education through vouchers disconnects parents from political activity and support for government, since they are no longer dependent upon a government institution to provide this important service. In other words, they claim that the school choice journey for inner-city parents starts with them being politically engaged citizens and then sends them "backward" to the unwanted destination of mere self-interested consumerism or narrow-minded tribalism. Supreme Court Justice Stephen Breyer has gone so far as to claim that school vouchers will "balkanize" inner-city populations along religious lines to the point of extreme civil strife.[28]

Although these competing claims about the impact of school vouchers on the civic and consumer behavior of parents are common in the scholarly literature, neither logic nor evidence appears to support them. As a distinct demographic group and market segment, low-income inner-city parents whose children are enrolled in neighborhood public schools have some of the lowest rates of political participation in the United States. Since means-tested school voucher programs are targeted toward the types of families that have traditionally been highly disengaged from politics, it seems unlikely that such school choice programs would decrease overall levels of political and civic activism among this group.

Conversely, other analysts have argued that social programs of this type are more likely to have an empowering versus a disempowering effect on participants. Mark Warren, for example, argues that if adults were given greater responsibility for important areas of their lives such as their workplaces and schools, "they would become more public-spirited, more tolerant, more knowledgeable, more attentive to the interests of others, and more thoughtful about their own interests."[29] In a phrase, they would become better citizens. Benjamin Barber speaks specifically of the empowering potential of school vouchers when he says:

> Their great virtue is that they are intolerant of state bureaucracies in that they mobilize parent/student constituencies in a fashion that also serves to mobilize citizenship...to care for and to act on behalf of one's own interests is the first step toward civic activity in a lethargic representative system where individuals are accustomed to deferring to politicians, bureaucrats, experts, and managers. Vouchers are a form of power, and power is the most effective catalyst citizenship can have.[30]

Barber's comments raise at least a couple of interesting questions. First, does this mean families that pursue vouchers will most likely place a value, real or perceived, on them that will motivate parents to exercise citizenship? In turn, does this suggest that effective parental school choice eventually produces citizenship empowerment?

Whichever viewpoint proves to be correct, this debate raises many questions about the wider impacts of participation in school voucher programs. For example, does the pursuit by parents of school options beyond the public schools in their own neighborhoods lead them to be less active in their communities or does the fact that they have exit options make their "voice" more influential in shaping public education? Moreover, does reduced dependence on government and increased levels of participation in their children's new private schools of choice by parents translate into enhanced political skills, self-confidence as public sphere actors, and an increased sense of responsibility to participate politically? Do the specific characteristics or previous experiences of different families and parents influence the ways in which this occurs? And what is the role in this process of program-related factors such as the specific design and methods of delivery of school vouchers? These and other similar questions, we argue, should be at the crux of the parental school choice debate in order to fully understand the potential impact of voucher programs on poverty in the United States.

Based on the theories and evidence regarding the nature of program delivery and its effects on participants in the fields of welfare, housing, and early childhood education programs outlined earlier in this chapter, we believe that parental school choice through vouchers is indeed likely to be more and not less empowering to parents. The degree of empowerment that occurs, however, is likely to depend on the types of resources that inner-city families bring to the experience, an issue that we explore in subsequent chapters of the book, and which is fundamental to our framework for better understanding school vouchers.

Conclusion

We began this chapter by explaining the intersection between urban poverty and education reform, highlighting the fact that voucher programs like the OSP place program participants in a unique situation from a service delivery standpoint. We discussed the often-ignored matter of how social programs are designed and the effects that design can have on the attitudes and behaviors of participants. Drawing from the literature on income-support programs, we have argued that interventions targeting disadvantaged families can be designed and delivered in ways that promote a passive "clientele" response, an active but individualistic "consumer" response, or a community-oriented empowered "citizenship" response from participants.

As we travel further along the school choice journey of our participant families, the concepts of clientism, consumerism, and citizenship will form the basis for a deeper understanding of the interplay between under-resourced families, social service delivery, and education reform. We will highlight the importance of participant characteristics in this process by showing how factors such as family structure, income, social networks, and family resources appear to interact with the design elements of social programs to produce a client, consumer, or citizen response. Finally, we consider the nature of parental school choice in relation to our theoretical framework, and examine findings from our OSP focus groups and interviews to assess the potential of such programs to empower participants.

2

The History of Vouchers and Education Reform in Washington, DC

The story of the OSP begins with a city's long-standing struggle to overcome persistent and concentrated poverty. In the District of Columbia, poverty wears a distinctive face. Nearly 16 percent of District of Columbia families live below the poverty level, compared with 9.8 percent nationally. The proportion of individuals in the District of Columbia who own the homes they live in is well below the national level, a factor the World Bank identifies as a significant contributing dimension of poverty. Less than 60 percent of the minority students, who account for a large proportion of the population of Washington's public schools, graduate from high school.[1] The young people who do not complete high school are much more likely to be poor than those who go to college,[2] a factor which may make programs like the OSP even more important to low-income students who take part in them.

In this chapter, we take a closer look at the relationship between various forces that have converged to create the OSP, including the concept of school vouchers and the special circumstances surrounding our nation's capital. We also provide an overview of our methods of examining the school choice journey experienced by the families in our study.

History of Vouchers

School voucher programs make public funds available to qualified families to cover some or all of the expenses associated with enrolling their child in a participating private school of their choosing. In other areas of public policy such as housing and nutritional programs (i.e. food stamps), vouchers are commonly used as antipoverty instruments.[3] One of the primary selling points of vouchers as opposed to direct government services is that vouchers allow recipients to select a product or service that best fits their particular needs. The Pell Grant program and the G.I. Bill that support college students are examples of education vouchers that are widely used. Although vouchers are popular in these other policy domains, they are controversial when applied to K–12 education in the United States. Teachers' unions and other organizations that represent the public school establishment are the most influential opponents of vouchers, often claiming that they do not benefit families and undermine the public school system.[4]

Discussions about school vouchers are as old as the United States itself. Thomas Paine, an intellectual leader of the American Revolution, argued for school vouchers in his 1791 treatise on *The Rights of Man*.[5] Paine claimed that the enlightened governments of the West should subsidize the education of the poor and that school vouchers are the best way to do so. Paine's arguments in support of school vouchers were later echoed by liberal English philosopher John Stuart Mill, who specifically argued that governments should mandate universal education and finance it for disadvantaged families, although government organizations should not educate students directly. He wrote:

> [The government] might leave to parents to obtain the education where and how they please, and content itself with helping to pay the school fees of the poorer classes of children…The objections which are urged with reason against State education do not apply to the enforcement of education by the State, but to the State taking upon itself to direct that education…That the whole or any large part of the education of the people should be in State hands, I go as far as anyone in deprecating.[6]

Long before school quality was acknowledged as an important social and economic issue, Mill was calling for parental school choice through government vouchers for poor families.

The modern case for school vouchers was advanced by US economist Milton Friedman in his 1955 article, "The Role of Government in Education."[7] Friedman agreed with Mill that government should finance but not necessarily operate K–12 education, and he extended the argument by claiming that a universal school choice program, through vouchers, "would widen the range of choice available to parents," and generate competitive pressures that would improve education for all students. Friedman's vision for government-financed vouchers available to all families, regardless of income or circumstances, has been a focus of the scholarly and policy debate over school choice, even though no "Friedman-like" universal school voucher programs have been implemented yet in the United States.

A brief review of the 21 school voucher programs that existed in the United States as of January 2014 reveals that they were designed to serve students with various disadvantages (see Table 2.1).[8] The urban school voucher programs in Milwaukee, Cleveland, the District of Columbia, and Racine are restricted to students with low to moderate family incomes.[9] Statewide programs in Indiana, Ohio, North Carolina, and Wisconsin also are means-tested, while the statewide program in Louisiana is eligible only to students who are both low-income and enrolled in low-performing public schools.[10] Ten statewide voucher programs—in Florida, Georgia, Louisiana, Mississippi (two programs), North Carolina, Ohio (two programs), Oklahoma, and Utah—are limited to students with disabilities.[11] The original statewide voucher program in Ohio, called

Table 2.1   Twenty-One Direct Voucher Programs in the United States: 2012–13 Enrollments

Location	Eligibility	Initiated	Students
Milwaukee, WI	Means Test	1990	24,027
Cleveland, OH	Means Test	1995	6,513
Florida	Disability	1999	25,366
Ohio	Disability—Autism	2003	2,241
Washington, DC	Means Test	2004	1,584
Utah	Disability	2005	672
Ohio	In Underperforming Public School	2005	17,057
Georgia	Disability	2007	3,227
Louisiana	In Underperforming + Means Test	2008/2012	4,963
Louisiana	Disability	2010	197
Oklahoma	Disability	2010	197
Douglas County, CO	Universal	2011	NA
Indiana	Means Test	2011	9,324
Ohio	Disability	2011	1,371
Racine, WI	Means Test	2011	500
Mississippi	Disability—Dyslexia	2012	13
Ohio	Means Test	2013	NA
Wisconsin	Means Test	2013	NA
Mississippi	Disability	2013	NA
North Carolina	Disability	2013	NA
North Carolina	Means Test	2013	NA
Total			**97,252**

Sources: Malcolm Glenn and Randan Swindler, *School Choice Now: The Power of Educational Choice* (School Choice Yearbook 2012–13). Washington, DC: Alliance for School Choice, p. 13. Friedman Foundation for Educational Choice, "School Choice Programs," accessed on January 4, 2014, at http://www.edchoice.org/School-Choice/School-Choice-Programs.aspx

EdChoice, exclusively serves students who attended underperforming public schools. Although the program in Douglas County, Colorado, a suburb of Denver, is in theory available to all students in that narrow geographic area, it has been barred by the courts from enrolling any students until the constitutionality of the program is determined. For now, to even qualify for school vouchers in one of the US communities which offers them, students must be disadvantaged in some educationally relevant way.

The existing school voucher programs appear to deliver on their promise to enroll highly disadvantaged populations of students. For example, more than 34 percent of the 97,252 students currently served by school vouchers are participating in programs limited to students with disabilities, more than twice the national rate of 14 percent of K–12 students diagnosed with disabilities.[12] John Witte, who led the first official evaluation of a school voucher program in the United States, reported that the Milwaukee Parental Choice Program (MPCP) served disproportionate numbers of students who were low income, African American, or Latino, and who came from single-parent families. Witte wrote, "The MPCP was established and the statute written explicitly to provide an opportunity for relatively poor families to attend private schools. The program clearly accomplished that goal."[13] In a follow-up evaluation of the Milwaukee program conducted from 2006 through 2011, researchers concluded that school voucher participants were slightly more likely to be low income and low performing than the average student in Milwaukee Public Schools.[14]

The voucher programs operating in the United States, all of which target students from underprivileged and disadvantaged circumstances, gravitate more toward the vision of John Stuart Mill than of Milton Friedman. Friedman's main argument, that universal school choice (including the ability to attend private schools) would generate competition among schools and improve education for everyone, was grounded in basic economic theory. Mill's claim that school vouchers should be provided only to disadvantaged students focuses our attention on the core question of what will happen to the families themselves once they receive this "opportunity." Building on Mill's claim, political philosopher Harry Brighouse and political scientist Joseph Viteritti, in separate but complementary works, argue that the means-tested school voucher programs that figure so prominently in the history of parental school choice in the United States represent a leveling of the educational playing field, since they provide poor families with private schooling options that otherwise might be the exclusive preserve of the rich.[15] Carolyn Sattin-Bajaj describes the experiences specifically of immigrant youth as they seek educational equity and economic mobility through school choice.[16] Our study examines this question of what happens to the participants in the means-tested OSP, especially from the perspective of the low-income families themselves who decided to take this school choice journey.

Do Vouchers Make a Difference?

This inquiry focuses on the school voucher experience and its effects on parents and students. A large research literature, in contrast, examines the effects that parental school choice has on the broader educational system including the students, teachers, and schools of the public sector.[17] While the system-wide effects of parental school choice through vouchers are certainly important, our interest first and foremost is with the nature of the experience of school choice for those who actually embark upon that journey.

Most of the school voucher programs in the United States have been studied using quantitative methods. From these studies, we know that parents who have received vouchers tend to be much more satisfied with their child's school than other parents. There is some evidence that students go farther in school as a result of school choice. Most of the rigorous voucher evaluations—those that use a random assignment research design to control for biases—conclude that some or all groups of voucher students benefit academically from their experience with parental school choice.[18] Those studies have not yet compelled a scholarly consensus on the effectiveness of voucher programs, but they have shifted the debate away from the issue of "do vouchers improve outcomes?" to questions of who benefits, by how much, in which academic areas, and why.

In every study that has asked the question, parents have reported being more satisfied with their child's school if they were given the opportunity to select it. As Brian Gill and his colleagues state in their summary of the research on this question, "the findings on parental satisfaction in voucher programs have been strongly and uniformly positive."[19] In John Witte's initial study of the MPCP, he reported that: "The results for Choice parents evaluating their child's private schools...were considerably more positive than they were for their child's prior public school."[20] In an evaluation of the Cleveland Scholarship and Tutoring Program, Jay Greene and his colleagues reported that: "Two-thirds of parents new to choice schools reported being very satisfied with the academic quality of their child's school, as compared to fewer than 30 percent of parents with children in public schools."[21] In a study of Florida's McKay Scholarship Program for students with disabilities, Jay Greene and Greg Forster found that parents were much more satisfied with the educational services their child was receiving in private schools of choice than they had been with the services the child had been receiving in his or her previous public school.[22] In a survey of parents across the country whose children attended private schools using partial-tuition, voucher-type scholarships, Paul Peterson and David Campbell reported that 72 percent of scholarship-using parents gave their child's school a grade of A compared to just 16 percent of parents in the control group.[23] There is a clear and consistent positive relationship between parental school choice and parental school satisfaction.

Parents might be more satisfied with schools of choice because they encourage students to obtain higher levels of educational attainment. Attainment refers to how far a student progresses through the educational system and is often measured by benchmarks such as high school graduation, college attendance, and obtaining a college degree. In separate studies, James Coleman and his colleagues and Derek Neal found that African American students who attended Catholic high schools were more likely to graduate from high school and attend college than were similar students who attended public high schools.[24] Joshua Cowen and his colleagues similarly reported that ninth graders enrolled in the Milwaukee school voucher program in 2006 were more likely to have graduated from high school, attended college, and persisted in college six years later than were a carefully matched group of Milwaukee public school students.[25] Although only a few quantitative studies existed regarding the effect of school vouchers on various educational attainment benchmarks prior to the launch of the OSP, they did suggest that such programs might help students go farther in school.

But do students learn more when their parents are allowed to choose their school, particularly a private one? Prior to the launch of the OSP in 2004, the largest rigorous evaluation of voucher-type scholarship programs examined the effects of privately funded partial-tuition scholarships in New York City; Dayton, Ohio; and Washington, DC.[26] Using experimental research methods, this three-city study found that African American students benefited academically from the school choice opportunity, while the smaller subgroups of white and Latino students in the study, on average, showed no achievement gains from the scholarships. The learning gains experienced by African Americans who used scholarships to attend private schools amounted to about one-third of the size of the notorious black-white test score gap, leading the study authors to speculate that school choice through vouchers could be an effective general strategy for closing that learning deficit.

Two other research teams used different methods to analyze the same data, with one team largely confirming the original results,[27] and the other team questioning them.[28] Moreover, the test-score gains for African Americans in the District of Columbia component of the three-city study, which were strong in the second year of the analysis, fell to zero in the third and final year of the study, as many students gave up their partial-tuition scholarships to transfer to one of the free public charter schools that had proliferated throughout DC. It was not obvious from this influential study whether voucher-type scholarships had delivered sustainable achievement gains for the District of Columbia students.

Other quantitative evaluations of school voucher or voucher-type programs also reached similar conclusions that the effects of such programs on student test scores varied from neutral to modestly positive. John Witte's original study reported no significant effects of the small pilot program on student achievement, while follow-up studies by Jay Greene and his colleagues as well as Cecilia Rouse used different research methods and concluded that students did benefit academically from the program.[29] Witte and his colleagues conducted a follow-up study of the much larger Milwaukee program starting in 2006, finding no effects of vouchers on student achievement until the final year of the study, when the scores of voucher students surged most likely due to a new high-stakes testing accountability policy.[30] Kim Metcalf and his colleagues reported few significant effects of the Cleveland voucher program on student test scores during their four-year evaluation, although a separate study of one network of private schools in the program reported voucher achievement gains.[31] Jay Greene reported achievement gains from a privately funded scholarship program in Charlotte, North Carolina, as did David Figlio from a tax-credit scholarship program in Florida.[32]

We also know from previous research on voucher programs that participation in parental school choice involves hard work that does not always pay off for families. When initially offered vouchers, typically between 20 and 30 percent of students decline to use them. Voucher use also tends to drop over time especially when students "graduate" out of elementary or junior high school and must find and enroll in a new private high school of choice. As a result, students who participate in voucher programs often end up switching schools frequently during their educational careers.[33] Parents provide a variety of reasons to explain why they decline to use school vouchers, either initially or over time: the school they most preferred was full, they had problems with transportation, they were disappointed with the quality of the school, or the school they initially selected proved a poor fit for their child.[34] The hard work of seeking out a school of choice for one's child, and moving them to a different school if their initial choice does not pan out, is a central element of what Bryan Hassel calls *The Charter School Challenge*.[35]

Prior to the establishment of the OSP, not much was known about what tends to happen to students when their parents are given new opportunities to select their school, particularly a private one. Parents sometimes struggle with the demands of making the school choice, and students often switch schools multiple times over several years. In spite of the challenge, parents consistently report being more satisfied with schools of choice than with assigned public schools, and initial research suggests that students graduate at higher rates from private schools of choice. There is not yet a complete research consensus on the achievement effects of school vouchers and scholarships, but many of the most rigorous studies indicate that at least some groups of students benefit from such programs.

There is almost no evidence to explain specifically why students might benefit academically from experiencing school choice through vouchers. One of us (Wolf) coauthored a study that identified an advantaged peer group, more challenging homework, and more caring teachers as three factors associated with academic gains from the privately funded scholarship program in Washington, DC that preceded the OSP.[36] The evidence was only suggestive, however, and not compelling. Howell and his colleagues were able to rule out many possible explanations for the pattern of achievement results that they observed in New York, Dayton, and the District of Columbia, but could not definitively rule any explanations in.[37] Private schools tend to be much smaller than public schools and have a reputation for promoting character traits such as grit and self-discipline, so school size and character outcomes could be the specific sources of the voucher effects we have observed to date—especially any attainment effects. At this point, both quantitative and qualitative researchers can only speculate regarding what specific elements of the school choice journey render it a rewarding experience for most but not all the families.

Such was the research base in 2004 when policy makers chose to launch a new government-sponsored voucher program in the District of Columbia. We knew a great deal regarding what happens generally when school choice is expanded to previously disenfranchised families through scholarships and vouchers, but no one could be certain what would happen in this particular case. Would the journey be smooth, uneventful, and impactful or rough, tumultuous, and disappointing?

The Opportunity Scholarship Program

Policy makers have been proposing a school voucher program for the District of Columbia for decades.[38] One clear motivation for increased parental school choice in the nation's capital has been the widespread dissatisfaction with the performance of District of Columbia Public Schools (DCPS). Fewer than 60 percent of DCPS eighth graders eventually graduate from high school.[39] An astounding 85 percent of those DCPS students who graduate and go on to enroll in the University of the District of Columbia require remediation.[40] These dismal results led observers to wonder if parental school choice might offer a better way to improve high school graduation rates and post- secondary success.

The first attempt to enact a school voucher program in the District of Columbia took place in 1981, when the Committee for Improved Education placed a voucher initiative on the ballot.[41] That initiative failed, as almost all contentious initiatives and referenda do, in the subsequent election. The District of Columbia school voucher debate then moved to the halls of the US Congress, since the federal government possesses the ultimate responsibility for funding and overseeing education in the District. Throughout the 1990s and early 2000s, Congressman Richard Armey (R-TX) annually proposed a school voucher program for the District of Columbia, only to see his efforts fail on largely partisan votes. With fellow Republicans in control of both houses of Congress in 1998, Armey's voucher bill passed but was vetoed by President Bill Clinton.

The school choice policy breakthrough in the nation's capital took place with the *District of Columbia School Choice Incentive Act of 2003*.[42] The *Incentive Act*, signed into law on January 29, 2004, established the first federally funded school voucher program in the United States. It was passed by a single vote in the US House of Representatives and cleared the US Senate only after being attached to a "must pass" emergency appropriations bill. The legislation was packaged as part of a "three sector strategy" (public, private, and nonprofit) to improve education in the district. The $40 million annual appropriation attached to the bill included an extra $13 million for educational improvements in the District of Columbia Public Schools, $13 million to increase the availability of facilities appropriate for public charter schools in the district, $13 million for a school voucher pilot called the "Opportunity Scholarship Program" (OSP), and $1 million for administration and evaluation of the voucher initiative.

The purpose of the new voucher program was to provide low-income students with "expanded opportunities to attend higher performing schools in the District of Columbia."[43] According to the statute, eligibility for entry to the program was limited to students entering grades K–12 living in the District with a family income at or below 185 percent of the federal poverty line (about $36,000 for a family of four in 2006). Participating students received scholarships of up to $7,500 to cover the costs of tuition, school fees, and transportation to a participating private school in the District of Columbia. Scholarships were renewable for up to five years, so long as students remained eligible for the program and in good academic standing at the private school they were attending.[44] In a given year, if there were more eligible applicants than available scholarships or open slots in private schools, applicants were awarded scholarships by lottery. In making scholarship awards, priority was given to students attending public schools identified as "schools in need of improvement" (SINI) under the *No Child Left Behind Act* (NCLB) and to families that lacked the resources to take advantage of school choice options. Private schools participating in the program had to be located in the District of Columbia and agree to the requirements regarding nondiscrimination in admissions, fiscal accountability, and cooperation with the government-sponsored evaluation of the program.

Most of the private schools in the District of Columbia have taken part in the voucher program. In 2005 there were 88 "general service" private schools operating in the district that could, conceivably, participate in the OSP.[45] Of these 88 general service private schools, 68 of them (77 percent) chose to be part of the program in 2005–6, the OSP's second year of operation.[46] Participating schools were diverse in terms of their religious status: 34 percent were Catholic, 24 percent were independent private schools (many of which have a loose religious affiliation or tradition), 22 percent were non-Catholic faith-based, and 20 percent were secular private schools.[47] The independent private schools that participated in the voucher program included many of the District's elite preparatory academies, including Sidwell Friends School, which has educated the children of Presidents Bill Clinton and Barack Obama.

Student participation in the OSP began with a modest initial enrollment that eventually grew to fill the program. The $13 million annual appropriation was sufficient to fund up to 1,733 vouchers at the maximum value of $7,500 in a given year. Since the program was launched late in the spring of 2004, after many families had already made their educational plans for the coming year, the OSP was only partially filled by 1,027 scholarship users in its first year (identified herein as Cohort 1). After a second year of recruitment, the program filled to near capacity with 1,716 scholarship users (Cohort 2) in the fall of 2005. The program had carryover funds from its initial years of operation, both because it was under-enrolled during that period and because the average payment to participating students was somewhat below the $7,500 maximum, allowing 1,930 students to enroll in the fall of 2007. About 10 percent of the eligible population applied for vouchers in the first two years of implementation.[48]

Early Assessments of the Program

From the very beginning of the OSP, observers wondered who would actually participate in the program. During our interviews with key community stakeholders, some critics of the OSP expressed concern that the program would "cream" very active families and academically talented students from the public school system. At the other end of the spectrum of concerns, some program proponents feared that many eligible families, particularly those attending public "schools in need of improvement" (SINI), would not take advantage of the scholarship opportunity because they lacked the motivation, commitment, and other intangibles necessary for their children to succeed in private school.

The data indicate that the OSP largely reached its target audience of disadvantaged students in failing public schools. The first cohort of eligible applicants, in the spring of 2004, scored around the 41st national percentile in reading and the 47th national percentile in math—levels approximately equal to the performance of the average student in DCPS who did not apply to the program. Initial applicants were equally likely to have a disability and more likely to be African American or participating in the Federal Free/Reduced Price Lunch Program for low-income students than the average student in DCPS.[49] For the first two cohorts combined, about 43 percent of eligible applicants to the OSP had been attending regularly failing SINI public schools, though only 11 percent were enrolled in the public schools at the bottom performance quartile across the district.[50]

The OSP statute required that independent researchers conduct a statistical evaluation of the program, under the supervision of the US Department of Education's Institute of Education Sciences. One of us (Wolf) led that longitudinal study while also assisting with the qualitative research that is the focus of this book. The results of the government-sponsored experimental analyses of the OSP after one, two, three, and four-plus years in the program were reported to the US Congress and published in a leading public policy journal.[51] In sum, the highly rigorous quantitative evaluation of the District of Columbia OSP found that students tended to benefit educationally, clearly in terms of educational attainment and possibly also in terms of reading achievement, from the opportunity to exercise school choice by way of a voucher. The reading achievement gains from the program were clearest for the subgroups of students who entered the program in Cohort 1, were in grades K–8, were female, transferred from a school that was not SINI, and were not in the lower third of the achievement distribution when they joined the program. Parents reported being more satisfied with their child's school if they had been given an

Opportunity Scholarship, and they viewed the voucher schools as safer than District of Columbia public schools. In contrast, the students surveyed for the evaluation did not share their parents' enthusiasm regarding the safety and desirability of the schools they were able to access through the voucher program compared with the schools of DCPS.

Politics Re-enters the Equation

In the spring of 2009, the OSP was facing its statutory sunset. The third- and fourth-year evaluation reports on the program, which documented the initiative's reading and graduation rate benefits, had not yet been released. Program supporters, led by Senator Joe Lieberman (I-CT) and House Minority Leader John Boehner (R-OH) wanted the program to be reauthorized and extended for an additional five years. Opponents, led by Senator Dick Durbin (D-IL), wanted the program defunded. In March 2009, Durbin succeeded in limiting the program to continuing students, prompting US Department of Education Secretary Arne Duncan to rescind 216 Opportunity Scholarships that had been awarded to new participants.[52] Thus began a process of political jousting and political activism discussed at length in chapter 6 of this book.

In February and March of 2011, the reauthorization of the OSP was the subject of several congressional hearings.[53] In April, near the conclusion of the negotiations surrounding revisions to the Fiscal Year 2011 Budget Reconciliation Bill, House Speaker John Boehner insisted that the reauthorization of the OSP be included in the final package, an arrangement to which Senate Majority Leader Harry Reid and President Barack Obama reluctantly agreed.[54] Seven years after its launch as a pilot project and two years after being closed to new applicants, the District of Columbia OSP was given a new lease on life, strengthened, and expanded.[55] Still, President Obama's FY 2014 budget proposed to zero-out funding for the OSP.[56] The District of Columbia's OSP remains the most politically controversial school choice initiative in the country.

Filling Research Gaps and Answering Burning Questions

Why did a clear political consensus in support of the OSP fail to materialize quickly, in spite of the substantial evidence that parents like the program and participating students graduate at higher levels as a result of it? Why did the OSP parents and supporters not bring enough pressure on national Democratic leaders to keep the OSP open to new applicants in 2009 and 2010? What was happening in the lives of the OSP families while the program was first implemented, then restricted, then threatened with extinction?

Even the rigorous and extensive government evaluation of the OSP has left many questions that are begging answers. Why are parents so convinced that the voucher program has landed their children in better schools, when the students themselves report similar levels of school satisfaction and safety whether or not they were offered a scholarship? How has the District of Columbia school choice experience played out at the grassroots from the perspectives of the parents and students who participated in this pioneering school choice program? Moreover, why do some types of applicants—Cohort 1, K–8, non-SINI, higher-baseline performers, and females—demonstrate statistically significant reading gains while others do not? Why are the achievement gains for voucher students neither large nor consistent across the areas of both reading and math? This qualitative study seeks to complement what we know from the government evaluation by providing some answers to these and other lingering and important questions about the OSP's brief but dramatic history.

Research Approach and Design

From the fall of 2004 through the spring of 2008, our research team engaged students and parents in an extended conversation about their experiences with the OSP, using a phenomenological approach. Phenomenological research examines the lived experiences of individuals and groups in an effort to understand and give meaning to relatively new or unknown phenomena, in order to gain understanding of the essence of an experience from the viewpoint of those engaging in the activity.[57] In this study, an annual series of focus groups[58] and personal interviews were the primary methods used to gather information from participating families about discrete aspects of their experiences with the OSP. Study participants were asked a variety of questions: How did you first hear about the OSP? What were the greatest challenges your family faced? What best explains your satisfaction (or lack thereof) with the OSP? The following sections provide a general overview of our research methods, including recruitment and sampling, data collection, and analysis. Fuller details about the research approach are included in Appendix I.

Study Sample and Data Collection Methods

This study focused on 110 families representing approximately 180 students who were offered Opportunity Scholarships in 2004 (Cohort 1) or

2005 (Cohort 2). The Cohort 1 component of the study included 60 families and around 100 students; Cohort 2 consisted of an additional 50 families representing approximately 80 students. Although the study is not a causal analysis or a quantitative program evaluation, we employed various techniques commonly used in such studies to enhance the credibility of the findings.[59] In particular, we used a stratified random sampling technique, stratifying on student grade level at application and language spoken at home, when drawing our study participants, as described in detail in Appendix I.

A total of 37 professionally facilitated focus groups were conducted with study participants over a five-year span (see Table 2.2). Twenty-nine of the focus group sessions involved parents and eight sessions were conducted with middle and high school students. The purpose of the focus

Table 2.2   Calendar and Composition of Focus Group Sessions, 2004–8

Group	Fall 2004	Spring 2005	Spring 2006	Spring 2007	Spring 2008	Total
Cohort 1 Spanish-speaking Parents	x	x	x	x	Combined cohorts	4.5
Cohort 1 Elementary School Parents	x	x	x	x	x	5
Cohort 1 Middle School Parents	x	x	x	x	Combined w/ high	4.5
Cohort 1 High School Parents	x	x	x	x	Combined w/ middle	4.5
Cohort 1 Parents of Former Users					Combined cohorts	0.5
Cohort 2 Spanish-speaking Parents			x	x	Combined cohorts	2.5
Cohort 2 Elementary School Parents			x	x	x	3
Cohort 2 Middle School Parents			x	Combined w/ high	Combined w/ high	2
Cohort 2 High School Parents			x	Combined w/ middle	Combined w/ middle	2
Cohort 2 Parents of Former Users					Combined cohorts	0.5
Cohort 1 Middle Students	x	x	x			3
Cohort 1 High School Students	x	x	x			3
Cohort 2 Middle Students			x			1
Cohort 2 High School Students			x			1
Totals	**6**	**6**	**12**	**7**	**6**	**37**

groups was to present topics and questions to parents and older students who had received the OSP scholarships and provide them with opportunities to share with us their thoughts, opinions, and experiences (See Appendix II for a copy of a sample focus group session guide).

We augmented our focus group data with information from 65 semi-structured interviews with parents (34), high school students (2), community stakeholders (12), participating school staff (13), and program administrators (4). A total of 25 interviews were conducted in 2005, another 27 in 2007, and 13 in 2008. We also administered surveys to all participating schools in 2008 and received 24 completed responses. The central purpose of the individual interviews was to provide participants and stakeholders with an environment, completely free from any possible peer influences, in which to discuss with us their experiences with the OSP and to share their views on the strengths and limitations of the program (see Appendix III for a sample interview script).

Finally, in 2008, we invited our study participants to a large meeting room in a downtown Washington hotel to "poll" them regarding their OSP experience. A total of 38 substantive questions were projected, one at a time, onto a display screen and each participant was asked to select a response from a fixed list using a handheld wireless keypad device (see Appendix IV for the polling script). This more precise and anonymous form of gauging participant responses, which is now commonly used in college classrooms, allowed us to associate a specific frequency with each response category and explicitly compare the distribution of responses by cohort and topical focus group.

We have designed our data presentation strategies to retain the authenticity of the qualitative data that study participants provided to us while also protecting the confidentiality of their statements. We quote participants literally. Although we attach formal names to interviewees who we profile at the start of each chapter, those names are fictitious. Our study participants were very real to us but, consistent with the norms and regulations regarding research on human subjects, they must remain anonymous to the public. Still, we think that these various qualitative data collection and reporting strategies allowed us to uncover the lived experiences of the OSP families and share the essence of their school choice journey with you.

Conclusion

School vouchers are a mechanism to allow parents to choose a private school for their child with the assistance of government funds. They have been controversial in the United States because they provide an alternative to the assignment of students to schools by address or neighborhood. As of January 2014, 21 school voucher programs existed in the US. All but one of them were targeted to students with particular education-related disadvantages.

One of the best known and most controversial school voucher program is the District of Columbia Opportunity Scholarship Program, enacted in 2004. During its pilot from 2004 to 2009, the OSP provided vouchers worth up to $7,500 to low-income District of Columbia parents to enroll their child in a private school of their choosing. Nearly 4,000 students were offered vouchers during the pilot, and nearly 3,000 students initially used their voucher. A rigorous statistical evaluation of the program concluded that the older students in the OSP graduated from high school at significantly higher rates as a result of the program. Evidence also suggests reading gains from the program, especially for certain subgroups of students, but there was no evidence that the initiative affected math scores. The OSP remained controversial and was closed to new applicants after its pilot period ended in 2009 but was reauthorized in 2011. Political disputes over whether or not to fund the program continue.

Given the unique nature of the OSP within the context of the US attempt to improve the quality of education and academic outcomes for low-income students, it is critically important that we understand the strengths and limitations of federally funded voucher programs through the actual experiences of those who participated in the OSP. The transition from traditional public to private schools for low-income families presents unique opportunities for the students and their families, as well as unfamiliar challenges. The more we understand about their experiences with this pioneering school choice program, the better prepared we will be in the future to discuss and implement other programs that seek to produce positive outcomes for students. As with all stories based on real-life experiences, however, this one reflects only those encountered by our narrators; others' lives or experiences may be different. Thus, *The School Choice Journey* that we present here was the journey of a particular group of people: over 100 parent and student participants in our nation's first federal private school voucher program. And so our documentation of the journey begins.

3

What Were Families Looking for in the Voucher Program?

This is the first in a series of chapters that illuminate many of the discrete aspects of the parental school choice journey for OSP families. In this chapter, we explore what motivated families to participate in the OSP, what families looked for in schools, and the importance of reliable information. Each distinct question forms a chapter section. In each section, we begin by providing an overview of the theoretical debates and prior research regarding the question. We then allow the study participants themselves to provide insights into their thinking and behavior, drawing upon the interview, focus group, and polling data that we accumulated over the course of our study.

Using personal interviews as an example of how the participating families informed our analysis, we would like to quickly share a summary of an interview we conducted with Joyce and Larry. They are married and appeared to be in their mid-40s during the time of our interview. They have been in the United States for about five years and are originally from East Africa. They both speak English with a heavy accent, yet Larry has a good command of the language. Joyce is soft-spoken and shy, and she said very little during the interview. Most of what was shared about their family was articulated by Larry. The oldest of their three children, who they describe as very hardworking, used the Opportunity Scholarship for three years and has graduated from high school. Their other two children were in private schools during the 2007–8 school year, however these students were transferred to another private school the following year. Joyce and Larry are leaving the current private school because they believe the teaching standards are declining, and they feel that dwindling resources are to blame.

Their primary reason for pursuing a private school for their children was to integrate religion into their children's educational experience.

Although they define themselves as Orthodox Christian, they consider Catholic schools as morally compatible with their religious beliefs. Also, Larry feels that private schools will provide his children an edge within an increasingly competitive global economy.

Joyce and Larry were considered middle class in their native country, but they were essentially starting from scratch in the United States. As relatively new immigrants, Larry often feels invisible and powerless over his economic situation. Therefore, he views the OSP as priceless. In fact, he notes that the scholarship relieves some of the discomfort he feels as a shuttle bus driver for a local university. He believes that the program is needed more now than before because it will take years to turn around the public schools in Washington, DC.

We learn three key lessons about the school choice journey from the interviews with parents and other data presented in this chapter. First, most of the families say that they are traveling to a destination more than escaping from a less-desired situation. They speak often of the prospective benefits of the schools they can access through choice, and they seldom mention the disappointing and discouraging conditions in their child's previous school. Second, families appear to have distinctive and evolving preferences regarding where they most want the school choice journey to take them. At the start of their experience with school choice, the families were divided into a large group that said academic factors were most important to them in choosing a school, a substantial minority that said safety factors were paramount, and a small remaining group of parents that listed a wide variety of school characteristics as the most critical including religion, foreign languages, ethnic diversity, and school location. Third, through the course of their school choice journey, parent priorities regarding the most important features of schools shifted in interesting ways. Ultimately, families expressed a need for some "directions" at the start of their journey. They saw information about school choice and schooling alternatives as critical to their ability to choose wisely.

Starting a School Choice Journey through the OSP

Participating in a means-tested publicly funded program entails a complex and sometimes intrusive set of procedures that often deters eligible families from pursuing such a program.[1] As we began to engage the families and learn more about them, it was clear that individually they were motivated to pursue the OSP for a wide range of reasons. Collectively, however, they shared some very similar experiences pertaining to their introduction to school choice. Prior to the launch of the OSP, the majority of families who participated in the study had not ventured outside their neighborhood public schools to explore other educational opportunities. Over two-thirds of the focus group families we polled in 2008 said that their child attended a traditional public school prior to participating in the OSP (see Figure 3.1).

Many of the participating families never imagined that they would have the means and opportunity to enroll their children in some of the most prestigious private schools in America. They expressed gratitude for the financial support that would afford their children the opportunity to increase their educational options. For instance, one parent who heard about the program through the Washington Scholarship Fund's (WSF) multipronged recruitment campaign said:

> I was constantly looking for financial assistance; I went to libraries, and I asked a lot of people. It was suggested that I apply to this program. Then I read the ads in the newspaper, which finally convinced me to take a shot and apply.[2]

This parent had been exploring school choice possibilities well before the OSP was established. Once she became aware of the OSP, she was finally able to pursue other school options.

Although the families were grateful for the opportunity to exercise parental school choice, many of them also seemed a bit daunted by the responsibility to choose their child's school. As low-income urban parents, few participants had actual experience purchasing major consumer items

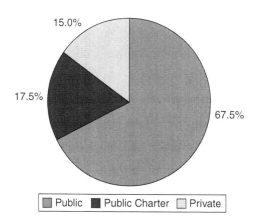

Figure 3.1   Type of School Children Attended Prior to the OSP

Notes: Based on keypad responses by 40 parents participating in final focus group session, May 2008, Washington, DC.

such as houses or even cars. As adult members of a capitalist system, they certainly engaged in consumer behavior on a regular basis; however, few of them were familiar with the process of evaluating multiple providers of a highly consequential product or service such as a school for their child. As will be discussed in more detail in chapter 4, many of the OSP families in our focus groups had family structures headed by a single parent, or alternatively by two parents but with a minimal support network. These families not only tended to lack experience with major consumer purchases, they also possessed limited resources in the areas of time and social networks that help consumers get what they seek from major purchases.

Previous Research on What Motivates Families to Seek School Choice

There is general agreement in the research literature that parents seek educational choices beyond their assigned neighborhood public school for a variety of specific reasons but with clear common themes. Most prominent among the motivations behind school choice appears to be that parents seek a better educational alternative for their children. Surveys of the literature on why parents choose schools suggest that a more effective educational program tends to be the most common reason given for exercising choice, followed by a religious educational environment and a better match between the cultural values of the family and school.[3] Milton Friedman's famous argument that universal school choice would generate competitive pressure on all schools to improve academically was at least partly premised on this expectation that the main parental motivation for engaging in school choice is to improve academic outcomes for their children.[4]

Prior research on parent motivations to use school choice has not been monolithic. One question is whether parents seek a better school in the absolute sense or a school that is a better "fit" for their particular child. Bruce Fuller and his colleagues conclude that parents look to match their children to schools that serve their specific needs: "When benefits are targeted to low-income families, many parents do actively choose a school that they believe better fits their educational preferences than does the neighborhood school."[5] As Jeffrey Henig writes:

> Even under the best of circumstances, the neighborhood public school will not adequately serve the needs of every neighborhood child. This can be due to the particular characteristics of the child, the particular limitations of the school, or a simple lack of fit between one and the other.[6]

Recent survey research by James Kelly III and Benjamin Scafidi confirms the distinctiveness of many parents' view of their child's educational needs, indicating that "the process of discovery is guided by a personal vision, and sustained by a personal conviction, of what is in the best interests of their child."[7]

There also is some disagreement in the research literature regarding whether school choice families tend to be primarily running away from a bad schooling situation or running toward a good one. Low-income parents and students in urban neighborhood public schools frequently report disturbing levels of violence in their schools and subsequent concerns about student safety.[8] At the same time, parents seem to be hopeful of finding an attractive destination on their school choice journey. In a sophisticated statistical analysis of the background factors that predict whether or not students participated in the Florida Tax-Credit Scholarship Program, which operates much like a voucher program, Cassandra Hart finds a mix of both push and pull. Participants were more likely than eligible non-participants to come from public schools with poor safety ratings and low test scores, signaling a push away from something bad, but also were more likely to have a lot of varied private school choices nearby, evidence of a pull towards something better.[9] Obviously, school choosers are looking for a change of scenery. Whether they are mainly seeking to escape from a bad situation or are simply interested in a distinct school that might be a better fit for their child remains an open question whose answer might vary across different choice programs and contexts.

What Specifically Motivated Families to Participate in the OSP?

The first year of the program was filled with new opportunities and challenges for the participating families. Most of them explained that they were excited about the chance to enroll their children in private schools. Their expressed motivations for exercising school choice tended to cluster around three themes: choice, academic improvement, and religion.

Several parents described their interest in the Opportunity Scholarship Program simply in terms of having more choices. Parents in separate focus groups made virtually identical statements to that effect when they said:

> What's most important is the education, the opportunity to have another type of education, an option.[10]

[The scholarships] give you the opportunity to choose from several schools. You know you're not just stuck with one school. They offer several schools to choose from—I think that's very good.[11]

From the statements of these parents, however, it is impossible to determine if they sought school choice as desirable in and of itself—simply due to the act of choosing—or because they were confident that many choices would enable them to match their child to an appropriate school.

A second motivation for using school choice that was expressed by families was academic improvement. As one parent stated:

This is what I tell my kids: "I tell them that this is an opportunity for you to strive. Do your best, take advantage of it." That's what I tell my children.[12]

A student in our focus groups echoed this sentiment, saying of the OSP that "It helps us get into a better school to help us learn more."[13] Another parent had a very specific academic reason for seeking parental school choice for her son: "He's very intelligent as well, and he needed to be challenged."[14] These OSP participants saw the program as offering them access to academic environments more challenging than they had experienced previously.

In addition to the academic characteristics of the school environment, some focus group parents mentioned access to a religious schooling environment as their primary motivation for seeking parental school choice. A married couple in our focus groups explained that "religion was very important for us because that helps for the culture of the child."[15] They proceeded to describe how they viewed religion as a force to shape the values of their children and wanted that moral formation to take place in school as well as in church and at home. Other parents said they were motivated to place their children in a school that included religious instruction because they associated religion with a well-disciplined school environment. For example:

I like my children to go to a school where religious education is taking place because I believe religion will discipline the children.[16]

Consistent with the theme of religion, one parent simply said about the OSP: "This is a blessing."[17]

A married immigrant couple said that their primary motivation to participate in the OSP was grounded in their strong religious beliefs and the chance to enroll their children in a Catholic school. Though they are not Catholic, they expressed the opinion that the Catholic religion complements their moral and religious beliefs. Their secondary motivation for participating in the program was their view that a private school would give their children the edge based on their understanding of what they called "today's complex global economy."[18]

Most of what we learned about what motivated families was captured during the first and second year of the program. By the fourth year, some parents offered a different perspective on what initially motivated them. It appears that hindsight and increased comfort with the focus groups helped some respondents to be more clear and precise about what spurred them to set out on their school choice journey. For example, one mother explained her decision to enroll her child in the OSP as an attempt to alter her daughter's attitude about education and learning. She explained that her daughter was simply not excited about school prior to the OSP and, as a result, was not performing well in the public system. The mother pursued the OSP because she hoped that private school would offer her daughter a different environment. She hoped that smaller class sizes and more individualized attention would improve her daughter's outlook and her chances for success. By the fourth year, she was confident she had made the right decision.

One mother, who was raised and attended school in Africa, participated in the OSP because the private school her daughter enrolled in offers a culturally rich curriculum. This particular mother had learned several languages during her upbringing and was adamant about her children having the same experience. The school she chose includes a dual-language immersion program. After just three years of study, her daughter speaks and writes Arabic fluently.[19]

As can be seen from the comments made by participants presented above, most respondents provided "forward looking" motivations for signing up for the OSP. They spoke of the many options available to their children through the program, especially schools with more academic rigor, religious and cultural diversity, and language programs. Their comments suggest that they were enticed by the OSP, not necessarily driven to it by intolerable conditions associated with the previous schools their children attended. Yet, a small number of participants suggest they were fleeing a bad situation. For example, a high school student indicated that the OSP served as an escape from feeling trapped:

> It [the OSP] gave you a way out of nowhere. You're not used to being on top of everything... you're not the one that got the killer jump shot, but you're still trying to go somewhere and go to school and get away from this environment and you've got that opportunity to use your scholarship.[20]

In the opinion of this student, the OSP offered a path to a much different and brighter future.

Choosing Schools

Once families decided to take the first formal step in the journey, the choice process began when parents completed the program application and began their research on prospective schools. The families were provided with a school guidebook, compiled by the WSF, which presented basic information about each school to help them start their search process. They learned, for example, that more than half of the private schools participating in the program in 2005–6 were faith-based schools.[21] The student population in these private schools was typically much smaller than in the public schools that many families were leaving, and the average student-to-teacher ratio was approximately 10 to 1.[22] In addition to the general information provided by the WSF, the government evaluation of the program found that participating private schools were not significantly different from their public counterparts in terms of the amenities they offered to students; both public and private schools offered similar access to special programs for advanced learners, libraries, gymnasiums, and an art program.[23]

The private schools that took part in the program were disparate in some seemingly important ways. Only a very small number of participating schools offered separate academic programs and services for students with special needs. The schools as a whole were less likely to provide their students with school counselors or a nurse's office. Only a few of them offered special classes for English-language learners.[24] We might expect these differences to alter the decision-making process for eligible families, but they were rarely mentioned during the focus groups.

The specific school preferences that choosing parents have is central to the debate about the efficacy and desirability of school choice programs. As Bruce Fuller and his colleagues argue, "choice schemes assume that the family is highly rational, acts from clear preferences, and is able to effectively demand action from local schools and teachers."[25] If parents do not really know what to look for in a school, or if they seek objectionable conditions such as racial uniformity, then their educational choices will be unlikely to result in educational benefits for their child or society in general.

The Fordham Institute recently released a report based on a scientific national survey of parents that offers important insights regarding what, specifically, parents look for in schools. Most parents expressed a "vanilla" preference for schools with high expectations for student achievement and behavior; a challenging curriculum that includes science, technology, engineering, and math (STEM); and some character-development and life-skills instruction.[26] Beyond that general consensus, the study identified the following "market niches" based on strong secondary preferences that were not universally shared by other parents in the sample:

- Pragmatists (36% of parents)—instruction in IT and vocational/technical topics;
- Jeffersonians (24%)—instruction in citizenship, democracy, and leadership;
- Test Score Hawks (23%)—high test scores;
- Multiculturalists (22%)—teaches about diverse cultures and how to appreciate differences in others;
- Bohemians (15%)—instruction in arts and music;
- Strivers (12%)—prepares children for a challenging college experience.[27]

Similarly, Kelly and Scafidi, in their more focused survey of private school choice participants in Georgia, found that nearly 40 percent of parents listed "better education" or "better learning environment" as their most important factor in choosing a private school, followed by a "religious education" (28%), "improved student safety" (7%), "smaller class sizes" (4%), and "better preparation for college" (4%).[28] Paul Teske and his colleagues, in surveying a representative sample of 800 parents in Milwaukee, Denver, and Washington, DC, reported that 45 percent of respondents list some variant of "academic quality" as the factor they most seek from schools, followed by a distinctive curriculum or theme (19%) and a convenient location (11%).[29] Jennifer Steele and her associates found that parents in New Orleans who enroll their children in public charter schools view a school's academic curriculum as the most important school feature (37%), followed by student achievement (32%) and discipline policies (27%).[30] A survey of over 1,000 parents we conducted in a study of school shopping in Detroit reveals that parents most clearly seek academic quality when selecting a school, "with secondary emphasis on safety/discipline, convenience, or extracurricular activities."[31]

These survey results regarding parental preferences for schools reflect a combination of "e pluribus" and "unum." Parents are unified behind the idea that solid academics and safety are important in schools but have very distinctive preferences for the curricular emphasis and culture of their child's school. Under such conditions, school choice programs would want to let "a thousand flowers bloom," provide some oversight of school quality, and place great responsibility on parents to fit students to the proper schools.[32]

The OSP serves a group of low-income urban families that are almost exclusively African American or Latino. What evidence do we have regarding the preferences of such distinctive families for specific characteristics in schools? Regarding the student demographics of the school, Laura Hamilton and Kasey Guin conclude that urban families tend to give little weight to race considerations but do factor school poverty rates into their decision.[33] They report that "Many parents believe that peer effects (the average ability of the child's schoolmates) and resources (e.g. class size) are important determinants of student outcomes and, therefore, are likely to emphasize these factors if they have information about them."[34] Mark Schneider and his colleagues go even farther in concluding that "Lower socioeconomic status and minority parents are more likely to value schools that perform the bedrock function of providing a safe environment and the fundamentals of education."[35] Their claims are consistent with two experimental evaluations of means-tested school choice programs in Washington, DC that have found that parents who choose schools are most likely to describe "academic quality" as the most important reason for their selection, with school safety, discipline, and location as additional important concerns.[36]

Do parent views regarding the most important features of schools likely change over time? We might think so, even though, to our knowledge, no one has explored that question in depth. Abraham Maslow famously theorized that humans face an ordered hierarchy of needs, from the basic physiological needs of food, clothing, and shelter, to the need for safety, then love, then respect and esteem, and finally, what Maslow called, "self-actualization." According to Maslow, people who lack a basic need will neglect all "higher" needs until that basic need is fulfilled. Thus, a starving person will risk their freedom by stealing bread; only secure people will seek love; and only people who are nurtured and loved will devote themselves to the kinds of career achievements and civic activities that will bring them public respect.[37] If Maslow's theory of human motivation is correct and applies to education, we might expect parents in the OSP initially to emphasize the features of schools that satisfy more basic student needs, such as school safety. Once those basic needs have been satisfied, we might expect parents to proceed to focus on higher-order student needs such as educational achievement and preparation for college.

What Families Reported in the Focus Groups
about Choosing Schools

In the program's first year, parents in the focus groups most commonly identified safety as their primary considerations in choosing the best school for their children. Some of them also suggested they wanted an educational environment in which learning was grounded in faith or values. Secondary to these two issues, they sought academic rigor, smaller classes, and an opportunity for their children to learn a second language. Their desire for language classes, as well as their focus on ethnic and racial diversity, suggests that some parents valued the richer cultural experiences and academic curriculum available in private schools. Interestingly, we uncovered substantial evidence that the preferences of families evolved over the course of their experience of the OSP, just as Maslow would have predicted, from a greater focus on satisfying basic student needs to a greater focus on satisfying higher-order student needs.

In their initial year of participation in the OSP, as noted, parents overwhelmingly mentioned safety as their top consideration in choosing a school for their child. In every initial parent focus group that we facilitated, including those in Spanish and regardless of whether the session involved the parents of elementary school, middle school, or high school students, the safety of the school was most frequently mentioned by parents as their number-one school choice consideration. When asked what school feature was most important to them, many parents simply stated "safety" and left it at that. Some parents did elaborate on the idea:

> [Safety because]...it's...hard for the kids to really...want to go...outside because the neighborhoods in which they live are unsafe.[38]

> The safety of the school and [a school] that's gonna nurture [the student]. Not to hold her back but to push her forward.[39]

One parent with limited English-speaking skills stressed the importance of safety and how it influenced her school choice decision:

> I think safety was a lot of reasons why most parents chose different schools was safety. Also that was a big issue for me...safety.[40]

The number-one concern of families in the initial years of the OSP was to use the school choice program as a way to get their children into schools that they viewed as safe.

Aside from safety, some families placed a strong emphasis on the moral environment of the school. Families of Hispanic descent, in particular, continued to look for schools that offered religious instruction as part of the curriculum and enforced moral norms:

> We feel like the values are important. We like to have the children respect God. We feel that that is very important because when the children are not taught about God, they do not believe and lack guidance and structure.[41]

Another factor is the state of the child himself. The environment is very important, what is going on in the school, how many girls are pregnant.[42]

One parent spoke of how the moral environment of the school is important not only to the students directly but also indirectly through its effect on the teachers:

They don't give you [the] entire background and history of the teachers. But I wanna know that they're personable, they're loving, they'll tend to the children's needs on all levels. Pretty much overall they're for the children, the children are number one, and [that they] will provide services for the children in the educational field, working with children.[43]

For a plurality of the OSP parents, the moral environment of the school, particularly if it was infused with religious values, was the most important characteristic of their school of choice.

When parents did mention an academic feature of a school that was most important to them, it tended to be class size. As one parent stated, "I was really, really interested in trying to get my son in a smaller class."[44] Another parent said, "I was looking for smaller classroom settings so they have better management over the classroom."[45]

Although many participants did not explicitly articulate their vision, most parents clearly wanted their children to have a learning experience that would better prepare them for the future:

The curriculum is very different, and the [complexity of the] language is very different. I looked at the difference, and I said to them that this school is preparing them to go to college and be executives versus...being blue-collar workers.[46]

Another parent argued that the smaller size of private schools, coupled with their moral environment, created the conditions needed for student success:

I'm interested in better education for my son, and I know that will be done not necessarily in public schools, but in private school in a smaller, more formal atmosphere.[47]

Some parents simply could not limit themselves to a single most important school characteristic. A concise example of this is the parent who said, "I believed private school [has] better discipline and academics."[48] A more effusive parent, when asked to describe the most important feature of her child's school, simply could not contain herself:

> I wanted structure 'cause where she came from, she'd been in public and charters all her life. I just wanted a change, a better structure, safety, a better environment, a better learning system for her, and I got that through the scholarship program. I love the school she's in.[49]

In the third year of our focus groups, we attempted to determine if parental views of the most important characteristics of schools had changed perceptibly. We had recorded on a flip-chart page, hidden from the focus group participants, the top three choices (with safety number one in all cases) from the initial year of the study for each specific focus group. We then asked the Year 3 focus group parents, many of whom had also participated in the previous two years of focus groups, to describe their current view of the most important features of a school, and we recorded their top three choices. We then revealed to each group what they had said in previous focus groups and asked them to comment on any differences.

The results of this exercise greatly surprised us. In all eight initial parent focus groups—four for Cohort 1 and four for Cohort 2 participants—the parents had most frequently mentioned safety as the most important school characteristic. By the third year of our study, however, safety was still rated the most important school feature by only one of the eight parent focus groups, the Cohort 2 Spanish language group. The seven other parent focus groups in Year 3 most commonly mentioned other school characteristics, such as a strong curriculum, small class size, academic rigor, or a religious environment as most important. Three of these parent focus groups did not even consider school safety to be among the top-three most important concerns. Such a stunning turnaround cried out for an explanation.

And in explaining why they no longer viewed safety as the most important feature of a chosen school, without any guidance from moderators, parents provided statements on the hierarchy of human needs that could have come directly out of Abraham Maslow's mouth. One example is the parent who said:

> Well I think once you pull your children out of public schools and you get comfortable with the private atmosphere, safety becomes no longer an issue because they are safe. So then you can focus on what is important, and that is the curriculum.[50]

Another OSP parent, when confronted with the dissonance between the safety obsession of the initial parent focus groups and the interest in almost anything except school safety in Year 3, responded:

> No, I understand...I share the same view now that they're in school the way school is supposed to be...Safety is always an issue; however, we feel more comfortable now, and we can look at other things our kids need in order to achieve.[51]

Perhaps the most complete statement of Maslow's hierarchy as applied to schools comes from a parent who said:

> I also think that private and charter schools are really pushing to raise the children's academic standards, but more than this for me security...is very important...It's useless if a school has a great academic program, but there are shootings outside.[52]

After direct experience with the schools, parents of high school students, in particular, appear to have readjusted some of the criteria by which they choose a school for their children. Once they were able to put their child in an environment that put safety issues to rest, having satisfied that basic need, they had a chance to focus on the academic concerns that have a profound impact on where their children go and what they do after high school. Still, one focus group participant explained how fundamental school safety concerns are to inner-city parents:

> I don't have to worry about him being...hit by somebody else fighting or throwing kids...I don't have to worry about the fighting in the school. They might have one or two little misunderstandings, but it's not an everyday occurrence like it was at [his previous public school]. At [his previous public school], they fought every day—it was always commotion—so safety is still number one for me.[53]

This parent could not let go of his concern with school safety even after his child's transfer to a safer private school—through the use of an Opportunity Scholarship—had satisfied that basic need.

The Importance of Information

Information is central to consumer activity in any context. For example, shoppers rely on clothing label information to assess the fit and quality of an outfit, and they look to food packaging information to determine its likely taste and nutritional value. Magazines such as *Consumer Reports* and countless Internet sites provide guidance and comprehensive consumer information to eager subscribers and Web-surfers. The general agreement is that informed consumers help make markets work properly. According to Hamilton and Guin, "A critical factor influencing parental choice behaviors is the quality of information available to parents on the schools that operate within the choice system."[54] High-quality and accessible information supports educational markets by avoiding or minimizing "information asymmetry" between suppliers and consumers.[55]

Well-informed consumers are more likely to match their children to appropriate schools. If parents are primarily interested in academic quality, the presence of a large group of well-informed choosers will pressure schools to improve the quality of their educational product. The main areas of disagreement surround the questions of what school-information sources are most helpful, how much information is enough, and how many choosers need to be well informed in order for schools to respond in desirable ways to their preferences.

The three most commonly discussed sources of consumer information about schools are information centers and guides, social networks, and personal site visits. Henig argues that general sources, such as information centers and school directories, are especially valuable because they are available to all parents, regardless of their personal resources.[56] Citing several previous studies, Hamilton and Guin suggest that "social networks, including extended family and friends, are a primary source of information about schools for many parents."[57] Amy Stuart Wells stresses the importance of school site visits, noting that school choosers who select a school without a visit are more likely later to express buyer's remorse.[58]

Although research has been unable to pinpoint exactly how much information is necessary to make an individual feel that he or she is an effective educational consumer, the general agreement is that more is better. Families that are able to gather information from multiple sources and visit several different schools likely will be able to separate the more reliable from the less helpful information and draw accurate contrasts between various educational suppliers, services, and products. Moreover, recent research indicates that parents have more accurate understandings of the key characteristics of their child's school if they have been given the opportunity and the responsibility to choose it.[59]

The Importance of Information to OSP Parents

From the very outset, parents identified high-quality and accurate information as critical to their ability to successfully select schools. As one parent stated:

> The level of communication—letters, phone calls, follow-up letters, follow-up phone calls—I mean sometimes we are busy, and we need that.[60]

The parents in this study reported receiving information from four main sources: (1) WSF staff, (2) school marketing materials often distributed during school fairs, (3) meetings with school personnel during visits, and (4) other parents. In the final year of the study, we asked parents which of these information sources had been the most helpful to them in making their school choices. School personnel and marketing materials from participating schools were rated as the key sources of information by the most parents, followed by the WSF staff, and advice from other parents.

In addition to ranking information by level of helpfulness, the final focus group allowed parents to describe the different sources of information they relied upon at various stages of their school choice journey. In fact, it was around the issue of school choice information that we, as researchers, first observed a clear distinction between families firmly grounded in a "client" mentality, those oriented as "consumers," and those willing and able to go the distance to citizenship activities.

The type, quality, and amount of information about the participating schools were a "work in progress" in the first two years of the program. In the first year, parents relied heavily on published information provided by the WSF and the participating private schools, especially the school directory, to narrow down the list of potential schools for their children. The WSF school directory included general information about each participating school: location, religious affiliation, facilities, transportation options, and other details:

> That packet of information gave us all the schools that were available and information about each school...where they were located, what facilities they had, if they had a gym or a library, [if] they had music, [a] language program, drama...My kids are artists, so I wanted a school that had all that.[61]

As their experiences with the program increased, parents began to provide more feedback and deeper insights about how information and communication could be improved. We viewed these developments as attempts by the parents to become better informed and thus more effective "new education consumers."[62] During the first year, for instance, one parent pointed out that information about the availability of school-based lunches at each participating school would be very helpful. Other parents requested clarification about specific program rules and regulations. For example, what happens if their family moves out of the District of Columbia? What happens if their household income exceeds the maximum limits? How are scholarship funds transferred to the school?

These questions seem completely reasonable within the context of the abrupt launch of the OSP in February 2004. Within three months after the federal legislation was passed, the WSF was selected as the program administrator, and the marketing and student recruitment processes began. The WSF was charged with managing the application process and helping parents identify schools. This combination of activities—the "launch" of the school choice journey, if you will—unfolded while private schools were finalizing their entering classes for the next school year, and it was quite a whirlwind experience for most families. Though the parents were initially excited about the scholarship program, they did not seem completely comfortable with their school searches based on the limited information that was initially available to them.

Increasingly, information about the OSP began to spread across the District of Columbia, which included derogatory rumors about the impetus behind the program. For example, a parent shared that

> Many people object to the program because they believe that the school from their neighborhood will stop receiving money, money that goes to my daughter instead. And that is not true.[63]

Having initially accepted whatever information they could get, mostly sporadic and on the fly, to make schooling decisions during the frantic initial implementation of the program, parents later focused on identifying credible and accurate sources of information.

By Years 2 and 3 of the program, parents acknowledged that while the information in the school directory often was helpful, it had two critical shortcomings. First, the description of the schools was not always accurate. As one frustrated parent conveyed to us:

> [I had problems finding] the location. I had a problem because some of the information in the directories, it is not accurate, as in they don't give the right information. And I tried the website. Still, what is on the website and when you go to see the school is also different. I try to ask friends,

teachers, and other kind of people, but I didn't get the exact information I wanted.[64]

Second, even when the directory information was accurate, many parents came to realize that it was not sufficient for making a decision as impactful as school choice. Once they had a year or two of scholarship participation under their belts, parents began to seek more evaluative information about the program's private schools as well as information about teacher qualifications and student outcomes.

> I think [what] you should do is to put academic performance, maybe the SAT-9, in the directory, where someone can look up and think…"This is a good school," or "This is not a good school."[65]

Over time, parents began to accumulate information from a variety of sources to make their school choice decisions. Many of them exercised the option to move their child from one school to a different one and, in order to make a sound decision, made several school visits and talked with parents of students in the target schools. This is in contrast to the swift judgments they had to make when initially entering the program.

Parents gradually shifted their emphasis away from printed information and began to rely more on school visits and face-to-face conversations with school administrators, staff, and other parents. The following third-year parent described the challenge and process of developing a holistic picture of the school:

> On paper, they can tell you that it's the best school in the world, but I think that visiting is important. For example, I went to visit the school while school was in session so I could see the interaction between the teachers and students, the directors…one gets a better feel about how the school operates…You can observe how the students behave or if the teachers are yelling at the students. Also while at the school, you think about other issues, such as security and location.[66]

A Spanish-speaking parent suggested that school visits are especially important when your family comes from a different culture:

> Well, when you first approach them, you sort of feel bad, because you know space is very limited and, being a foreigner, it's different, so it helps to talk with the directors and other parents, to discuss the program and student life. This helps you to feel not like an outsider. You know you are being given this scholarship in this school, so these conversations help bridge

the cultural gap. You want to be part of the school. If they treat you bad, then you know.[67]

It took time for families to grow familiar with the ins and outs of parental school choice and with the challenges associated with making an informed decision. By Year 4, many parents had become more experienced in evaluating educational options, and they were able to offer advice to others who were just beginning the journey. One parent who had withdrawn her child from the program suggested that school shoppers observe firsthand how teachers and administrators handle the daily business of working with students before they make their school selection:

> They need to go visit that school and make sure that what they're saying is what they're offering, what they do have, and actually see it, go there. Go during the time of day that it should be given to make sure that it is being done.[68]

Although this parent had "buyer's remorse" regarding her school choice, she indicated that the problem stemmed from the choice process that she followed. A more thorough school selection process could have produced a better outcome, she reasoned.

The major divide that we observed regarding the families in our focus groups were between those who thought that non-parental organizations should play a stronger role in ensuring the quality of private school choices and those who thought it was entirely the responsibility of parents to choose wisely. We view the former group of parents as having a "client" perspective regarding the OSP. Parents with this client perspective offered recommendations such as

> I think WSF—if they would check into these schools you know just make sure they up to speed. Because if they on the same level as the public schools, why should you pay them this amount [of tuition]?[69]

Or they simply stated, "They need to evaluate some of those schools."[61]

The staff at the WSF did not perceive their role as including rating the quality of schools beyond ensuring that they were actually operating and properly managing their finances. The WSF staff also did not think that they should be matching students to schools on behalf of the school choice families. As one WSF administrator explained:

> I think that our role is more to educate [the families] about what to ask and who to ask than to actually give them the information, because we

can't play a subjective role...Often they ask us "Well, what do you think?" "What's the good schools?..." What we'll say is that it depends on what your family needs, which is the right school for you...Have you asked these questions. Did you go to our school visit? Did you send your child to the shadow visit? Did you ask them what they're teaching, and how their kids are doing? Did you ask them that if the children take the...test that the kids in independent schools take?[70]

Families with a client disposition on school choice tended to be disappointed with the limited amount of direction provided by the OSP at the start of their school choice journey.

Families with a "consumer" perspective on school choice were a better fit for the OSP compared to those who were more client focused. School choice consumers accepted that it was their responsibility to ensure that the school they selected was of high quality and a good fit for their child's needs. Parents with a consumer orientation toward choice tended to describe to us an extensive school choice process that relied more on personal interactions with school staff than on school publicity or the judgments of program officials. As one consumer-oriented parent said:

It was very helpful to visit the school and talk to the admissions people and to get information about what the school offers; the program, it did help me.[71]

Consumer-oriented parents also sought input from other people, including their child as well as members of the parents' social network.

She was there at the school to [inter]act with the kids and see if she liked it...at the end of the day the principal called me and told me how she did and when she got home I asked her and she said she liked it, so I told her that I would be applying for her to go to that school the next following year.[72]

Word of mouth...word of mouth; I have a friend whose children have gone there before, and they let me know certain things.[73]

Certainly some of these savvy parents entered the OSP with well-developed consumer skills and the confidence to deploy them in their school search; yet, it was apparent to us that other OSP families began their school choice journey with more of a client perspective and transitioned to more of a consumer orientation due to their experiences in the program, some of which involved hard lessons.

According to political scientist Robert Putnam, social capital "refers to features of social organizations such as networks, norms, and social trust that facilitate coordination and cooperation for mutual benefit."[74] In the frantic period of program implementation, there was little time for communal activities to promote social capital among the OSP participants. To respond to this challenge and to improve the flow of information to parents, the WSF facilitated the creation of the "Parent Empowerment" group in the spring of 2005, led by Virginia Walden Ford, who is one of the leading school choice advocates in the country. The empowerment group met monthly and discussed matters of general concern to the OSP families such as clarifying what school fees are covered by the voucher, what resources are available to help parents select schools, and what responsibilities families have to participate in the government-mandated statistical evaluation of the program. Once the continuation of the OSP became uncertain in spring 2009, the empowerment group served as a mechanism for activating parents to communicate with politicians and ask for their support of the program.

In addition to the official Parent Empowerment group, participants in our study found the focus groups themselves to be an invaluable source of support and information. Throughout the project, we witnessed parents exchanging tips and sometimes even telephone numbers after focus groups had officially adjourned. Some parents asked us to convene the focus groups more frequently so that they could have more opportunities to share their experiences and hear about other families' school choice journeys. During our final data collection session in 2008, we asked participants if the focus groups permitted them "to thoughtfully express" their experiences with the OSP. The overwhelming majority of respondents strongly agreed with that statement. Although it was not intended by us, our focus group research project apparently ended up serving as an instrument of networking and social capital for participants in the District of Columbia Opportunity Scholarship Program.

Conclusion

This is the first in a series of chapters that illuminate many of the discrete aspects of parental school choice for the OSP families. In this chapter, we explored (1) what motivated families to participate in the OSP; (2) what families looked for in schools; and (3) the importance of information about the participating schools. These experiences either reinforced previous thinking and behaviors or empowered parents in ways they had not previously demonstrated.

The families in this study described their motivations for participating in the OSP primarily in terms of simply having a choice of schools, securing future academic improvement for their child, or adding religion to their child's educational environment. Although some parents expressed concerns about safety in their child's previous public school, most of them tended to express their core motivation for their school choice journey as being drawn to something positive instead of fleeing something negative. As such, the recent development of targeting private school choice opportunities to students in perennially underperforming public schools, as encapsulated in the Ohio EdChoice and Louisiana statewide voucher programs, appears to be a poor fit for parental motivations at least as expressed by the District of Columbia OSP participants. They suggest that the school choice journey is more of an opportunity and less of an escape.

When asked what specific feature was most important in the schools they chose, parents initially listed safety and religion. Several years later, parents emphasized safety much less and were more likely to reference academic considerations such as teacher quality and class size. When challenged to explain this change, many parents spoke clearly in terms of Maslow's hierarchy of human needs. Having secured a safe schooling environment for their child, they now could focus on higher-order needs such as educational achievement.

The importance of reliable and easily accessible information is one of the most consistent concerns expressed by all parents. Parents indicated that accurate information is important to making an informed school choice and crucial for finding a good match for their children. By the second year of the program, parents began voicing concern about the accuracy of the representations made by participating schools in the directory that was distributed by the WSF. Parents proceeded to request evaluative information, rather than merely descriptive information, about the schools, so that they could be better-informed educational consumers. Some parents demonstrated a "client" perspective in suggesting that the WSF should carefully monitor and guarantee the quality of the schools participating in the OSP. Other parents exhibited more of a "consumer" perspective in recognizing that they were primarily responsible for ensuring the quality of the educational service they were seeking for their child. For parents with a client perspective, repeated personal interactions with school staff, primarily through school visits, were central to their information gathering approach.

The process of sharing information about the OSP also included opportunities for parents to network in ways that might expand their personal level of social capital and empower them to be more active citizens in the community. The WSF partnered with District of Columbia Parents for School Choice to organize an OSP parent-empowerment group to

serve as a means for sharing information about the program and mobiliz-
ing support for its continuation in the face of political opposition. To our
surprise, we realized that the focus groups themselves became a valued
means for parents to express themselves and learn from the school choice
journeys of others.

In addition to understanding what motivated parents, we gained
insights into what deterred some of them from embarking on a school
choice journey based on conversations with a small number of parents
who were offered but never used an Opportunity Scholarship. These
parents doubted that their school choice journey would be a fruitful one
because most of the schools that were high on their list had limited or no
seats available. In other cases, many of the participating private schools
did not offer the appropriate services for students with special needs.
Some parents said they would expand their search to include public charter schools and other schools outside the District of Columbia that had
such programs. The high school students, on the other hand, were most
likely to report the prospect of leaving their friends behind as the single
greatest reason for not using an Opportunity Scholarship.

It appeared to us that family resources played a role in whether or not
a family got off to a good start in their school choice journey. Families
headed by two parents (or by one parent with a substantial support network) described engaging in more extensive information-gathering activities than did single parents without a strong support network. Better
information likely revealed more attractive schooling options for the first
type of family and led to a smoother and more successful launch to their
school choice journey. Many of those parents with little social support,
on the other hand, were left standing on the dock, took only a short trip,
or had to change their itinerary in midstream. There were exceptions:
we certainly observed some single parents with minimal resources who
made the school choice journey a success and were grateful for the opportunity. Nevertheless, it is generally true that launching and navigating the
parental school choice journey was a greater challenge for such families.
The identification of different "types" of families in relation to the school
choice journey was a key finding of our study and one that underpinned
the development of the model discussed in the following chapters as we
continue to recount the experiences of our research participants.

4

What Major Challenges Did Families Experience Using Private School Vouchers?

Every journey most likely presents the traveler with challenges. In one of the most famous journeys ever described, *The Odyssey*, tremendous challenges defined the trip and claimed the lives of all but the cleverest and most motivated of the travelers. The most significant challenges that families reported encountering on their school choice journey were disappointment with various aspects of their child's new school, unexpected obligations, the stigma attached to the scholarship program, and the difficult schoolwork demanded at the new private schools. In many cases, the challenges associated with implementing or participating in the program were modest and fleeting. In other cases, these experiences proved to be overwhelming for some of the families, as well as for participating schools.

We get a sense of some of the challenges that families in school choice programs face from a single parent we interviewed who we will call Kate. Kate is a native of a South American country. She speaks fluent English and describes herself as a "college student." She was inspired to come to the United States by the potential economic opportunity. She has been most impressed by the way the United States places children first. She feels education is important because of the comfort and confidence it provides when communicating with others. She also feels that in the United States going to college is necessary because of the type of job opportunities that are available to people with a college degree.

She has one daughter and getting her into the program was very difficult. When Kate applied to the school of her choice, her daughter scored low on the placement examination. She pleaded with the school to allow her daughter to retake the exam, and the girl passed on the second attempt. Kate indicated that while she has some concerns about the private school her child now attends, she is pleased overall with the academics and the way parents are allowed to participate in the social life of the school through events and field trips. Her major concern is the miscommunication she experienced with the WSF and the schools about what expenses are or are not covered under the scholarship. Also, she sometimes feels that as scholarship recipients, parents are stigmatized by some of the school administrators because they are seen as poor. However, the teachers, she indicates, are excellent and more than make up for her dissatisfaction in other areas.

When asked if she thinks the program should be continued, she expressed that it should. However, she would recommend that the amount of the scholarship decrease each year to participating families so that more families could enter the program, and the parents in the program would learn to "save money for daily life…and they will try to do better."

This chapter describes the challenges that families were most likely to experience along their school choice journey. Most of these challenges involved an interplay between the participating families, the participating schools, and the program administrator—the WSF. The OSP created a new set of challenges for all of its direct participants—families, schools, and program administrators. For parents whose children were previously assigned to neighborhood public schools, the transition to private schooling represented a significant change.[1] At the same time, the OSP schools and the WSF also faced new issues and challenges as they adapted to the requirements of the program and the needs of participating students and their families.

Perhaps the most dramatic change that took place during our study involved the Center City Consortium of Schools (CCCS) of the Catholic Archdiocese of Washington. In 2004 the CCCS was an organization of 12 Catholic parochial schools in the District of Columbia with a history of serving disadvantaged students. Evidence from the government evaluation of the OSP suggests that schools in the consortium enrolled nearly a thousand students with Opportunity Scholarships from 2004 through 2008.[2] In the fall of 2008, however, due to funding challenges, 7 of the 12 schools dropped their Catholic and private school affiliations to form the Center City Public Charter Schools.[3] The hundreds of OSP students attending those schools in the spring of 2008 had to decide whether to switch to a different private school in order to remain in the OSP, or surrender their scholarship in order to remain in the school they initially chose through the voucher program, which was no longer private. Either way, the fall of 2008 brought yet another transition to the OSP students attending those seven schools.

The combination of families and private schools involved in the OSP produced a range of experiences that would have been difficult to predict. Thus, the focus groups and interviews provided us with a unique opportunity to analyze the ebb and flow of the families' experiences and, to a lesser degree, the experiences of the other program stakeholders, by thoughtfully examining their comments about the challenges and any concerns these experiences might have engendered.

While formulating the focus group and interview questions for this study, we assumed that moving from public to private schools would require varying degrees of adjustment for the participating families. We, therefore, designed questions that would capture the most significant differences between public and private schools from the perspectives of the students and parents. We also focused on documenting the specific student and family adjustments that were associated with the transition into private schools. For example, in the first year, we explicitly asked parents and students what support they would need to succeed.[4] In year three, we asked them less-direct questions about what they saw as their most- and least-positive experiences with the OSP.

This chapter illuminates many of the challenges experienced by each of those groups and how they were managed by the respective stakeholders, especially the participating families. In particular, we use the research findings to describe two key aspects of the families' transition into private schools. One dimension of the transition involves negotiating the short-term challenges associated with the differences between their children's public and new private schools. For some families this involved, for example, the challenge of coordinating transportation from remote areas of the District of Columbia to affluent neighborhoods on the other side of the city. The second dimension of the transition consists of the adjustments that the families, schools, and program administrator had to make over time as the program evolved.

As we describe in greater detail below, over the course of the study, participant experiences began to fall into discrete categories that were clearly linked with the structure of the family and the resources available to the parents. Their school choice journey was perceptibly influenced by resources. It became apparent that these factors were strongly influencing the way families were engaged with the schools and the program, as well as their ability to manage the challenges and adjustments commonly associated with switching schools. We conclude the chapter with a discussion about the potential relationship between family structure, family resources, and student outcomes, and incorporate these factors into the theoretical model that we started to build in earlier chapters.

The New School Environment

There are several well-documented aspects of switching schools that show that transferring from one school to another often has a temporary disruptive effect on student learning, especially for students who are disadvantaged in various ways.[5] Switching schools often entails separation from friends at a familiar school and the need to befriend strangers at the new school. The transition usually involves the need to adjust attitudes and behaviors, which is especially challenging for students during the initial stage of the process. Private schools are well known for offering demanding curricula and assigning more frequent homework than public schools.[6] Parent and student reports that have been documented by other studies note that private schools are more likely to require school uniforms, practice strict discipline, and include religious activities and instruction during the school day.[7]

Previous research also suggests that private schools tend to require more of parents. High levels of parental involvement are either mandatory or at least informally expected, and parents are seen as responsible for assisting with homework and participating in more frequent home-school communications.[8] Researchers commonly view these factors as positive features of private schools. Mark Schneider and his colleagues, for example, point out that the increased parental involvement required when schools are chosen by parents presents a great opportunity in addition to presenting challenges. Parental school choice can bring parents who are highly motivated or who have specific preferences out of isolation and place them in touch with one another in freely chosen schools, creating a contagion of parental involvement, and consequently, improving school performance on behalf of all students.[9]

Various commentators describe the process of building supportive educational communities from multiple perspectives. For example, from a voluntary institutional perspective, John Brandl writes that private schools have significant potential to develop a vibrant community capable of effectively nurturing young children.[10] George Akerlof and Rachel Kranton write of the importance of a culture of achievement at contemporary high schools.[11] If it is cool to be smart, then peer-pressure works in a positive way to encourage more students to achieve. Samuel Bowles and Herbert Gintis report on the ways in which community experiences that are both frequent and intensive tend to reinforce positive social norms such as cooperation toward shared goals.[12] Their game-theoretic analysis is easily applied to the case of private schools that require substantial community involvement.

The successful involvement of parents in their children's new schools is likely to be influenced by factors such as the degree of enthusiasm with which they and their children are welcomed into the school community. Sociologist Amy Stuart Wells warns that existing school communities tend to be wary of newcomers, stigmatizing students perceived to be outsiders.[13] Any exclusion or stigmatization of new students or parents likely would alienate them from their new educational environment and present a barrier to the type of supportive community envisaged by Brandl and others. This suggests that the different expectations and requirements of the private school sector are likely to require some measure of adjustment for students and educators as well as parents.

For parents whose children were previously assigned to public schools, as were the overwhelming majority of participants in our study, selecting and having their children attend a private school can represent a significant change. From both a personal and a practical perspective, participating families had to transition into relatively new learning environments that required adjusting their previous thoughts and behaviors on multiple levels. Though there is a dearth of literature about the transition process for low-income families moving from public to private schools, Wells has written extensively about the adjustment challenges faced by students who switch from inner-city to suburban schools of choice, and her work provides insights that are instructive. She notes that low-income students are active participants in their educational environment, at times resisting the change in expectations that others place on them. She further observes that students who transferred to a choice school at an earlier age were more likely to embrace the culture of their new school and remain in their suburban choice school than were older students who made the same change.[14] The continuing role of parents in this process is also highlighted by Wells, who reports that the parents of students who initially tried school choice but then returned to neighborhood schools "were frequently involved in the initial choice of a suburban school but less involved in helping their children cope in the new setting."[15]

Although previous research on "school choice adjustment" is quite sparse, the few studies that exist imply that adjustment can be more difficult for older students because they tend to be less adaptable than younger students and further behind their new private school peers in achievement. Also, the mutual adjustment of families to schools and schools to families is more likely to be successful the longer that students remain in a school of choice.[16] We were particularly interested in examining the challenges faced by participating families and how they dealt with them from both a short-term and a long-term perspective.

From year to year, it was difficult to determine a discernible pattern in participant experiences that could be attributed to the program design, the readiness of participating schools, or other factors that might be associated with the families. However, when we compared and contrasted the families' experiences over a five-year period, it became possible in general to classify their challenges and concerns as either "short-lived" or "persistent" issues. Following our review of the transcripts and previous reports, we sorted and selected the types of challenges highlighted below into categories, based on whether relevant responses were expressed only a few times or repeatedly across multiple participant subgroups and years. Identifying the "persistent" challenges is important because these are most likely to diminish the academic outcomes for the participating students, as well as inhibit the types of experiences that could lead to the acquisition of the consumer and citizen-related skill sets we described in chapter 1.

Initial or Short-Lived Challenges and Concerns

The short-lived challenges were generally identified by small numbers of students and families within a specific focus group, or alternatively by large numbers of participants, but in only one year. Some of the short-lived issues we identified through our research were addressed and resolved by the schools, the WSF, or Congress. Most importantly, many of the short-lived challenges appeared to be a natural part of transitioning to a different school and experiencing the limitations of a newly created federal program. These matters were like the minor glitches that everyone encounters on a long journey—a flat tire, temporarily getting lost, a bad meal at a restaurant—that are bothersome but do not, themselves, define the experience of the journey.

For example, throughout this study we attempted to understand how welcoming the teachers, parents, and other members of each private school were to the OSP families, specifically whether families felt isolated, alienated, or stigmatized. According to the participants, cases of stigmatization cropped up early on in the implementation of the OSP but, in the end, the overwhelming majority of parents described their new school communities as very welcoming.

Early in the study we also heard stories from the OSP parents indicating that they or their child had been identified as a scholarship participant and were treated differently as a result. As one parent stated, "There is elitism in the parent organization 'cause I went to a meeting, and I...pointed out some issues, and a parent just said—"Why don't you leave?"[17] Several parents also described situations in which teachers or administrators made comments in public that suggested their scholarship would be revoked:

> I had an incident with one teacher in the second grade where the teacher was saying something about where if you continue to misbehave your mother will lose her scholarship. So I felt like that wasn't right. I think all us are saying we didn't appreciate the principal or the secretary furthering that information to the teachers.[18]

Incidents involving perceived stigmatization were discussed in our initial focus group report on the OSP.[19] At that time, staff at the WSF communicated to us their desire to ensure that all private schools participating in the program implemented sound policies of anonymity regarding the OSP students. As a parent in the Spanish-speaking focus group quite simply stated, "If you let them know, that's when you get treated differently. If you don't, if you act like everybody else, then they won't know."[20] In later focus groups, we received some reassurance from parents that incidents of stigmatization were becoming rare and that school personnel had devised protocols to minimize the risk of such problems recurring. As one parent related:

> When we first started, I just felt that some of the schools looked at us differently like it was a handout, and to me they didn't know what to expect from us. They just treated us different, and I guess y'all acted on that or said something about it 'cause now they treat us just like we're paying . . . I think they've really changed.[21]

Another parent explained how her child's private school maintained the anonymity of the OSP families:

> Your check is in the rectory [administrative office] please go sign it—nothing at school, you know [the rectory is] a different building. People are going in and out of the building all day so it's not like you're pinpointed.[22]

The stigmatization incidents voiced by several OSP families called for a course correction early on in their school choice journey. Based on statements to us by both parents and the WSF administrators, that course correction was made swiftly. To test this claim and explore the broader question of whether the communities at the private schools became more or less welcoming of the OSP families over time, we asked the participants in the final focus group session a series of questions pertaining to this matter. First we asked them, "How welcoming were parents of other students when you first started in the program?" Using handheld response devices, the OSP parents gave a variety of responses ranging from respondents who said "Not very welcoming" to respondents who said "Very welcoming." Based on this pattern of responses, we detected an apparent difference between the experiences of the first cohort of the OSP participants, who reported feeling more welcomed initially, and the second cohort of participants, who reported feeling somewhat less welcomed (see Figure 4.1). It is possible that existing private school parents were more enthusiastic about new passengers embarking on their school choice journey when the "ship" was half empty but were somewhat less happy about the new passengers when the second wave filled it to capacity.

To gauge whether parents felt that their new private schools became more or less welcoming of the OSP families over time, we asked the participants in our final focus group: "How welcoming are parents of other students now?" Their responses showed a much clearer tilt toward a welcoming attitude after four years compared to initially, as only one parent responded that their child's private school now was "Not very welcoming" of new scholarship students, building steeply to a near majority of parents who gave the most favorable response of "Very welcoming." Breaking the responses out by cohort, we see that, surprisingly, the second cohort of OSP parents were more universal than the first cohort in saying that their new private schools (which were no longer so new at this point) were welcoming of other students (see Figure 4.2).

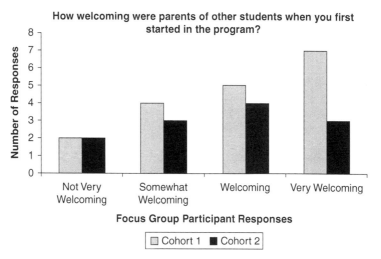

Figure 4.1   Initial Sense of Being Welcomed by Existing Private School Parents, by Cohorts

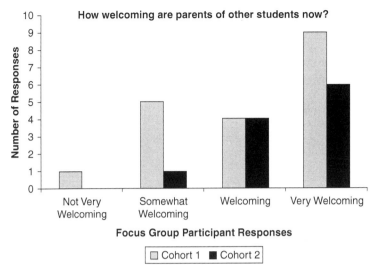

Figure 4.2   Final Sense of Being Welcomed by Existing Private School Parents, by Cohorts

A second serious challenge reported by many middle and high school students and their parents in the early stages of OSP implementation involved student discipline. Some parents whose children were involved in fights and other violations of the student code of conduct at their new private schools were concerned that their children would be expelled from their new school before they had a chance to demonstrate that they were capable of meeting the school's standards in this area.

> My first-grader…she got suspended Friday, three days, cause she hit a child back. Now in her school last year, they said fight 'em back…and this year it's different. I teach her at home you can't hit back, but last year that's all she was taught at school, to hit back. That's their rules, but they should have a little more tolerance to know that these kids come from different backgrounds; you have to work with them.[23]

These parents thought their child's new private school should provide some leeway and accommodations for the OSP students while they adjusted to new behavioral expectations, a nuanced approach that would be impossible to implement if the OSP students were anonymous to teachers in the private schools. Moreover, some focus group parents took strong exception to the suggestion that the new private schools should in any way accommodate the bad habits of the OSP students transferring from public schools. The position of these parents was best captured by an OSP father who stated, "Our kids need to come up; we don't need to bring our standards down."[24] A compromise position between excusing the behavior of new OSP students and holding them absolutely to strict standards was articulated by another parent:

> Even though it's her first year…they give you the first chance, and then you have to learn what you can and can't do. You get demerits…for chewing gum, talking in the assembly, things like that. So [the student] was getting in trouble for things like that.…[25]

So long as one or two strikes would not result in expulsion, most of the parents in our focus groups indicated that they would rather have their children forced to rise to the challenge of stronger behavioral norms in their new private school than have substantial accommodations made for the fact that they might have brought bad habits with them to their new school.

How could their children change those habits and accommodate themselves to the high disciplinary and academic standards of their new private schools? The answer that our focus group parents overwhelmingly provided was that the adjustment mechanism involved a heavy dose of parental involvement. In fact, our parent focus groups generated more "significant statements" about increased parental involvement, 19, than about any other focus group theme. When we asked parents how their lives changed once they had embarked on their school choice journey, they responded with a chorus of statements along the lines of: "I had to get more involved in my child's education."

The increased parent involvement that would be necessary for students to succeed in private school was described by most parents as a welcome step toward securing a better education for their children. The following statement by a parent was echoed, almost verbatim, by several others:

> You have to be a part of your kid's life, and sometimes it makes it harder 'cause they're stricter than the public school, and there are more demands, you still have to be a part of the kid's life. Go to the school. Go to the meetings. Don't just throw your kid there and say that they have a scholarship so everything is okay.[26]

By the end of their second year in the program, however, this requirement of greater parental involvement had become a short-term challenge for most parents, especially those with children in elementary and middle school:

> We're even challenged…to be more involved and not that we weren't involved before, but the level of even our commitment and challenge has

gone another level as far as us making sure that the kids got their home-work, school on time, and this and that and all because it's more the teach-ers expect you to have these things.[27]

The message from the OSP parents regarding parental involvement in their child's education was clear: involvement is both very challenging and extremely important. The older students in our focus groups largely confirmed that their parents were now more involved in their education.

> My mom, she helps me with my homework. She encourages me to keep trying and do my best, like when I was doing the Stanford 9 and stuff like that, she cut off the TV and stuff. I couldn't talk on the phone, so I just stayed in my room all day studying and trying to improve.[28]

The most serious concern reported by parents in the second year was the threat of "earning out" or being disqualified from the means-tested pro-gram because of modest increases in their income. As one parent said about the income restriction:

> Money is a big issue if you make a little bit more cause it's going to put you in a different status as far as your income, and it might make a whole lot of parents pay tuition.[29]

This topic was raised indirectly by parents in four of the six focus groups we operated during the second year of the program. In addition to expressing their concerns about "earning out," these parents described the variety of strategies they used to maintain eligibility. It was important to them to remain eligible for the program, so some of them eschewed entrepreneurial activities because the results of modest economic advances might have been the loss of a $7,500 Opportunity Scholarship. Turning down job promotions, cutting back on work hours, or forgoing improved housing opportunities in better neighborhoods outside of the District of Columbia were all among the examples parents shared about the sacrifices they made or were prepared to make in order for their child to remain eligible for the OSP. Some voiced a frustration that eligibility rules do not take into consideration other family financial obligations:

> I know it's a minimum requirement as far as the money you make. I mean like for, when I first applied, I made this amount. It's growing. I like private school, and I will do whatever I have to do to keep it there. But what happens just because my income change[s]? I think the requirement is like $32,000. So if I make [$35,000] to me it doesn't mean that I can afford to send my child to private school. It just means that I've got a little bit...more. But

that doesn't mean that I'm going to see it per se, because you know if that goes up, everything in my household going to change. But I don't want to be kicked to the curb just because of a $3,000 change when I know, we all know, $3,000 on your annual income don't mean a whole lot of change.[30]

Our focus group parents were delighted to hear that Congress and President Bush modified the OSP statute in 2006 to allow families to earn up to 300 percent of the poverty line and remain eligible for their scholarships once they were already in the program.[31]

The challenges associated with student discipline and concerns about students being "singled out," like other short-lived challenges, were rarely mentioned after the second year. By the third year of this study, the parents were primarily concerned about more persistent challenges.

Persistent Challenges and Concerns

Initially it was not clear whether the information that the families shared, particularly their concerns about how they might influence their children's experiences with the program, were fleeting or continuous. As a result, beginning in the third year of the study, we allowed the participants to revisit their responses from previous years in an attempt to help the research team sort and select their experiences into the appropriate category. Several of the challenges that were cited in the first and second years of the program were also repeated by some individuals and subgroups in the third and fourth (final) years of the study. When this occurred, we classified the relevant challenge or concern as "persistent," suggesting that it will likely be a long-term or permanent aspect of the families' experience with the program.

In the first two years, the question of tutoring and other forms of academic support for students who began their OSP experience at the high school level was a consistent topic in the focus groups. Because some parents were reluctant to discuss their personal challenges and concerns regarding school teachers and administrators out of concern that their child might be penalized, many of the focus group sessions ended with a question that asked parents to make recommendations to the WSF, policy makers, and others who are interested in helping their children succeed. Their suggestions sometimes revealed issues that they had not explicitly shared or discussed during the interviews and focus groups. For example, during the first two years of the study, parents frequently recommended or requested tutoring and mentoring for their children. During the last two years of the study, based on the families' direct experiences with tutoring and mentoring, the recommendations became more concrete with regard to these support services. They began to point to specific subject areas in which their children needed support. They also identified dates and locations that they saw as ideal for receiving support services.

On the basis of lessons learned from the high school students in the first year of the program, the WSF formed a strategic partnership with Capital Partners for Education (CPE)—another local scholarship program that specializes in granting scholarships to high school students from low-income backgrounds living in the District of Columbia who have demonstrated exceptional academic capabilities.[32] Despite the WSF's attempt to address the needs of high school students through this relationship, difficulties in the area of tutoring and mentoring persisted. This is reflected in part by the fact that CPE and the WSF ended their partnership after just one year, with CPE reporting that OSP high school families had needs that exceeded those of their typical ninth-grade families. Nevertheless, although CPE elected not to extend services to new families, they continued to provide services to the high school families that entered and remained in the OSP from the second year. As one parent described:

> Well, with me, CPE program has been excellent with my daughter. Her mentor is…she's great. I mean…if my daughter…has an assignment and sometimes she has even called her and asked her, you know, on some subjects that's in her field and will help her.[33]

Parents whose children in the OSP had access to tutors and mentors were grateful for them. Those whose children did not have access to those supports often told us that their child would benefit from tutoring and mentorship.

One of the most persistent issues expressed by parents was their lack of participation in school-based organizations. Several of the participating schools, unlike public schools, have mandatory parental participation requirements that are strictly enforced. In the first year, parents appeared happy to volunteer at their children's schools and typically did not have trouble meeting the time requirements associated with these activities, with the exception of a small minority who mentioned the difficulty of attending parent-teacher conferences because they were scheduled at inconvenient times:

> I am working in the daytime—excuse me—and they want to have a meeting with the teachers in the daytime, and I can't get out [of] my job every time they call and set up an appointment.[34]

Indeed, the majority of participants reported a significant increase in their level of parental involvement in their child's new school compared with their previous school. However, if we make a distinction between parent "involvement" and "participation," and we strongly argue that this distinction should be made, a significant difference in the findings emerges. We define *parent involvement* as those activities directly related to student academic development, and *parent participation* as activities related to school decision making, which include parent organizations and other activities that do not directly involve their children. Although parents reported increased interaction with their children and teachers, they reported little participation in school-based activities and associations such as parent organizations.

> But I'm going to be honest, after working all day, I don't have time to work with the WSF parent organizations. I hear this from other people [parents] who can't find the time either.[35]

It appears from the focus group study findings, therefore, that the OSP parents are far less likely to *participate* in school-based matters than to be involved in student-centered school activities such as parent-teacher conferences and assisting with homework.

During the personal interviews, many parents provided additional insights that help to explain why parent participation and involvement were challenging. Most parents, particularly the single parents, reported that they faced significant challenges with balancing work and the increased demands placed on them by many of the schools. For one Latino parent, language was a huge barrier to participation and involvement, and overcoming it would require a greater commitment to learning English so that he could help his daughter with her homework. He shared the following example:

> For us there was a significant change more than anything because we were forced to go to English school to learn English…when I realized all the homework was in English. So I had to stay awake all night with a translator and a dictionary.[36]

That is clearly an example of extraordinary parental involvement in the school choice journey.

The accuracy of the information provided by some of the participating schools was also a persistent concern. In the third year of the study, with several years of experience and hindsight to draw from, parents became increasingly concerned about the differences between what they initially learned about a school and what they experienced after their child was enrolled. Some of these parents claimed that certain schools misrepresented various aspects of their programs or offerings.

> They always seemed like they're [good schools] with their open house, but after you get your child there, it's not the same. Everything is just totally different, just totally different.[37]

Parents who voiced this concern often felt the OSP needed an "independent entity" that could verify the information provided to them by participating schools and would also be responsible for monitoring the schools during the academic year.[38] The elementary school parents who entered the program in the first year were particularly concerned about school quality and thought the OSP could be improved if participating schools were evaluated to ensure that they met a minimum set of standards. Generally speaking, the recommendations suggest that the parents realized that thoroughly assessing and monitoring schools was important, yet it exceeds their individual and collective capacity. They felt that filling this void might ultimately require information and support that did not exist. Called on to be the navigator of their family's school choice journey, these parents requested support analogous to a global positioning system device to help them decide where to turn.

The dearth of high school slots was another consistent concern, initially for families that had students in the upper grades and eventually for families with students in the middle and elementary grades. Families with children who enrolled in the first year were particularly concerned about high school slots. Only one in five of the participating schools offered high school options.[39] Among focus group families, 62 percent of all first-year students were seeking slots in the seventh grade or higher. Nearly all of these students—90 percent of all students who entered the program in 2004—would be entering high school by the beginning of the fourth year of the program. To further complicate the concerns about high school slots, most of the students who would be eligible for the program in the fourth year were better prepared than the students who enter private high schools directly from the public school system. Hence, there would be much stiffer competition among the OSP students for a smaller number of slots. Some parents expressed their concerns:

> [Students are] out of the school because you no longer are eligible, or there's no space? My daughter...I had to pull her out [of the OSP] because of a space issue...it was a space thing—I couldn't find a high school.[40]

Only problem I had was with this difficulty in finding a school once she's in high school—if I put her in the scholarship program in high school. They didn't really offer too many choices to go to. You really wouldn't have a choice in high school. And then we're having to see if pretty much we can deal with that.[41]

The supply of high school slots for the OSP students did not expand during the course of the pilot program, even as greater numbers of the OSP students became high school eligible. As a result, many families like these were forced to abandon the program.

School Challenges

Results from a survey completed by, and interviews conducted with, school representatives suggest that many of the participating schools that accepted large numbers of the OSP students were seriously challenged by the academic and social needs of the families. School representatives consistently expressed a need for additional resources, primarily in the form of tutors and other academic support services for the students. Representatives from the participating high schools were especially likely to recommend these academic supports. Also, most school representatives held the belief that parents could benefit from attending workshops and other activities before applying to the OSP, to provide them with a better understanding of the different and often unfamiliar types of school models, as well as other subtle differences associated with the private schools. According to a number of the school representatives, some parents select a school without a full awareness of the pros and cons associated with that school.

Ultimately, many of the chosen schools were not a good fit for particular students because the student's interests and needs were inconsistent with the school model. One school representative shared an experience about an OSP family that illustrates this point. He noted that the mother was very excited that her son would be attending his high school. However, her son was very disappointed when he discovered that the school does not have a football team and does not place a significant emphasis on athletics beyond good exercise habits. The student's disappointment over the lack of athletic programs spilled over into other areas, and his mother begrudgingly removed him from the school. The school representative thought this incident could have been avoided if the mother had discussed the unique features of the school with her son beforehand.

Program Challenges

The WSF was selected to manage the day-to-day business of the OSP, and leadership and staff there were perhaps in the best position to share insights about the more general challenges faced in administering a program that targets students from low-income families. Representatives of the WSF were interviewed at the end of each year of our study or after we had developed the first draft of each year's report. Following our interviews and focus group conversations with the participating families, we often shared with the WSF some of our key findings. During these meetings, they frequently confirmed much of what the families shared with us, as well as offered additional information or insights about key events that had transpired. The WSF specifically noted a need for "wraparound services" for some of the families. Consistent with the information that participants shared during their interviews and focus groups, the WSF interviews confirmed that some families had needs that extended beyond the scope of the program. In particular, the WSF representatives stressed the importance of assisting families with understanding the hidden and unanticipated costs (in terms of time, energy, and money) that may be associated with enrollment in a private school. For example, the costs of transportation to and from school, field trips, and school meals are not covered by the scholarship in every case.[42]

In addition to nonacademic or social support services, the WSF staff quickly realized that high school students needed a variety of academic and social supports to help them transition into and succeed in their new schools. Because some schools did not provide tutors or allow private tutors on their campus, the WSF had to facilitate efforts to provide tutorial services and other resources near to students' homes. WSF's relationship with the East of the River Family Strengthening Collaborative, a social service collaborative located in a high-poverty area of Washington, DC, was one example of their attempt to connect families with the resources that they needed.

The WSF interviewees had also observed that many OSP parents seemed isolated from the school community and had expressed an interest in meeting other parents who were participating in the program. As a result of this observation, the WSF facilitated the creation of Virginia Walden Ford's parent empowerment group.[43] In addition, the WSF formed partnerships with other organizations that could provide tutorial services and other resources to address family needs that were beyond the administrative scope and resource capacity of the WSF.

The participating families often praised WSF for exceptional support or what might be called customer care, and they were especially thankful for the timely modifications and improvements that were made in response to their concerns and feedback. As one parent stated:

> I think by me being in the program as long as I've been...I think it has, like, improved each year you know as far as they, Washington Scholarship has been great. They ask for your input, you know, after every test session and I think they've improved in every aspect as far as testing. And, any information you need, any help, they will actually provide it and I think they have, like, little incentive projects for the children sometimes.[44]

These program enhancements strengthened the relationship between the WSF and the families and largely explain why the parents consistently expressed high levels of satisfaction with the program, despite experiencing difficulties with some aspects of participation.

Family Types and Student Outcomes

For the OSP parents in general, their views on the success of participation in the program might be best understood in terms of a series of events that take place over the course of their child's education. To some extent, the variation in the ways that parents define success can be explained by the grade or developmental level of their children. In this study, for example, high school parents were more concerned about a safe environment and preparing their children for life beyond the OSP, whereas elementary school parents generally took high school graduation as given and were more interested in college preparatory school options. We also found evidence from the focus groups and interviews, however, that the challenges and opportunities available to participating families were strongly influenced by the family structure and the resources available to each family, and that these factors also had a powerful influence on how parents evaluated the success of the program for their child.

We must reiterate here that, since the OSP was targeted at low-income families, they all had relatively low levels of financial resources. What emerged quite clearly as we became familiar with the participant families in our focus group study, however, was that there was considerable variation among them in terms of resource availability. Resources were defined more generally to include time, practical support from extended families, and their own skills and knowledge, such as fluency in English. These types of resources were very important in enabling parents to deal with some of the short-term and persistent challenges of the school choice journey, such as the ability to *participate* in their child's school or increase their *involvement* with homework.

Moreover, we discovered that in many cases the level of resources available to a family appeared to be closely associated with the structure of the family unit. We also found, most importantly, that certain "types" of families could be identified based on the combination of family structure and family resources and that each family type was likely to be associated with a focus on particular levels of student outcomes, as discussed below and conceptually depicted in Figure 4.3.

Type 1 families are typically headed by a single parent (often a mother), who has weak or very limited family support. In many cases, she must focus primarily on providing the basic necessities to her family. When this type of parent is focused on finding the best school for her child, a safe and convenient location will be her first priority. Her limited resources and family support will make it difficult for her to be as active as she would like to be in her child's formal academic development. She is most interested in the immediate outcomes for her child, which include good attendance, making passing grades, and staying in school.

Type 2 families are also typically headed by a single parent, who is most likely a mother. She has a relatively strong support structure around her, however, and lives in a stable environment and has viable employment. Her modest level of resources and support allow her to consider a wider range of school options outside of her immediate surroundings. She

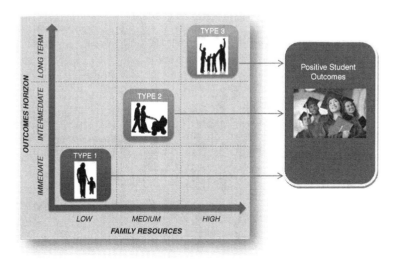

Figure 4.3 Family Resources, Outcomes Horizon, and Student Outcomes

has the time to be more hands-on and active with her child at home and attends most events related to her child at school. Time and other commitments do not allow her to participate in parent organization meetings and other school-based activities that are not directly related to her child as often as she might like. She demands that her child would do well in school, and she is more likely to discuss student outcomes that include post-secondary possibilities.

Type 3 families have either two parents or a single parent with an extremely strong social support network. Though these families have roughly the same level of resources as Type 2 families, at least one parent or caregiver is able to devote considerably more time to supporting the child. These families are very ambitious when selecting schools and often consider the very best options regardless of where they might be located and without considering factors that might deter families more pressed for time. Type 3 families are heavily involved in their child's development and are more likely to participate in school-based activities. These families take graduation from high school as a given and are most likely to discuss student outcomes from a long-term perspective that includes a discussion about what the child will one day contribute to the family or broader community.

Conclusion

Building on the discussion in the preceding chapter about the families' experiences with the OSP, this chapter describes the interplay between the participating families, participating schools, and the program administrator—the WSF. From completing eligibility forms to participating in school-based activities, families were challenged to assume greater roles and responsibilities associated with their children's academic development.

Many of the participating families, single parents specifically, had to overcome challenges associated with moving from marginal and relatively inactive roles in the academic development of their children to playing more active roles within private schools that expected and demanded more from them.[45] Consistent with other studies that focus on the transition from middle to high school, the older students appeared to have the greatest adjustment challenges.[46] Moreover, the parents of these students, particularly in families with multiple children or especially those that we define as Type 1 families, appear to have the least amount of time and resources to support the high school students. We discovered that most of the families increased their involvement in their children's development after receiving an Opportunity Scholarship, but they also were less likely to participate in school-based activities and organizations.

Most of the OSP families we spoke to had requested and received assistance at various stages in the process of choosing a school and adjusting to the new educational environment. Most of them also remarked that more assistance would have been welcomed, particularly in the form of better information about schools and access to other support services such as tutors. Most of the parents who were interviewed provided additional insights about the challenges and the sources of the problems they were experiencing, and their comments revealed that most of their concerns or challenges could generally be classified as short-term.

As we analyzed the qualitative data from the fourth-year of this study, it appeared that many of the persistent or long-term challenges were associated with cultural and language differences. For a number of parents, however, the persistent challenges had less to do with the schools and the program and more to do with providing their children with basic necessities. In fact, the challenges they faced outside of education directly impeded their ability to be more actively involved in school-based activities. When we attempted to group the comments that participants made about the schools into one category and their references to the program into another, we found that many parents did not make a clear distinction between the schools and the program. Thus, it appears that the combination of their positive experiences with most of the participating schools and the ongoing support they received from the WSF best explain their consistently high levels of satisfaction—a topic we explore in greater detail in chapter 5.

These findings are significant because, as we have noted in previous chapters, many of the families rely on other public agencies, including the traditional public schools, to provide them with access to necessities like food, housing, and employment. In many of these cases, families who need this support are displeased with the service delivery they or their close contacts had experienced. In a separate study, commentator Megan Cottrell, for example, described the roadblocks and frustrations experienced by her married friend who was several months pregnant and recently laid off from her job. Her friend completed an online application for Tempoary Assistance for Needy Families assistance and then waited for a call from the agency that never came. She eventually called the local TANF office and left several messages that were never returned. Taking matters into her own hands, she finally paid a personal visit to the office, at which point she learned no one was available to help her because she did not have a caseworker.[47] "Clients," as we call them, of social services agencies are fully aware of the imbalance of power in their relationship with caseworkers. One anonymous welfare recipient shared her views on this matter in another welfare study: "This is your life…and these people got you on a string, and you're their puppet." Recipients suggest that caseworkers have a tendency to view them through a lens of old stereotypes and prejudices and to look down on them: "They don't like us; they don't respect us as human beings."[48]

During the adjustment period of these families' school choice journey, many of them strove to develop and exercise consumer skills in the educational arena. They reported becoming more involved in their child's education and in interacting regularly with their child's educational provider. When these families encountered especially difficult challenges, however, some of them, particularly those with relatively few family resources, fell back upon client approaches to service provision. They requested that an independent organization verify the quality of the schools and the programs that they offered. Those parents were willing to surrender some of the power and responsibility that they had attained through the OSP to an outside organization. They quite reasonably asked that their child not be stigmatized as a scholarship recipient the way that welfare recipients had been labeled in the past. They worried that they might earn extra money that would disqualify their children from continuing to receive an Opportunity Scholarship. The school choice journey of these parents, launched by way of a government program to promote parental choice, demonstrated elements of both personal empowerment and personal dependence. Some parents asked to take the wheel and command the ship. Other parents felt the need to put their school choice journey on autopilot.

5

How Do Families Measure Student Progress, Satisfaction, and Success?

The fundamental goal of the OSP is to improve academic outcomes for children from low-income families, with a specific focus on students who previously were attending low-performing public schools. Measurement of the progress and achievement of students participating in the program, however, was not a straightforward matter. There is considerable debate surrounding the role and responsibility of schools in driving student achievement and how to objectively assess and measure student progress. The controversy surrounding this is reflected in the movement behind standardized testing, site-based accountability, teacher merit pay, the Common Core National Standards, and a growing number of reforms that many commentators feel are necessary to improve traditional public and public charter schools. Although it is less commonly discussed, private schools face their own particular challenges in terms of defining, monitoring, and reporting student progress, particularly in light of the frequently cited claim that differences between the performance of private and public schools disappear when analysts control for student socioeconomic characteristics.[1]

It is important to acknowledge, however, that student progress and achievement can be measured in many ways other than standardized test scores. Here is yet another way in which the school choice experience mirrors a journey. The main point of a journey is to reach an objective; yet, different travelers seek different destinations. In the example below, Fatima was most interested in her daughter mastering multiple languages. Having multilingual children was the primary objective that she sought from her parental school choice journey. Moreover, various conditions of the journey make the trip itself pleasurable for some travelers but not necessarily for others. For some journeymen, the speed of the trip is important. For others, beautiful scenery or interesting traveling companions are critical signs that a journey is going well. Parental expectations of a school choice program and the resulting levels of satisfaction with outcomes are likely to evolve over time as the very experience of participating in the program influences the ways in which parents think and behave, much as the objective of a journey can change during the course of travel. In both travels and parental school choice, the quality of the experience itself may be at least as important as achieving the goal, and the process and the destination exist in a dynamic relationship with each other.

We get a sense of the nuances surrounding how parents judge student success and their own satisfaction with a school choice journey when we consider the insights of one of the parents we interviewed, who we will call Fatima. Fatima is a single mother who is a first-generation US citizen. She identifies herself as a Muslim and was born in an East African country. She has four children, and one of her daughters is attending a private middle school as part of the OSP. She notes that her primary reason for pursuing the scholarship and her vision for her daughter is that she should learn multiple languages, specifically Arabic.

Although Fatima now plays this role in relation to her daughter, it is customary in Fatima's native country for the men to oversee and manage the children's education. She describes her education in Africa as "strict" yet stresses that she really benefitted from learning several languages. When asked to explain why she selected a particular school for her daughter, she said: "This was a school that really had a unique program. They had dual language, and, for me, I was very, very interested because, you know, coming from Africa, we speak many languages."

As a result of her personal experiences as a student, she strongly believes that children have the right to feel safe and nurtured in school, whether it is a public or private institution. When asked how her daughter is doing now, she explained: "She can read in Arabic like someone who has been learning all their life." She feels strongly that ending the program would be a "disaster for the children." Her support for the program is best reflected by the fact that she has referred at least three families whose children are now enrolled in the OSP.

In this chapter, we describe how the parents in this study defined and measured student progress and their own satisfaction with the OSP, and how the basis for their satisfaction changed over time. Using our theoretical framework, we examine how satisfaction with the program appeared to be related to the empowerment parents derived from participating in the program, the pleasure of being more actively involved in their child's development, and the level of support available through their family structure and resources.

How Do Parents Measure Progress or Success?

In education, it is important to distinguish between various measures of quality or success. The way this matter is approached in the public administration field is instructive. Measures of success tend to be classified broadly as inputs, outputs, intermediate outcomes, and end outcomes.[2] *Inputs* are the resources available to an organization. For a school, these would include resources such as funding, facilities, location, teachers, and the characteristics of the student body. Outputs include measures such as instructional time and the curriculum. Intermediate outcomes for schools include school safety and student motivation to learn. End outcomes are the desired final results of effective organizational operation. For schools, end outcomes include student mastery of skills, achievement gains, and graduation rates.

Most evaluations of parental school choice programs have focused primarily or exclusively on end outcomes. In particular, newer school choice options like voucher programs and public charter schools are judged to be a success or failure based in large part on the extent to which they increase student performance on standardized tests.[3]

This focus on end outcomes is justifiable in many respects, given that the ultimate objective of school reform is to improve academic achievement. However, our research findings suggest that most OSP parent participants were not looking primarily to standardized test scores in order to assess their child's progress or success. In fact, during the focus groups and polling exercises, rarely did parents mention or select standardized test scores as a means by which they assessed student progress.[4] For these parents, most of whom interact with their child intimately on a daily basis, subtle changes in behavior and attitude were found to be more important than test scores as indicators that their child was doing well or at least demonstrating that reasonable academic progress was imminent. Many of the OSP families believed that these behavioral and attitudinal changes only happen in safe and orderly environments, and this was often the single, most important reason they were excited about the program.

It has been well documented that student attitudes toward learning, particularly attitudinal changes following transfer to a new school environment, provide important indicators of future success. Some researchers have claimed that positive school cultures produce desirable student behaviors that eventually manifest themselves in student achievement and attainment gains.[5] In the case of a relatively new school choice program such as the OSP, however, it may take several years before consistent and reliable data are available to assess the intermediate and long-term relationship between the program intervention, student attitudes, and academic success. In fact, as described in chapter 2, the statistical evaluation of the pilot program produced somewhat mixed findings, with clear evidence of higher high school graduation rates for the older students in the study, some suggestive evidence of reading gains, but no findings of improvements in math achievement.

The focus group discussions with parents provided valuable insights into the ways the OSP families were measuring their children's progress in real time. Their comments could be generally placed along a continuum. At one end of the continuum were "immediate" outcomes such as safety and positive attitudes toward school and learning; this is followed by "intermediate" outcomes such as good study habits, reaching grade level, and improved grades; and finally by "long-term" outcomes such as graduating from high school and attending college. In turn, parental levels of satisfaction appear to be influenced by the extent to which these expected outcomes are being met. Figure 5.1 demonstrates the types of immediate, intermediate, and longer-term outcomes that parents in our study were using as indicators of their child's success or progress in the program, and the inputs that were seen as being the essential preconditions for each of these types of outcomes.

In the first few years of this study, the research team was cautious about discussing topics with parents that addressed measures of progress and success. We believed that such topics were premature at that stage given some of the more pressing issues facing the families, such as

Immediate	Intermediate	Long term
Inputs:	*Inputs:*	*Inputs:*
Safe environment	Smaller class sizes	Mentors
Effective student discipline	Quality teachers	Advanced learning opportunities
Tutors and academic supports	Rigorous curriculum	Scholarships and other financial support
Outputs:	*Outputs:*	*Outputs:*
Student excitement about attending school	Improved student grades	Improved high school graduation rates
Improved student attitudes and behaviors	Student performance at grade level	Higher college attendance and completion rates

Figure 5.1   Types of Student Outcomes over Time

whether they had in fact selected the right school and how they would adjust to their new responsibilities in relation to these schools. Therefore, questions about academic progress were not discussed directly with the focus group participants in the first year of the study. It is worth noting, however, that during the first year of focus groups, parents rarely spoke voluntarily of test scores or formal assessments when addressing more general questions related to what they found to be the most and least satisfying aspects of their new schools or the program.

During the second year of focus groups, parents were asked directly how they determined whether things were going well academically for their children. Their responses provided the first signs that they were not thinking about or measuring academic progress in formal or conventional terms. They mainly focused on immediate outcomes such as their children's improved attitude toward school and their studies, behavioral changes, and the work that they were producing:

> He can really write some beautiful stories…he's able to express himself now. His teacher is telling him he's a great writer.[6]
>
> She's changed tremendously…she entered the third grade. She couldn't read that well—she probably was reading on a kindergarten level. Now she's on her level and her attitude has changed. So, yeah…the private school has done a great deal for her.[7]
>
> My child is having the time of his life. The first thing I noticed when my son started going to [his new school] when I went to pick him up he was not ready to go home…you have to pull them off the playground to go home in the evening…They feel so comfortable around their teachers and administrators [that] they are in no hurry to go home.[8]

These comments also reflect the type of expectations parents had when choosing a school, which were largely centered on the school environment rather than on its academic record. The most commonly cited parent indicators of success for their child involved greater commitment to schoolwork, use of a more advanced vocabulary, and apparent feelings of safety and comfort in the school.

By the third year of focus groups, some elementary school parents continued to cite immediate outcomes, such as the degree of motivation and enthusiasm their children expressed toward school, as their litmus test for student academic progress:

> Success is measured at all levels, different levels, if the child has to learn what he has to learn in each class. So my measurement of success is he's all the time engaged in school, in classes, and homework and then learns

what he has to learn in each class. So that's what I measure. So I think he
has learned what he should learn in each class.[9]

As far as attitude, my children's attitude has changed…They have so
much involvement in school where by the time they get home all they have
time to do is study then get ready to go to bed.[10]

At this stage, however, after three years of participation in the program, several parents also listed "excelling at grade level"—an intermediate outcome—as their preferred measure of success. Others continued to
focus on more immediate outcomes relating to factors such as student
enthusiasm, feelings, and self-esteem:

My youngest, her reading skills had went up tremendously. Before she got
to [her new school], she was the type of child, she didn't socialize a lot. She
was quiet, didn't participate when it came to teacher asking, "Raise your
hand." But now since she attended [her new school], she participates, she
raises her hand, she reads a lot.[11]

As well as the shift in focus from immediate to intermediate and
long-term outcomes over the duration of the program, the focus on
different types of outcomes varied between groups of parents, depending in part on factors such as the age of their children. For example,
from the beginning of the study, the first cohort of high school families
expressed a sense of urgency, often bordering on desperation, about the
importance of addressing the developmental needs of their children and
better preparing them for life beyond high school. Like other parents,
this group initially emphasized immediate outcomes associated with
school conditions, such as safety, and student attitudes toward learning,
as their indicators of success. However, as their children approached
high school graduation, these parents in particular began to shift their
focus to intermediate and long-term outcomes such as student grades,
graduation, and college preparation as measures of student and program success. We also observed a strong tendency for Latino parents,
compared with parents of other ethnic groups, to focus on long-term
outcomes for their children. From the outset, Latino parents generally
identified factors such as a rigorous curriculum, safety, and student
interest in a school mainly as stepping-stones toward a strong academic
foundation associated with long-term outcomes, regardless of the age of
their children.

By the fourth and final year of the study, a larger number of parents
across the whole sample began expressing interest in longer-term outcomes. They began to place a greater emphasis on student academic development or progress, as well as the students' interest in pursuing college.

The increased focus on long-term outcomes is captured by the following high school parent quote:

> She's doing good in school, and she says, "Mommy, I want to continue...and, when I finish, I want to go to a university." She's very interested in college. I don't have to tell her, "You have to do your homework, or you have to learn something." Every time she's coming back home, she starts to do her homework, and she's doing it on the computer...she's learning, learning, learning![12]

In addition to the focus groups, the study used interactive polling to gather information about the importance of different types of indicators of student success on the program. Participant responses to the polling questions confirmed that attitudinal and behavioral indicators were, on the whole, more important to parents than standardized test scores. More than two-thirds of the parents who participated in the interactive polling said that general attitudinal and behavioral indicators were the primary means by which they evaluated the educational progress made by their child and no parent reported that standardized test scores were their primary measure of schooling success (see Figure 5.2).

It is not clear why few parents use standardized test results as a source of feedback about their children's progress. One possibility is that positive attitudes and behaviors are seen by the parents as precursors to student success that later will be captured by standardized assessments. Or, their responses may indicate that these parents do not place much confidence or credibility in test scores to measure and assess student academic progress. These are but two possibilities. Given the significant investments that are made in purchasing and administering standardized tests, and the near obsession with test scores as a metric of schooling success in

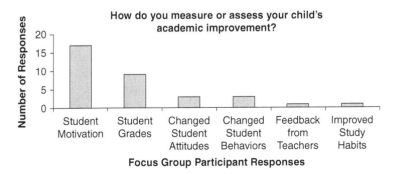

Figure 5.2   How Parents Assess Student Progress

many educational evaluations, this is an issue that demands a greater level of attention but exceeds the scope of this study. Our original finding that parents tend to rely very little on student test scores when assessing academic success, however, was recently confirmed in a report by James Kelly and Benjamin Scafidi based on Georgia survey data.[13]

A Critical Look at Parent Satisfaction

Every evaluation of school choice programs that has asked the question has reported high levels of parental satisfaction with choice schools, especially in the initial year of enrollment in the school or program.[14] The literature suggests that satisfaction with the new schools of choice may be higher in the first year either because the dissatisfaction with previous schools is freshest at that point or because the charm of the new schools has a tendency to wear off somewhat over time, particularly as parents become more aware of their organizational shortcomings.

Over the course of the study, we observed high levels of satisfaction with the program but were in no position to explain levels of parent satisfaction from one year to the next. Our analysis of program participant responses over the whole four years of the study revealed, however, a somewhat more complex picture in which parental satisfaction with school choice appeared to be multidimensional and to vary over time as particular elements of the program became more or less important to the families. For example, satisfaction with the opportunity to choose their child's school and with the school choice program in general were found to represent two distinct dimensions of overall satisfaction. When their child first entered the new school, most parents were particularly concerned about aspects of the school environment involving safety and discipline, and the presence of these factors immediately contributed to high levels of satisfaction. Over time, other aspects of the school environment such as the standard of teaching became more important to many of the parents, and if their expectations in relation to these characteristics were not met, their levels of satisfaction with the program declined. These results are consistent with research showing that parents pay attention to school "brands" and have buyer's remorse when their brand expectations are not realized.[15]

In general, a combination of factors was found to best explain overall levels of satisfaction or dissatisfaction, but our detailed analysis of the focus group material revealed some interesting findings about the relative importance of different factors in contributing to overall satisfaction with the OSP. It might have been expected that if parents were dissatisfied with the school they had chosen for their child, they would also be dissatisfied with the program that was the vehicle for making that choice. Upon closer analysis of our data, however, we discovered that some parents who reported being dissatisfied with the school they had chosen were still satisfied with the OSP itself. Indeed, throughout the four years of the study, families expressed consistently high levels of satisfaction with the parental school choice program, even though they may have been dissatisfied with some aspects of the schools that their children were attending. This indicates that a clear distinction must be made between satisfaction with a school choice program, on the one hand, and with specific schools selected through the program on the other. As one parent stated:

> We'll keep the scholarship, but we'll just transfer her from where she is to a different school. She's been in this particular school for two years, and it seems like she's regressing instead of progressing.[16]

This finding, that satisfaction with a school choice program can be distinct from satisfaction with a school of choice, is particularly pertinent to the understanding of how to improve the delivery of school choice and improve outcomes for families. For example, the nation's largest urban voucher program, in Milwaukee, signs students up for the voucher program through the private school that they have already chosen.[17] Under that atypical program design, the school choice program and the school of choice are virtually one and the same. As a result, students who leave "schools-of-choice" in Milwaukee rarely remain in the school choice program. Instead, most of them return to Milwaukee Public Schools.[18]

The high levels of parental satisfaction with the OSP that we identified in our study provide further support for a consistent finding across previous school choice studies and one that is particularly important to our theoretical framework. Previous studies of parental school choice and satisfaction, including a growing body of research in Milwaukee that the authors were involved in,[19] have indicated that when families have an opportunity to choose the schools their children attend, regardless of the specific program involved, most report high levels of satisfaction. For example, Greg Forster and Christian D'Andrea reported that families in Florida who were given the opportunity to select their child's school reported significantly increased levels of satisfaction on a wide variety of topics. More specifically, they noted that parents were pleased with their student's academic progress, the amount of individual attention their student received in the school of choice, and the quality of teachers in the chosen school.[20]

The findings from our qualitative study of the OSP regarding parental views on the program were similar to those found in Florida. Sources of satisfaction with the program among the parent participants were found to span a broad idiosyncratic spectrum. If parents said that they were satisfied with the OSP, we asked them to specify the main source of their satisfaction. Most were pleased that their children were now attending safer and more disciplined schools. For some, satisfaction stemmed from improved communication between home and school; for others it was a reflection of their approval of the smaller class sizes and one-on-one interaction with teachers and administrators. Only a very small number of parents said that their satisfaction was based primarily upon academic quality.

Understanding the Broad View of Parental Satisfaction

By re-examining the comments made over the full four years of the study, we have been able to examine the deeper sources of parent or family satisfaction with the OSP. Moreover, the multiple techniques used to gather data provide valuable insights into how participants' views on the program and the schools were changing over time from the perspective of the participants themselves. Because parents were encouraged to revisit their earlier responses or comments in subsequent focus groups, which allowed them to reprioritize or modify their previous positions, we can explain why their views changed or persisted over the duration of the study. Additionally, in the fourth year, participants were asked to reflect upon how they and their families had changed as a result of participating in the OSP. The pattern of responses revealed a great deal about their relationship with the program, the aspects of the program they liked most and least, and how their views on the program and the schools were influenced by the personal changes they underwent on their school choice journey.

Halfway through the program's first year, many parents and students were clearly thrilled with their new schools and were more than happy to describe what they perceived as the benefits of attending private school. As one parent said:

> I thought it was going to be downhill for me...you're going to give me this money to send my child to school, what exactly do you want? Am I going to have to send pints of blood every month? But nothing; they don't...it's a whole lot better than I imagined.[21]

As a high school student commented in the first year of our study:

> It's just more opportunity than public school. I guess that's why ya'll call it the Opportunity Scholarship.[22]

The general disposition of parents in particular changed over time, however, as they grew more familiar and comfortable with the processes, policies, and procedures associated with participation in the OSP and the specific private schools their children attended. Increasingly, their early, lofty positive attitudes toward the program and participating schools began to grow more matter-of-fact, and their comments began to reflect a certain level of discomfort with the changes inherent in starting out on the new venture that was their school choice journey. During our discussions, parents described the challenges they encountered when they left their neighborhood public schools, as well as the sometimes-difficult process of adapting to private schools. While students needed to grow more accustomed to new and often more stringent student codes of conduct, their parents needed to refine their support role, and some had to learn how to support their children in the new, private school environment.

> When my son first got there, he said to me one day, "Mommy, I don't feel like I belong here." And that struck a real chord in me that he wasn't feeling comfortable.[23]
>
> Some of that stuff—I forgot a lot of that stuff. You know, it's made me have to brush up on things, and once I started getting into it with them, then it brings me back...all those math fractions and algebra and stuff like that. It takes me back, but it's still much harder...than what I had to do.[24]

A more detailed review and analysis of their comments revealed some patterns in terms of both satisfaction and frustration with schools. For example, the families repeatedly remarked about the positive aspects of smaller class sizes found in their new private schools, from the one-on-one attention their children received to the orderly atmosphere found in those classrooms. On the other hand, frustrations also took a similar course among many of the participants. Family resource limitations were perhaps their greatest source of consistent frustration, and this was the aspect of their OSP experience that was most uncomfortable. Many families quickly realized that enrollment in private school brought with it unanticipated expenses and consequences, including fares for transportation to and from schools, and the need to arrange trips to school that were in some cases longer than families had initially realized. Many parents also had to provide lunch for their children, make payments for extracurricular activities, and provide other costly and time-consuming support. The following are quotes from parents in the first and second year of the program, respectively:

> I have four kids, and it's to and from school—it's $50, actually, a week for them to get back and forth...that's like $200 a month extra.[25]

> When I had my parent-teacher conference, that's what her teacher brought up to me, that she worries about [the student] sitting alone, reading, eating by herself. So she doesn't have that...peer interaction like she probably should, because we can't afford to do a lot of the extra things they do.[26]

A number of families quickly recognized that they were responsible for filling resource gaps that had not existed when their children were attending public schools, as the $7,500 voucher only covered transportation expenses and school fees if sufficient funds were left over after paying for the private schools' tuition. Some parents, for instance, learned that there was no additional support provided by some schools for their child's learning disabilities; others found that tutoring was either unavailable or available only at additional cost.

> Many of the schools don't offer services for special-needs students. My grandson is borderline emotionally disturbed...so I had to bring my therapist, bring my psychologist, bring my mentor, and bring my family. I had to bring it 'cause they didn't have it in the school...when they call me and say he's throwing chairs, I can come up there, but I really had to get them to understand he really is a special-needs child, and you're really going to have to work with him.[27]

One concern that increased consistently among parents from year to year was the shortage of high school slots, as discussed in chapter 4. The District of Columbia has a severe shortage of quality high school options across both public and private schools and, as a result, many parents were worried that the handful of private high schools in the program would not be able to accommodate their children as they advanced from elementary and middle school. Some families even left the program for that reason.

> I think they need...a lot more high schools that accept scholarships...it's so hard to find anything after the sixth grade.[28]
> We have to have some place for our children to go when they get into high school. We have to have more choices. We have to![29]

Another concern, one that many families feared would threaten their children's continued participation in the OSP, was the prospect of "earning out," also discussed in chapter 4.

By Year 4, instead of focusing mainly on their own personal challenges, many of the parents were assessing the schools their children attended with a more critical eye. As one parent noted:

> I've been in the program since the program started. When we first started, the classes were much smaller; the teachers were more...aggressively

teaching the kids. Now, as we're going on, every day it seems like the school has a different group of teachers, and I just found out recently that most of the teachers don't even have degrees.[30]

They also raised questions regarding where their scholarship funds went and how the funds were being spent. By the third year, a number of parents even began to wonder whether some of the participating schools were motivated by scholarship funding:

It's like the school is taking advantage of the money they get from the scholarship...They just raking in money all kinds of ways—they get it from the scholarship fund for the tuition and the before and after care, and they turn around and get it out of you if you running late.[31]

Satisfaction with the Opportunity Scholarship Program

Though families provided a long list of reasons why they were satisfied with the program itself, most of the comments could be placed into one of three categories: (1) they felt lucky and proud to receive a scholarship, (2) they appreciated the support they received from the WSF, and (3) they were pleased that their children would receive a quality education.

Given the random selection lottery that is associated with the program, many parents felt fortunate that their children received a scholarship.

I said, "If they stay up until 12:00 doing their homework, I'm going to stay up 'til 12:00. You're going to get it done. I be tired the next day, but you're going to get it done, 'cause this is a blessing to get the scholarship."[32]
   It makes a lot of kids feel very important...I think it's fantastic that they have private schools for these kids...It makes their ego—they feel more important, they want to learn more, and they feel like they're not going there to waste their time.[33]

Almost all the families experienced adjustment challenges as a result of their move from the public to private school sector. The WSF anticipated many of their needs and helped to make the transition as smooth as possible. For example, the mere process of completing the official application, which ran 19 pages including a baseline survey, could have been a major obstacle for parents and guardians who had limited literacy skills. However, the WSF assembled a large group of volunteers who provided families with one-on-one assistance to complete the application and to ensure that all supporting documentation was included. This level of "customer service" was consistent throughout the parents' experiences with the program.

> I went through the process, which was absolutely wonderful to me, 'cause I was clueless as to the whole procedure…And each time, I was contacted verbally through the phone and through the mail. So I had no problem going to any of the locations…And any time I called, the people are very attentive.[34]

Parents were also impressed with how issues were managed when they expressed frustration and disappointment with schools. Over the course of the four years that we engaged with the families, parents expressed fleeting forms of frustration with a wide range of experiences. For example, during Year One, it was unclear to families which expenses their students' scholarships would cover. They missed some of the supplemental learning opportunities their children previously received in public schools, particularly tutoring and assistance for special-needs students. Ironically, the way these issues were managed by individual schools and the WSF became an additional source of satisfaction.

> I made a comment at the bottom of the renewal form, the survey form asking how you think the school was…and I went to her school one day…there was a panel from the WSF there…they were there with their clipboards…and I was like, "Oh, it does work. You make a comment, it does help."[35]

The OSP represents an opportunity for students that most parents never had. Many of the families associate "private schools" with a better education. In the minds of the parents who hold this view, the OSP essentially guarantees their children a "better" education.

> It's a wonderful program. It gives opportunity, and the children can go to a wonderful school and be challenged even more and do very, very well—even better than if they stay in public school.[36]
> My mom didn't finish high school. I was an honor roll student, no one even talked to me about college…And now I'm 37 years old, and I'm a college student, when I could have gotten it [a college degree], and it could have been over with…Now I'm back in school, raising kids, helping them with work, when it didn't have to be that challenging. I don't want my kids to experience the same thing, so I'm already speaking to them—"You can be whatever you want to be."[37]

Sources of Satisfaction with the Schools

In chapter 3 we discussed why parents sought to participate in the Opportunity Scholarship Program and what they sought in their child's private school at the front end of their school choice journey. Here we share the specifics of how parents explained and justified their general satisfaction with their journey while it was well underway.

Access to private schools was obviously the primary reason why families pursued the OSP. Like the families' sources of satisfaction about the OSP in general, most of their comments about the specific schools their children were attending could be placed into three general categories: (1) improved school safety and student discipline, (2) improved academic or learning environment, and (3) noticeable signs of improved student attitudes and behaviors toward learning.

Safety and student discipline were two of the greatest concerns identified by the parents in the early years of the program.

> In the private school, I never have to worry about my children…My friend was going to public school—they would wait one hour in line to be searched, to go through the metal detectors, to be searched for school. But the private school where my son goes, they just walk in. They don't have to worry about students coming in with guns.[38]
>
> They're just not allowed to do these things in Catholic schools that they do in public schools…They stop that at the door, which is great, 'cause in public schools, kids get hurt every day…This child has an apple; they want to take the child's apple—you try that in Catholic schools, it's going to be a problem.[39]

Over time, the parents' focus shifted from school safety and student discipline to the conditions for learning, a development that we discuss in greater detail in chapter 3, and it was clear that they were using subjective assessments of their children's attitudes about learning and study habits as indicators of their academic progress and development. Smaller class sizes, improved instruction, and challenging curricula were all considered essential conditions for effective learning by these parents, a majority of whom felt that the schools their children were attending through the OSP offered all or a combination of these attributes. As one parent noted:

> He functions better in small settings, and that was my main concern—to find a school that had a smaller setting that he could adapt and get the education that he needed, so that he would have a better chance when he finishes school, going out in society to work, and not have to do manual labor.[40]
>
> The teacher is excellent. The intensity of the curriculum they have at her school is excellent—they have these pre-K kids doing fractions.[41]
>
> In DC public school, they didn't have art, so I never knew that my daughter could draw. She has art in [her choice school]. And two weeks

ago, she got a scholarship to Corcoran for the pre-college program, and I was really surprised, 'cause she had such a talent, and she went through the whole DC from pre-K to eighth grade and never knew she could draw.[42]

Scores from standardized tests and other formal methods of measuring student progress were seldom referenced by parents when they were asked to share information about how they measure their child's progress. However, some parents did express the view that formal academic assessments do not happen frequently enough and that, when they do, the validity and reliability of the findings are either not clear or not trusted. Instead, it was apparent that most parents were looking for signs like their child's willingness to go to school in the morning or complete their homework in the evening without prodding. By these standards, parents noticed significant positive changes in their children's attitudes and behaviors toward learning.

> Even my co-workers have commented on how much she has changed…her outer appearance, the way she walks and talks, and how she interacts with other children. It's much different than when she was going to public school or charter school. Now, her whole being is completely different.[43]
>
> [The student] didn't have much respect for authority in the very beginning, before she started Catholic school, but now she's very respectful. She respects me to the utmost now.[44]

Most parents indicated that when safety, discipline, positive conditions for learning, and improved student attitudes and behaviors are present, more formal signs of progress are inevitable:

> My kids increased their grades with the curriculum and academic standards at the school. Their grades were able to come up.[45]
>
> Honor rolls last year and this year…She's consistent with her learning…her studies have become better…they got technology, they take computer classes, and they go on their lunch break. They all have the same things in common and want the same things out of life…it lets you keep going on instead of going backward.[46]

One parent said of her child in the OSP, "I can see her happier, and she has learned much more, even to read and write pretty well."[47] Her child's happiness was her primary concern. The additional learning that she had observed seemed, to this parent, almost as an afterthought.

Empowerment as a Key Source of Satisfaction

As discussed in earlier chapters, we identified patterns of refined and growing consumer behavior among the parent participants in the OSP, which led us to tentatively theorize that certain aspects of the program had an empowering effect on families. By the third and fourth year of the study, participation in the program appears to have transformed many of the parents from passive recipients of services, or clients, into more active and discerning consumers.

The development of observable consumer behavior among parents began from the outset of their involvement with the program. In the first year, we witnessed the OSP parents working to develop additional consumer skills to complement those already acquired during the application process. The practical steps they took to gain initial access to the program, such as making visits to several schools and consulting various sources of information before making their school choice, should not be underestimated.

These consumer skills were developed further in the second year of the program and enabled parents to make decisions such as whether to remain with the school their children had initially entered, transfer to a different school within the OSP, or exit the program. By the end of the second year of data collection, it became very clear to us that the vast majority of the families were moving in practical ways away from a marginal role as passive recipients of school assignments to a role of active participants in the school selection process. For example, they were being challenged to collect information about several schools, review this information to refine their choices, and eventually visit schools and engage teachers and administrators in a completely new fashion.

Another clear example of parents taking ownership of their school choice journey was the case of financial reporting by the schools. In the first year during the focus groups, several parents commented that it was not clear to them exactly which education expenses were and were not covered by the scholarship, in general or for their particular child.[48] In essence, they were saying that they did not completely know what they were buying. Moreover, the parents said that they felt a fiduciary responsibility to monitor the expenditure of scholarship funds at their child's school, to make sure that taxpayer dollars were being spent appropriately. In response to their complaints, the WSF clarified the financial policies of the OSP and encouraged the schools in the program to share expenditure information with parents. In the second year of focus groups, parents expressed appreciation for these changes, as one commented, "Now we get letters in the mail stating how each dollar was spent for our child and if we have any difference we can voice our opinion."[49]

A key question here is whether the experiences of the OSP families differed significantly from those involved in other school choice programs in terms of empowerment. Although we can only speculate about this, since our research focused on the OSP participants, we would argue that their experiences probably differed in some respects but not in others. On the one hand, as it relates to families' direct experiences with participating schools, other research on this topic indicates that families participating in other school choice programs have had very similar experiences to those in the OSP.[50] However, on the other hand, with regard to the program itself, it is arguable that the OSP pilot initiative was different from public charter schools and represented an improvement over other voucher programs, particularly in relation to the level and types of support provided to families by program personnel.

Previous research, discussed in detail in chapter 1,[51] has shown that social programs that are well designed and effectively delivered often provide recipients not only with tangible resources but with the attitudes and skills needed to become more astute consumers and active citizens who can promote their own interests in society. This often happens when participants have positive rather than negative experiences of participating in a program and interacting with program personnel, and when they are provided with accurate and helpful information. Among parents who remained in the OSP, interpersonal communications with program and school personnel were reported to be the most helpful sources of information about schools. Having accurate and comprehensive information was found to be a key source of satisfaction with the program, and we believe that this was because it enabled parents to carefully analyze school options and find a good match for their children. In doing so, they were refining their consumer skills. Even the minority of families that decided to transfer schools or leave the program due to dissatisfaction with their experiences used their newly developed or refined consumer skills to identify and visit alternative schools, meet administrators, sit in on classes, consult other parents, and in general make a better-informed decision.

However, we also found that some families were unable to complete the transition to fully effective consumers, exhibiting some aspects of consumerism but also elements of a client-like mentality. On one end of the spectrum, many OSP parents jumped in and fully embraced the private school marketplace by visiting numerous schools, asking many questions, and setting clear expectations of the schools that they ultimately chose for their children. On the other end of the continuum, some parents appeared to remain relatively passive participants in the school search process and in relation to the school that their children entered. These parents considered only a small number of schools or a single school, and they did not conduct school visits. They tended to defer accountability to others, for example recommending that the WSF provide more oversight and quality control of the schools in the program, making it virtually impossible for parents to choose a "bad" school for their child. Since many of these parents viewed inadequate evaluative information about schools as one of their sources of dissatisfaction with the OSP, this finding lends support to the argument that the ability to become sufficiently empowered to seek information and evaluate schools independently is likely to drive satisfaction with the program.

Conclusion

This chapter has examined how parents defined and measured student progress and their own satisfaction with the OSP, and how this changed over time as some developed more consumer-like behavior and became more discerning in their expectations of the program and of schools. Previous studies have indicated that parents from low-income and ethnic minority groups have different priorities in relation to educational environments compared with other parents, focusing for example on the provision of a safe environment, which is seen as fundamental to learning.[52] In this study of low-income families, we also found evidence of an early focus on immediate outcomes that reflected the participants' initial values and expectations of OSP participation, such as a safe school environment and attitudinal adjustments on the part of their children. Over time, however, as the families became more empowered by the program, and developed or improved their consumer skills, many parents began to place a greater emphasis on intermediate or longer-term academic outcomes, and became more critical of aspects of schools that hindered or failed to demonstrate progress in these areas. In this respect, it can be argued that the OSP has been particularly successful in generating high levels of parental satisfaction as a result of quality service delivery and high levels of support provided to families, which have had positive effects and influenced the parental school choice journey movement from clients to consumers. On the other hand, some parents did not successfully make this trip; they continued to rely heavily on the WSF to provide information and support and so some remained stagnant in a client-like disposition.

Although the data generated from this study did not allow us to fully investigate why some families were more empowered by the program than others, it is possible that preexisting experiences and levels of family resources may have contributed to their different experiences with the program. According to our theoretical model, the ability of families to benefit from the potentially empowering effects of the OSP and to make the transition from clients to consumers is likely to be influenced by their family structure and the associated levels of resources available to them. Resources are defined broadly in terms of factors such as time, existing knowledge, and practical support from social networks. As discussed in the previous chapter, our three identified family "types" have varying levels of resources available to them, and are typically associated with an emphasis on different levels of student outcomes described as immediate, intermediate, and long term (see Figure 5.1). In this chapter, we have described further the interaction between parental expectations of the program and parents' levels of satisfaction with it, and have begun to show how characteristics of the program appeared to have had an empowering effect on some of the parents but not on others.

As noted above, some participants displayed few consumer skills from the outset, relying on the WSF for substantial direction in choosing schools. Their failure to properly evaluate school options may have been one of the factors contributing to their dissatisfaction with schools at a later stage. This is especially the case in relation to the unanticipated additional costs for transportation, lunch, or extracurricular activities, which surprised some families but should have been identified before enrolling their child in the school.

For other participants, satisfaction or dissatisfaction with the program was increasingly determined by the extent to which their child was perceived to be progressing toward long-term outcomes. After the first year or so, the focus of attention of these parents shifted from their own personal challenges, such as resource limitations or the difficulty of helping with homework, to a critical examination of schools in relation to the desired longer-term outcomes for their children. It can be argued that having more personal resources at their disposal facilitated this, as hypothesized in our theoretical model. In some cases, parents started to question the standard of teaching in their child's school, or even the motives of the schools for participating in the program. In this way, they were exhibiting clear signs of consumer-like behavior.

As conveyed in Figure 4.3 (chapter 4), we hypothesize that some types of families experienced a shorter or longer journey to their target destination of positive student outcomes, depending on the resources that they brought to the trip. Intact families and single-parent families with extensive support systems had the extra person-power to navigate the consumer demands of parental school choice more quickly and effectively, we surmise, expediting their child's progress along the path to self-confidence and achievement gains. Families that lacked such resources could still travel the path—and many such families in the OSP undoubtedly did—but the journey was longer for them, as they had to be concerned with a number of additional "stops" along the way.

This was not the end of the journey, though, as some parents continued to make the transition from clients to consumers. The ultimate stage in the process of empowerment of low-income families is the difficult transformation into active citizens. Did many OSP participants reach that final destination? We explore that crucial question next.

6

School Vouchers and the Empowerment of Urban Families

Families chose to participate in the OSP because they were interested in an education option for their children that they believed they could not access by way of traditional public or public charter schools. In essence, they were pursuing and entering a different educational and social community. A critical element of community is reciprocity. When a new educational opportunity is provided to families, usually something, whether explicitly or tacitly, is expected of them in return.[1]

Parents and students in the OSP appeared to be surprised when they learned that one thing that would be expected of them was to fight for the continuation of the program. And many observers, including us, were surprised at the strength of their response. We get a strong flavor of the fight that was in the OSP participants when we consider the case of Ronald Holassie. Ronald is an African American teenager raised in a low-income single-parent family who attended Archbishop Carroll High School in Washington, DC as a result of the OSP. In this exceptional case, we use Ronald's actual name and school because he and his family were not direct participants in our research study and he has spoken publicly about this issue, in testimony before Congress, in interviews with the media, and in a 30-minute documentary about the OSP called *Let Me Rise*.

Ronald describes his life before the OSP as irresponsible and directionless. He bounced around various District of Columbia public schools and says that he "wasn't doing well academically."[2] Ronald was among the early applicants to the OSP and won a scholarship in the lottery. His mother selected Archbishop Carroll as his high school because she thought the structured Catholic school environment would give Ronald more of an academic focus. After an initial adjustment period, Ronald thrived in his new school. He became involved in student government and ultimately was appointed the deputy youth mayor of the District of Columbia for legislation.

When the US Congress closed the program to new applicants in 2009, and the Obama Administration revoked the scholarships of 216 new program participants, Ronald felt that he needed to get involved in efforts to save the OSP. After Ronald testified before a US Senate committee about how he attributed much of his personal success to the scholarship program, Senator Roland Burris (D-IL) questioned him sharply, claiming that a smart, motivated young man like him would have turned out just as well if he had attended a District of Columbia public school. Ronald countered that Senator Burris was mistaken, as several of Ronald's friends who were much like him had gone to their assigned public high school and dropped out or were expelled.[3] In *Let Me Rise*, Ronald states that "the way for a young man to rise is to improve himself any way he can."[4] That certainly is not the statement of a person with a clientist perspective. At least partly as a result of the political activism of Ronald and the other OSP participants, the District of Columbia Opportunity Scholarship Program was saved from extinction and continues to this day.

In this chapter, we discuss the level of willingness of the OSP parents to join other members of the school community in activities that express their opinions about the program—to exercise their voice in being active consumers and empowered citizens. Given the highly political nature of the OSP, the research team thought it would be worthwhile to assess how the parents might share their experiences (beyond the focus groups and personal interviews) and express their opinions about the program with others. In fact, their eventual willingness, after some hesitation, to more publicly and directly engage Congress, President Obama, US Secretary of Education Duncan, and other influential stakeholders arguably determined the fate of the OSP.

Lower-income and working-class urban individuals and families traditionally have relatively low rates of political activism.[5] In some respects this is understandable, as such groups tend to face major life challenges and experiences that diminish their willingness and ability to be actively involved in the broader community.[6] Though perhaps understandable, the lack of political activism demonstrated by most lower-income urban adults is regrettable because it is specifically linked to the inability of such groups to shape public policy in ways that serve their interests.[7] Having participated in the OSP for the past three or four years, and having expressed high levels of satisfaction with the program, a logical question emerged for us in our research: Are OSP parents sufficiently motivated to take action to support the program's continuation?

Parents were first asked about their willingness to share their experiences with the OSP publicly and with decision makers in Year 3 of the data collection. The elementary school parents, in particular, were very receptive to expressing their views of the OSP to policy makers. This higher level of potential activism among parents of younger students may have been because their children would be grade eligible for the program for a longer period of time than high school students. The parents of elementary school students had many more years of school choice at stake.

Over the course of this four-year study, a core group of the Cohort 1 parents of elementary school children consistently attended the focus groups. The parents in this core group appeared to experience a noticeable change in their concerns about the OSP from school selection issues toward advocacy for the continuation of the OSP. In 2007 and 2008, elementary school parents in both cohorts indicated that they would be active in making their voice heard on the pending reauthorization of the District of Columbia Opportunity Scholarship Program as the end of its pilot period approached in 2009. The parents in Cohort 1 were particularly enthusiastic about influencing OSP policy. As one parent stated:

> We still need school choices for our children until things are better as far as the public school is concerned. So we're going to have to lobby.[8]

When asked what kinds of public expressions of support parents would be willing to make, most focus group participants said that they preferred to write letters and testify before Congress or the city council rather than participate in other forms of expression like demonstrating and voting. Three years into their school choice experience, parents said that they appreciated the opportunity that has been provided to them and their children and would be most comfortable expressing that appreciation through individual acts of testimony to decision makers.

At the end of our data collection for this study, in the spring of 2008, we reviewed all the evidence we had collected from our interactions with 100 OSP families over the previous four years and determined that only a small percentage of them had made the full school choice journey from clients to empowered citizens. We made that judgment, at that time, because even the highly committed parents who consistently participated in our focus groups described their lives as very busy and focused on their own family needs, including the educational development of their children. If the program's continuation were imperiled and would require parent support, the evidence suggested that most OSP parents would not publicly fight to save it.

The Politics of School Choice and the Battle over the OSP

School choice programs are politically controversial because they challenge the ideal of the common school. It is a major aspect of American lore that neighborhood public schools are open to all—common—and forge effective democratic citizens out of diverse groups of students.[9] Although some contemporary scholars have revealed this idyllic view of the common school to be largely a myth,[10] the US public continues to possess what Terry Moe calls a "public school ideology."[11]

Public opinion regarding school vouchers is decidedly mixed, as levels of support depend on how much respondents know about the topic, how the survey question is worded, and whether or not the respondent has a school-aged child. Survey researcher Paul DiPerna finds that only 43 percent of US adults support school vouchers when they are asked the question out of context. Support for school vouchers increases to 60 percent when respondents are provided with a straightforward definition of vouchers before being asked the question.[12] Support for vouchers remains below 50 percent when vouchers are described as allowing "parents to choose a private school to attend at public expense" but often registers above 50 percent when characterized as allowing parents to choose from among public, private, and parochial schools for which "the government would pay all or part of the tuition."[13] Support for school vouchers tends to be somewhat higher among African Americans, Hispanic Americans, and parents of school-age children.[14] Dick Carpenter has found that Americans express higher levels of support for private school choice programs funded by tax-credits than they do of voucher programs that are directly funded by the government.[15]

As we mentioned in chapter 2, after the five-year term of the OSP pilot expired in the spring of 2009, political opponents of the program took action to end it. The main political opponent of the OSP was the country's teachers' unions, which, along with the National School Boards Association, fiercely oppose private school choice.[16] The teachers' unions are the single largest campaign contributor to the Democratic Party, so their opposition to vouchers in general, and the District of Columbia's OSP in particular, is often (but not always) re-enforced by the votes of Democratic lawmakers.[17] This political reality was reflected in the opposition to the OSP, which was led by US Senator Dick Durbin (D-IL) and Delegate Eleanor Holmes Norton (D-DC), with encouragement from President Obama. After Democrats took control of both houses of Congress and the presidency in the wake of the 2008 elections, OSP opponents sought to shut down the program entirely by the fall of 2010 through language inserted in the Fiscal Year 2010 Budget.[18]

This legislative development provoked editorials, in both liberal and conservative newspapers, opposed to ending the program.[19] A bipartisan coalition of political leaders, including Senators Joe Lieberman (I-CT), Susan Collins (R-ME), Robert C. Byrd (D-WV), and Dianne Feinstein (D-CA); House Minority Leader John Boehner (R-OH); and Mayor Adrian Fenty (D-Washington, DC) spoke in opposition to ending the program and in support of its reauthorization.[20] The school choice journey of District of Columbia parents and children was being threatened with premature cancellation. How would parents and students respond?

The first of several participant rallies to save the program, sponsored by a network of grassroots organizations including DC Children First, DC Parents for School Choice, and The Voices of School Choice, took place on May 7, 2009.[21] Journalist Joseph Lawler, who covered the rally, estimated the crowd size to be 1,400 participants including parents, schoolchildren, and teachers.[22] As the editorialists of the *Washington Post* wrote, "Hundreds of children, outfitted in the uniforms of the private schools they attend through vouchers, sat in rapt attention as one of their own read a poem he had written" pleading with policy makers to continue the program.[23] In response to the rally, President Obama announced a compromise that would permit existing OSP participants to continue to use their scholarships until they graduated from high school but close the program to all new entrants, including 216 low-income students who had just been awarded scholarships through the annual program lottery.[24]

Less than a week later, on May 13, supporters staged another rally in advance of a hearing in the Senate Committee on Homeland Security and Government Affairs entitled "The DC Opportunity Scholarship Program: Preserving School Choice for All." The Government Affairs committees in both the Senate and the House had jurisdiction over the OSP because Congress has ultimate authority over much that happens in the District of Columbia, including its educational programs. One of us (Wolf) was called to testify at the hearing, as he was lead author of a government-sponsored statistical evaluation of the OSP that reported clear achievement gains for scholarship students in reading but no significant improvements in math after three years.[25] Other witnesses at the hearing were former Washington, DC, Mayor Anthony Williams, Sidwell Friends Head of School Bruce Stewart, OSP students Ronald Holassie and Tiffany

Dunston, and OSP parent Latasha Bennett.[26] Much like the character at the center of the movie *Won't Back Down*, in fighting to save the OSP, Bennett was transformed from a single mom trying to secure a better education for her child to a political activist crusading to save a government program and a scholarship for her daughter, one of the 216 scholarships revoked by US Department of Education Secretary Arne Duncan.[27] All six witnesses spoke in favor of the OSP while six witnesses invited to testify in opposition to the program, including leaders of the national teachers' unions, all declined to appear before the committee.[28]

On May 23, House Minority Leader John Boehner (R-OH) introduced legislation in the House to reauthorize the OSP. Although the leaders of the political caucuses in the House generally refrain from serving as the lead authors of bills, in this case Boehner made an exception to highlight the importance of the issue to him. He was joined as lead author of the proposal by Representatives Howard "Buck" McKeon (R-CA), Chair of the House Education Committee, and Darrell Issa (R-CA). As Issa stated to journalists covering the story, "The reasons to continue funding the D.C. Opportunity Scholarship Program are convincing...It's working for students, and it's wanted by parents."[29] Senator Lieberman followed by introducing his own reauthorization bill, called the Scholarships for Opportunity and Results (SOAR) Act, coauthored by a bipartisan group of his fellow senators.[30]

After two rallies, a highly publicized Senate hearing, and the introduction of reauthorization legislation in both the House and Senate, the status of the OSP remained the same: available only to continuing students (funding permitting) and closed to any new applicants including the 216 students awarded scholarships in March of 2009. On August 18, supporters held a third rally in front of the US Department of Education, specifically to protest the revocation of the 216 scholarships. It was smaller than the first two rallies, including 70 parents, students, and activists according to media reports.[31] Senator Durbin (D-IL), an opponent of the OSP and Chair of the Senate Appropriations Subcommittee responsible for funding the program, held a hearing on September 16 that was limited to testimony from the program administrator and leaders of the Washington, DC traditional public and public charter schools. The hearing raised concerns about possible "stealth students" funded by the program but unaccounted for in participating private schools, as well as possible "storefront" private schools in the program that lacked physical features traditionally associated with schools, such as cafeterias and gyms.[32] The Washington Scholarship Fund later provided to Senator Durbin documentation of private school enrollments for all 1,718 students funded by the OSP during the 2008–9 school year and argued that facilities are less important than the educational environment of a school.[33]

A fourth major rally in support of the OSP was held on September 30 on Capitol Hill, in the wake of further committee hearings on funding for the program. Journalists' estimates of the size of the crowd varied from "more than a thousand" to "some 1,500" parents, students, and activists.[34] OSP parent Latasha Bennett was a featured speaker at the rally, and more than a half-dozen parents were interviewed by various media outlets regarding their support for the program. According to one of the accounts, "The battle has pitted a growing number of local Democratic African American parents, community leaders, and national conservative education reform groups, against congressional Democrats backed by teachers' unions and other voucher critics."[35] In the wake of this largest rally in opposition to the cap on the OSP, opinion writers were divided regarding whether or not the citizenship activities of hundreds of empowered parents ultimately would save the program, with the *Wall Street Journal* claiming that the activism of parents meant that the program has "a brighter outlook in Congress" while a *Washington Times* reporter claimed that "students may lose out" and the *Washington Post* editorialized that "Optimism that the district's federally funded school voucher program will be allowed to flourish is fading."[36]

Enrollments and Hope Begin to Wane

The battle to save the OSP continued through the fall of 2009 and all of 2010, and program opponents appeared to be winning. An appropriations bill passed by Congress in December 2009 codified the compromise that the Obama administration proposed. Continuing students were funded, but new applicants were excluded from the program.[37] Due to students who graduated or left the program, enrollment dropped from 1,714 in 2008–9 to 1,322 in 2009–10, consistent with the strategy of opponents to eliminate the program by attrition.[38] Enrollments dropped further, to 1,012 students, in 2010–11. The Washington Scholarship Fund, the nonprofit organization selected by the US Department of Education in 2004 to run the OSP, bowed out in the spring of 2010 to protest the political opposition to the program. Program administration responsibilities were shifted to the DC Children and Youth Investment Trust Corporation, a unique independent nonprofit organization established in 1999 to improve the way services are provided to children and youth in the District of Columbia. Senator Lieberman proposed the reauthorization of the OSP in an amendment to a government spending bill on the floor of the Senate, but his proposal was voted down, 55 to 42, with 38 Republicans and 3 Democrats joining Lieberman in supporting reauthorization.[39]

On June 22, 2010 the US Department of Education released the final report from the statistical evaluation of the OSP. The study found, in the end, "no conclusive evidence that the program affected student achievement," as reading gains that were statistically significant after three years just missed the standard threshold for significance in the final year.[40] The final analysis did report that the program had large positive impacts on the likelihood of students graduating, as the effect of using a scholarship was to increase the odds of graduating by 21 percentage points, from 70 percent to 91 percent.[41] The mixed results from the government study—clear and large graduation rate gains but statistically insignificant achievement effects—provided ammunition to both supporters and opponents of the school choice program.[42]

The Battle Lines Shift

The 2010 congressional elections gave hope to supporters of the OSP. Republicans, who tend to be more consistent supporters of private school choice than Democrats, took control of the US House of Representatives and gained six seats in the US Senate. John Boehner (R-OH), the school choice advocate newly installed as Speaker of the House, invited dozens of the OSP parents and students to be his personal guests at President Obama's State of the Union address that kicked off the new legislative session in January of 2011.[43] Both Boehner and Senator Lieberman introduced a bill to reauthorize the program, again titled the "Scholarships for Opportunity and Results (SOAR) Act, and hearings on the legislation were held in the Senate in February and in the House in March.[44] The SOAR Act passed the House on a vote of 225–195 on March 31, but opposition to program reauthorization from many Senate Democrats and President Obama continued.[45]

Although the new House of Representatives had succeeded in passing the SOAR Act, the previous Congress and President Obama had failed to pass a federal budget for the fiscal year ending in September 2011. That meant that the government was operating under a continuing resolution, which simply extended the approved spending from fiscal year 2010 into 2011 while congressional leaders and the president negotiated a new budget for the five remaining months of the fiscal year. On April 9, 2011, they announced their compromise agreement. To the surprise of many, the deal included reauthorization of the OSP through adoption of the

SOAR Act.[46] The program received another five-year lease on life, the maximum value of the Opportunity Scholarship was raised to $8,000 for elementary school children and $12,000 for high school students, and the requested annual funding amount of $20,000,000 would support around 2,000 participants.

The reauthorization victory sparked renewed interest in the OSP on the part of low-income District of Columbia families. After holding a series of application sessions in the late spring and early summer of 2011, the District of Columbia Investment Trust Corporation supported 1,615 new and continuing scholarship students for the 2011–12 school year.[47] All 216 students whose scholarship awards had been revoked by Secretary of Education Duncan in 2009 were offered new scholarships. A total of 1,584 students enrolled in private schools through the OSP in 2012–13.[48] As is made clear by the trend lines in Figure 6.1, if the OSP had not been reauthorized, it soon would have disappeared.

The battle surrounding the District of Columbia Opportunity Scholarship Program continues. President Obama has proposed that funding for the OSP be zeroed out for fiscal year 2014, which began October 1, 2013.[49] If low-income families in the District of Columbia want to continue their school choice journey, it looks as if they will have to keep fighting for it.

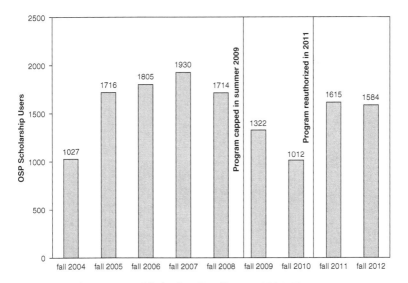

Figure 6.1   Opportunity Scholarship Enrollments, 2004–12

Source: Wolf et al., 2010, Table 1-1, p.3, updated with information publicly released by the District of Columbia Trust in 2010, 2011, and 2012.

Conclusion

The four-year battle to save the District of Columbia Opportunity Scholarship Program has produced important revelations regarding the politics of education reform and the parental school choice journey. First, the politics surrounding school choice initiatives such as the OSP are atypical. After all, the two political leaders who saved the program were the Democrat's candidate for vice-president in 2000 (Lieberman) and the Speaker of the highly partisan, Republican-controlled US House of Representatives (Boehner). Instead of simply pitting Republicans against Democrats or conservatives against liberals, the politics of school choice tends to involve a coalition of groups from the right and left tails of the ideological spectrum against most Democrats and some Republicans in the center.[50] Most support for school choice comes from Republican politicians who believe that free markets tend to do a better job of delivering services than do government monopolies, and from liberal Democrats and low-income parents who view school choice as an issue of social justice, civil rights, and empowerment.

These strange bedfellows may disagree on almost every other major policy issue, but they agree that parents and not government officials should decide which schools their children should attend—traditional public, public chartered, or private. Opposing the school choice political coalition are centrist or establishment Democrats and Republicans, and both groups tend to have strong ties to organized labor in general and to the powerful teachers' unions in particular. School choice opponents, such as Senator Dick Durbin (D-IL), argue that parents and students who are looking for other options should remain clients of their local public school system while the government continues its efforts to improve the quality of the public school monopoly for them. School choice supporters argue that parents should be informed consumers of their child's education, able to select the school that best fits their child's needs from among distinct educational alternatives.

Whether or not the OSP parents would be forced to revert to educational clients or would have the opportunity to continue their experience as educational consumers would end up depending on the extent to which they were willing and able to become empowered citizens capable of shaping outcomes in the political arena. Based on our knowledge of political science, which holds that adults with low levels of income and education tend to be less-active citizens than their better-resourced peers, and our interactions with the OSP parents through our qualitative research, we were somewhat skeptical that a substantial number of the OSP participants would commit the time and effort to actively advocate for the program, and that their voices would have much influence. Our academic training suggested that they would not, but we were obligated to remain open to being convinced otherwise.

When the battle over the OSP began in earnest, shortly after we had completed our collection of the qualitative data that informs this book, our own roles shifted from that of social science researchers leading focus groups and conducting interviews to that of participant-observers. Both of us, Stewart and Wolf, were asked to discuss the results of our research on the OSP at various policy forums, including congressional hearings, and we used those events as opportunities to observe the extent to which the OSP parents themselves were playing the empowered citizenship roles that might complete their school choice journey.

We were surprised by what we increasingly saw. In the hearings, rallies, and media coverage of the issue from 2009 to 2011, the pleas and testimonials of the OSP parents played a prominent role in shifting public opinion and support for the program. Latasha Bennett, Patricia Williams, Joe Kelly, Betty North, Lydell Mann, Elaine Cousins, and other OSP parents provided personal testimonials to policy makers and journalists. All four of the congressional hearings on reauthorization of the program unfolded before rooms packed primarily with OSP parents and students. Rallies that included an estimated 1,500 participants took place in support of a program that was serving only about that many families at the time. Not all rally participants were OSP parents and students, but every media account mentioned that these groups attended the rallies in force, as empowered citizens advocating for their cause. This was a level of citizenship activism that we did not observe during the first four years of the program, when participants assumed that the OSP would continue because it was serving disadvantaged families and, in their view, doing so effectively. It was only when some Washington politicians took steps to end or at least cap the program that the OSP parents became empowered as citizens, clamoring for their school choice journey to be continued.

7

What Lessons Were Learned That May Help Future Travelers?

In conducting the phenomenological research that informed this book, our original intent was to augment the official quantitative evaluation of the District of Columbia OSP by documenting and describing the first-hand experiences of participating families. We soon realized, however, that the findings that emerged from the four qualitative annual reports we produced had considerably wider implications, particularly in the context of an emerging body of research that is illuminating the potential impacts of social programs on the political empowerment and economic advancement of low-income families. We began to focus on this issue in greater depth in our investigations and, as a result, developed a framework for thinking about and understanding school choice programs like the OSP and publicly funded schools more generally as social service delivery agents that can disempower or empower low-income families.

As discussed in chapter 1, three key concepts, drawn in part from the existing literature, undergird our emerging theoretical framework: clientism, consumerism, and active citizenship. These concepts refer to the different types of relationships that can exist between public agencies and social program participants, and they have been found to be associated with specific attitudes and behaviors on the part of participants. To quickly recap our earlier discussion about how these concepts help explain these relationships, public agencies demonstrate a *client* approach to engaging participants and delivering services when they place a low premium on soliciting input from program participants about their needs and preferences. These agencies often view participating individuals and families as little more than recipients of public services with no right to select or mold what they receive or how it is delivered to them.

The term *consumerism*, on the other hand, connotes a more symmetrical relationship between public service recipients and the agencies charged with providing them with such services. It often entails providing program participants with opportunities to express their needs and preferences, and it uses this information to help shape program or service delivery. Effective consumerism requires that the recipients have the relevant skills and knowledge that will enable them to make well-informed choices and "vote with their feet."[1] Finally, empowered *citizenship* is defined as a form of political participation in which low-income individuals and families are able to represent their own interests and collaborate with others who are interested in protecting and advancing those interests.

Well-designed public programs can provide recipients not only with material resources but also with the attitudes and skills needed to become more astute consumers and empowered citizens who can advocate for their own interests in society. Conversely, social programs that are poorly designed and delivered can have disempowering effects on recipients, often reinforcing their disadvantaged situation and circumstances and generating an attitude of defeatism.

It became clear from the literature, however, that there are substantial knowledge gaps in this area generally, and there has been no previous research on the broader family effects of participation in means-tested school choice programs. The specific nature of voucher programs raises interesting questions about their likely impact on the parents as well as the students involved. On the one hand, most publicly funded school voucher programs are means-tested and limited to families with income near the federal poverty level. Under such circumstances we might expect that clientism would characterize the relationship between recipients and service providers. On the other hand, school choice programs are designed to rely on the effective participation of parents to make them work. Parents are expected to seek out information about new or expanded school options and to find among those varied options one that is of high quality and a good fit for their child's needs. This raises questions about whether or not program participants are initially equipped to exercise parental school choice, and whether the program itself is designed to provide the information and other resources that can help these families make informed school choice decisions and become effective education consumers. In the context of our conceptual framework, it also raises the question whether participation in the OSP ultimately results in the achievement of empowered citizenship through political participation. Does school choice help to facilitate a journey that goes all the way from clients, to consumers, to empowered citizens?

We discovered through focus group discussions with our sample of parent participants in the OSP that they reported levels of satisfaction with the program that seemed unusually high given their children's experience with the participating schools. This suggested that something was happening that distinguished this experience—their school choice journey—from other programs that the participants may have encountered that were characterized by clientism. We therefore began to investigate whether the participants' positive experiences with the OSP were promoting consumer or citizenship-type behaviors that might have beneficial impacts not only on their child's academic outcomes but on their lives more generally.

The remainder of this chapter summarizes the main findings of our research relating to family experiences with the OSP, along with the experiences of the program administrator, participating schools, and a number of key citywide stakeholders.[2] The lessons learned and corresponding recommendations arising from the findings are set out, and our proposed conceptual framework for the study of school choice is described. By synthesizing the major findings of this study, and considering their implications for the OSP and other school choice programs, we argue that well-designed school choice as an education strategy offers clear potential for raising student academic outcomes and helping to fight intergenerational poverty in the United States.

From Clientism to Consumerism and Empowered Citizenship

One of the objectives of this study has been to explore how a well-designed parental school choice program might constitute a powerful antipoverty tool over and beyond any immediate educational benefits bestowed upon the children of low-income families, by facilitating the development of the skills needed by parents to become more astute consumers and assertive citizens. So what were the main conclusions of our study regarding the transition of the OSP participant families from clientism to citizenship?

Our research findings only partially supported the argument that a well-designed school choice program can help transform "clients" into effective consumers and active citizens. Although a large number of the OSP participants did indeed develop effective consumer skills during their period of participation in the program, some retained a client-like mentality. Although a surprisingly high number of OSP parents and high school students engaged in active citizenship in support of the program, the overwhelming majority of those efforts took place only after the program was threatened with extinction. It was often the fear of losing opportunity to attend the private school, and not the program as designed, that motivated the OSP families to travel the full distance to empowered citizenship.

From Clientism to Consumerism

The OSP presented families with new responsibilities that challenged them to assume more demanding roles in the education marketplace than ever before. Prior to their application to the OSP, the majority of families who participated in the study had not ventured outside their neighborhood public schools to explore other educational opportunities and had never been called upon to demonstrate the types of consumer skills that would be needed to select an appropriate private school for their children. As low-income urban residents, few of the participants even had experience in making large consumer purchases such as houses or cars and therefore had not developed the skills needed to compare and evaluate high-value and complex products from multiple providers. Over time we noticed, however, that participation in the program appeared to be transforming many of the families from passive recipients of services, or clients, into more discerning consumers.

Even during the first year of the program, we observed that many parents were working to develop their skills in assessing and comparing distinct features of their children's new schools. This consumer confidence was demonstrated in the ways they began to proactively volunteer more feedback and deeper insights about how the program might be improved. For example, they began to express a desire for more reliable information about discrete aspects of the schools. Many parents learned that not all private schools are well resourced. As time went on, these parents became even more discerning, seeking information about aspects of private-school education such as teacher qualifications and whether the schools really could deliver on the services they had advertised. Some parents even exercised their newly heightened consumer skills by moving their child from the initial private school they had chosen to a different one within the program. Making that switch often involved conducting several school visits and engaging teachers and parents of students in potential new schools. Indeed, by the end of the second year of data collection, it became very clear to us that the vast majority of the participating families were moving from a marginal role as passive recipients of school assignments to a role of active participants in the school selection process.

However, a minority of families failed to make this transition to effective consumers. These families appeared to remain relatively passive participants in the school search process and in relation to the school that their children attended. They considered only a small number of schools or a single school, and they did not conduct school visits. They tended to defer accountability to others, often requesting that the WSF provide more oversight and quality control of the schools in the program, to guarantee that they all would be high quality. These families tended, on the whole, to be disappointed with the OSP, perhaps because their child had enrolled in a school that was not necessarily a good fit for their needs.

From Consumerism to Citizenship

Initially we surmised that very few families would make the full hypothesized transition from clients to active citizens. As might be expected in the case of low-income families, a high proportion reported in our early focus groups that they were not politically active, a finding that gave us the opportunity to investigate any growth of political awareness and activism resulting from participation in the OSP. When asked, many of these families indicated that they would be willing to help "save the program," and the majority said that they would prefer to do so by "direct testimony" rather than other forms of political advocacy or support such as voting or protesting. In our final set of focus groups during spring 2008, it appeared that few families were monitoring the rapidly changing political environment and, locally, none of the political leaders who had strongly supported the OSP remained in office. The OSP Parent Empowerment group, established by the WSF in the spring of 2005, remained focused on program implementation topics, such as choosing a good school and adjusting to a different school environment. Although this issue fell outside the immediate scope of our research project at the time, only two of our focus group participants reported that they had attended Parent Empowerment meetings related to supporting the continuation of the program.

The relatively low level of political activism that we observed among the OSP participants from 2004 to 2008 changed dramatically after the program was capped and threatened with extinction in 2009. As discussed in chapter 6, hundreds of OSP parents and students joined political activists in multiple public rallies in support of continuing the program. More than a dozen parents shared personal stories of their school choice journey with journalists covering the battle to save the OSP. Opportunity Scholarship parents and students provided some of the most compelling testimony provided in four congressional hearings on the program. Certainly the persistent efforts of political leaders such as Speaker John

Boehner (R-OH), Senator Joe Lieberman (I-CT), former Washington, DC, Mayor Anthony Williams, former Washington, DC, City Council Member Kevin Chavous, and former Washington, DC, Mayor and current City Council Member Marion Barry were crucial to the successful reauthorization of the program. As these leaders said throughout this process, they persevered in their quest to reauthorize the OSP because so many parents and students were demanding it. If many of the parents had not gone the distance in their school choice journey, from clients to consumers to empowered citizens, then their journey would have come to an abrupt halt.

Explaining the Findings

The reasons why many low-income Washington, DC parents and students committed so much time and effort to saving the OSP seem clear. These families felt they were receiving something of great value, and they were therefore motivated to fight to preserve the program when it was threatened, even though only a small number of these families had been politically active previously. One noteworthy finding from political science research highlights that constituents punish politicians more when benefits are taken away from them than they reward politicians when benefits are given to them.[3] Nothing calls a political constituency to action more than the threat of losing a government program that they value. It appears that, in the case of the battle over the OSP, the fear of losing the program trumped the influences of background demographics and empowered a surprisingly large number of the OSP parents to rise up and help rescue the scholarship program.

Still, not all the OSP parents made the complete school choice journey from clients to savvy consumers to active and influential citizens. Although the data generated from this study did not allow us to fully explore why some families were more empowered by the program than others, the findings did suggest that preexisting experiences and levels of family resources may have explained some of the differences between the families. As discussed in chapter 4, we established three broadly defined family "types." Each family type has varying levels of resources available to them, which typically appeared to influence the different types of outcomes envisioned for their children, as well as the ways in which the parents engaged with the program.[4] As we discovered, a high proportion of the parents headed what we termed Type 1 or Type 2 families, which had low levels of support and resources available to them, and were often preoccupied with long hours of work and daily economic survival. It is unsurprising that fewer of the parents associated with these types of families had the time or energy to research schools effectively or become politically active. These factors also strongly influenced the ways that families engaged with the schools and the program, as well as their ability to manage the challenges and adjustments commonly associated with switching schools. In the context of the wider body of literature on the impact of social programs on low-income recipients, this is an important finding that recipients' family structures and characteristics interact with program design to influence the attitudes and behaviors of participants.

Parental school choice has always existed for parents with sufficient financial wherewithal. [5] The OSP provided the families in this study with the financial support they needed to pursue the private schools participating in the program. To some extent, our research participants were demonstrating some fundamental consumer behavior when they took action and applied to the OSP. Of the roughly 40,000 students eligible for the program when the OSP was established, only 10 percent of them applied to the program in the first two years.[6]

In this respect, the OSP families may be atypical of low-income families more generally. But the high levels of demand for scholarships, once information about the program was disseminated, suggest that many low-income families can and do exercise school choice when presented with the opportunity. Beyond being accepted into the program, however, we found considerable divergence in the extent to which different families were able to effectively pursue the opportunity they had been given, in terms of researching, selecting, and adjusting to a suitable school for their child.

At one extreme, some families displayed active consumer behavior from the outset, making visits to several schools and consulting various sources of information before selecting schools. These parents were generally able to articulate clear reasons for pursuing the OSP and the specific characteristics they were looking for in schools, some of which reflected long-term aspirations for their child's education. Many others, however, simply wanted out of what they considered "bad schools" and did not clearly base their school selection on a full understanding of the educational needs of their child or the ability to effectively research school options. These families almost exclusively relied on the school directory published by the WSF, collateral material provided by individual schools, and other more generic information when making their school choices. In fact, some parents gave the impression that they believed that all private schools are "good schools," and we learned through their experiences there were some subpar private schools in the program.

This initial assumption of some parents that all private schools would be well-resourced clearly generated some disappointments. Some parents were surprised to discover that not all the participating private schools had the facilities, programs, or services previously available at their child's public school, such as supplemental programs for students with special needs, language classes for non-English speakers, or breakfast and lunch programs. Like the unanticipated costs for transportation, lunch, or extracurricular activities, some parents failed to identify these factors or take them into consideration in their initial school choice decision. In many cases, this resulted in major challenges for the students and their families following enrollment in the private schools, including practical issues such as managing the logistics and costs associated with transportation to and from school, as well as academic challenges associated with a more-demanding curriculum. The participating schools and the program administrators also faced challenges in dealing with or trying to accommodate the students' and families' needs.

Among those families who successfully overcame the initial challenges of participation in the program, we saw a clear development of consumer skills after the first year or so, with the focus of attention shifting from immediate concerns such as safety and their own personal challenges in supporting their child's education to a more critical examination of schools in relation to the desired longer-term outcomes for their children. This key development was commented on by the program administrators in an interview:

> The families who come in here…are just happy because their kids don't have to walk through metal detectors and aren't worried about safety. [They] are just happy to be out…[but] in a year or two, that school that they picked in year one is not good enough because they don't offer Chinese or whatever it is as they become more sophisticated.[7]

After several years of participation in the program, we found that many parents had settled quite comfortably into their roles as education consumers and that, as their comfort level increased, they became more precise about describing their experiences and the impact of the program on their family. Some even began to display elements of empowered citizenship by indicating that they would push aside their desires for anonymity and publicly advocate for the continuation of the program.

On the other hand, those parents who did not achieve this level of comfort with regard to consumerism and active citizenship tended to defer accountability to others for the problems and challenges they were facing in the program. When asked what recommendations they would make to address this concern, they suggested there should be an independent entity that would verify the information provided to them by participating schools, as well as to monitor the schools during the academic year. These parents indicated that inadequate evaluative information was one of their main sources of dissatisfaction with the OSP.

Finally, we were surprised to discover that, in many cases, the students themselves had not been involved in the selection of schools, even if they were high school age. This was in part because the participating high schools all were oversubscribed. Many parents did not want their children to be disappointed if they were not successful in gaining admission to their school of choice. Therefore, parents often withheld information about the school selections from their children until they received formal notice from the school.

In the case of the OSP, the inability of some families to make the journey to effective consumerism or empowered citizenship may have reflected limitations of the program itself. As the OSP administrators recognized, the program resources were inadequate to meet the unanticipated high demand for advice and support that many families needed when they first entered the program. Although the provision of even more information and advice by the program administrators might have reinforced clientism among these families instead of promoting consumer skills, it is also possible that additional support in the early stages of program participation might have given the families a firmer foundation and greater confidence as they moved into subsequent phases of the program. This might have included, for example, training workshops or printed and audio and video guidance on what to look for when selecting schools and how to go about the school search process.

Recommendations for Program Improvement Based on Lessons from the Families

The families that shared with us information about their school choice journeys taught us a number of important lessons about how urban parents experience choice programs. Drawing upon those lessons, we offer the following suggestions to individuals and organizations that may be interested in providing educational options or supports to low-income families:

- Use a targeted approach involving more personalized support for families who exhibit limited facility with identifying their child's longer-term needs or independently researching and evaluating schools. Our conceptual framework highlights the potential need for high levels of support for families with low levels of available resources (time, employment status, parent education level, etc.) including an emphasis on young single-parent families.

- Determine which consumer skills will be necessary to effectively navigate a school choice initiative and provide families a preprogram orientation about not only the opportunity but the challenges that might be associated with the new program. More generally, funds might be allocated for parent workshops on parental school choice, as well as the development and publication of school selection guides and other resources specifically targeting low-income families.

- Given scarce program resources, funds should be targeted to providing high levels of support and guidance to families at the school selection stage of their involvement in the program, helping to avoid poor initial decisions that have subsequent implications for the families concerned, as well as for schools and the program administrator.

- The school selection process might be modified to encourage parents to involve older children in those decisions. This might include, for example, allowing the school representatives to informally interview the students to investigate the likely mutual fit.

- Parents who have successfully negotiated the school choice process have much to share with other parents. These parents should be recruited and offered as a resource to parents who are new to or have very limited experience with school choice.

The Role of the Program Administrator

The program administrator, the WSF, faced a unique set of challenges in delivering what was essentially a new program concept that differed markedly from the design of previous parental school choice programs.[8] Implementation involved a complex set of activities that included building an organization that could effectively engage prospective families and participating schools and manage multiple and sometimes competing stakeholders. Implementing the OSP did not simply involve processing applications and handing out vouchers.

Despite some early growing pains, in our opinion, the WSF delivered a program that represents a significant improvement over other voucher programs, specifically regarding the level and types of support provided to families by program personnel.

Initially the program got off to a quick start and neglected some administrative issues when it came to implementation. A lot of that was corrected as soon as folks found out about...the issues that families were having when it came to eligibility and participation in the program.[9]

In interviews, representatives of the WSF were very positive on the whole about the perceived success of the program, which was largely attributed to its specific design. Although these comments must be understood as the subjective evaluation of the implementers themselves, they certainly conveyed a sense of personal pride and satisfaction with the positive outcomes that had been achieved:

> We've watched lives change by this program. Kids who told me five years ago that they would be...oh, they don't know what they'd do...they probably wouldn't go to college. They'd probably sell drugs...or drop out of school. Now these same kids are saying to me...we're looking at several [colleges and universities]...I think that's just outstanding.
>
> There needs to be an acknowledgment that it takes time to grow a program. And, when we were awarded the grant, everyone said, "You can never do it, you can never do it, you can never do it; there's no time." We ended up with 1,000 students in school that first year, and the response was "only a 1,000?" What happened to you? Can't do it?[10]

The support and assistance provided by the program administrators, and the ways in which they interacted with the participating families, clearly contributed to the ability of OSP families to make effective use of this school choice opportunity. The families often praised the WSF for exceptional support, or what might be called customer care, and they were especially thankful for the timely modifications and improvements that were made to the program in response to their concerns and feedback. For example, during the first year, the WSF discovered that the transition for families with high school students was very challenging. Many of these families voiced a need for tutoring and other academic support services that many schools did not offer. Based on this feedback, the WSF entered into a strategic partnership with Capital Partners for Education (CPE). Although this relationship ended after the second year of the program, it provides an example of the various program enhancements that were made in response to family needs. It strengthened the relationship between the WSF and the families and largely explains why the parents consistently expressed high levels of satisfaction with the program.

However, the unanticipated needs of some of the families overstretched program resources, as well as the ability of some schools to address the challenges faced by the OSP students and their parents. Other than knowing that the participating families would have household incomes below the poverty level, it appears that the designers of the OSP did not have a clear understanding of other key characteristics of the families that entered the program:

> Because of the extremely low-income nature of the low-income threshold identified in the legislation, the families we were serving had different challenges than the families that we served in our privately funded program—so more challenge, we had less resources.[11]

Perhaps one of the least expected challenges encountered by program administrators was that many of the families did not have the experience or knowledge required to research and make well-informed choices about schools, often focusing on the need to move their child from a school that was perceived as bad rather than focusing on the particular merits of alternative schools.

> They literally come with generations of...failing public schools...(the) idea that different schools would have different missions is sort of outside of their understanding of how education works.[12]
>   When I hear parents talking about exercising school choice, whether it's within DCPS or the charter schools or whether it's the private schools, what I hear is, "I wanna get my kid away from those other kids," and that's for two reasons. One is discipline and security, and the other is what they perceive—and I'm afraid is often right...a downdraft of expectations and negative peer pressure.[13]

The program administrators also faced practical challenges when attempting to place children in appropriate schools since many of the popular schools were in areas of the District of Columbia that were not easily accessible by public transportation.[14]

> You look at a map of the district and you look at where the low-income families reside, most live in northeast or southeast. All of the private [high] schools, with the exception of one, are in northwest and upper northwest, also in Ward 3.[15]

Despite their successes, it was clear that the capacity of the program administrators to effectively manage the OSP was hindered by resource limitations. The authorizing legislation limited administrative costs to 3 percent of program expenditures, which totaled $390,000 per year for the $13 million program. The WSF reported that the resources allocated for program administration were inadequate. Moreover, the ability of families to participate effectively was constrained by the lack of scholarship resources to assist them with the hidden and unanticipated costs that may be associated with enrollment in a private school, such as transportation to and from school, field trips, and school meals. Scholarship funds could only be used for such school expenses if tuition at the private school was below the $7,500 scholarship cap, and this was not the case for the majority of students, especially at the high school level.

> The voucher has to be big enough...and there needs to be money in the...legislation for administration of the program.[16]

Policy makers recognized that the original voucher maximum was both too low and too rigid in applying to students at all educational levels; so the bill that reauthorized the program included a two-tier voucher maximum of $8,000 at the elementary level and $12,000 at the high school level.

Recommendations for Program Improvement Based on Lessons from the Program Administrator

- School choice programs should build on the model of the OSP in terms of "customer care" but should offer more resources per family, even if this means reducing the overall number of scholarships awarded. The administrative costs of implementing such a program should also be adequately covered, in light of the emerging lessons about family support needs.
- Families likely to require higher levels of support and assistance in order to participate effectively in the program should be identified at an early stage, and these families should be eligible to receive specially targeted services and supports. According to our findings, this group of families may include single-parent families that lack extended family support.

Experiences of the Participating Schools

The success of a school choice program, as well as the experiences of participating students and their families, ultimately depends on the schools that agree to participate in the program. This study included a survey of the private schools that took part in the OSP and interviews with school representatives to capture their experiences with the participating families and to solicit feedback about the challenges and opportunities they encountered in the program. Overall, the schools reported very positive experiences, with 17 out of the 24 school representatives surveyed (approximately 70 percent) reporting that they regarded the OSP as "very successful," and expressing praise for the program administrators:

> The program works splendidly—it is very easy for both schools and families. Staff of the program is extremely helpful.[17]
>
> This program must be saved. Students are finally succeeding. The earlier we get them, the better they do. Start in pre-K.[18]

A number of school representatives indicated that their involvement in the program generated positive impacts on students in their school more generally.

> It provides the student body with diversity, which may not have been achieved by any other means. Along with the diversity, students are enriched by the various cultural experiences.[19]

The results also revealed that many of the schools were heavily challenged by the academic and social needs of their OSP students and their families. Like the WSF, some schools had not anticipated these challenges and, in many cases, were under prepared to cope with them.

When asked to identify the greatest challenge they faced, around half of all school leaders cited factors that related primarily to academic or other transitional difficulties that the OSP students encountered upon entering their new school. They reported, for example, that the students were not used to coping with the demanding workloads and the high expectations made of them. Several school representatives remarked that some of these students had academic challenges that the school found difficult to accommodate. School representatives consistently expressed a need for additional resources, primarily in the form of tutors and other academic support services for the students, particularly for high school students, but also for more practical purposes, such as "More money...for uniforms and field trips" and "food and clothing subsidies."[20]

Several schools cited family-related factors as their greatest challenge in relation to their participation in the OSP. They believed that parents could benefit from workshops and other activities before they apply to the program in order to help them better understand the different and often unfamiliar types of school models, as well as other subtle differences associated with the private schools. According to some of the school representatives, some parents selected a school without a full awareness of the pros and cons associated with that school or school model. Many of these schools were not a good fit for the child because the student's interests and needs were inconsistent with the school model. It was noted by one school representative that some students had behavioral problems that were attributed to the lack of adequate parenting skills. Other schools referred to the parents' inability to follow school policies or to meet the additional demands of private schooling.

The perceived importance of equipping parents to provide adequate support and participation in their child's education was reflected in the school responses to the question: "With more resources, how could your school better serve OSP families?" Although the largest single category of responses from school leaders related to direct support for students, such as after-school tutoring or homework clubs and mentoring and counseling services, a substantial number of schools highlighted additional types of help and support for parents and families. These recommendations ranged from increased financial support to workshops intended to provide parents with the knowledge and skills needed to better support their child's education and become more involved in the school:

> Assist parents in understanding the learning process and the living process...strengthen the ability of parents.[21]
> Provide workshops for parents and give them required tasks so it's not a handout.[22]
> Require that parents perform tasks and get involved in PTA.[23]
> Parent accountability—scholarship cannot be renewed unless all school obligations have been met.[24]

Recommendations for Program Improvement Based on Lessons from the Participating Schools

We offer the following suggestions to individuals and organizations that may be interested in providing educational options to low-income families:

- The findings of this study and other school choice research should be used in developing advice and guidance for schools on participation in means-tested school choice programs and the likely needs of students and their families.
- Parent workshops should be incorporated into the OSP and other school choice programs that include sessions on supporting

their child's private school education through involvement and participation.

- There is a pressing need for school choice program designers to consider how best to meet the requirements for additional student academic support and family assistance, prior to entry into the program, in order to relieve the burden on individual schools. This might include summer school to solidify an entering student's skill base and prepare him or her for the school's expectations regarding academics and student behavior.[25]

What Were the Major Student Outcomes?

The commonly stated goal of parental school choice is to improve academic outcomes for students from low-income families. In order to maximize academic success for the children, it is important that families are able to understand their educational needs, envision desirable short- and long-term outcomes, select an appropriate school for their child, and support their child's education by participating in school activities and homework.

Parents who thoroughly understand the needs of their children and can therefore effectively maneuver the education marketplace are far more likely to focus on and work for positive academic outcomes for their children than those who do not. We found that the families' focus on different types of outcomes fell along a continuum that begins with immediate outcomes (e.g., students feel safe in school environment and have a positive attitude toward school), proceeds to intermediate outcomes (e.g., students develop good study habits, students reach grade level, and students improve grades), and concludes with long-term outcomes (e.g. students graduate from high school, students attend college, and students learn to give back to their family and community). In general terms, we discovered that family types identified in our study were typically associated with an emphasis on different levels of student outcomes, which we described as immediate, intermediate, and long-term and which were used by parents to gauge the success of the program.

The empowerment of families through their participation in a well-designed school choice program such as the OSP appears to be associated with an increasing focus on longer-term outcomes. Most of the parents focused largely on immediate outcomes when they first entered the program and rarely spoke of performance measures such as test scores and formal academic assessments. However, we observed that those families who initially brought greater levels of personal resources to the program were more effective education consumers relatively early on in their school choice journey, were more likely to begin to emphasize the importance of intermediate and longer-term student outcomes, and were more discerning about the capacity of schools to deliver these outcomes.

Since the OSP targeted low-income families, all of the participating families had relatively low levels of resources in a strictly financial sense. What emerged quite clearly as we became familiar with the participant families in our focus group study, however, was that there was considerable variation among them in terms of the nonfinancial resource availability. We defined *nonfinancial resources* more generally to include time, practical support from extended families and their own skills and knowledge, such as fluency in English. These types of resources were very important in enabling some families to select an appropriate school for their child and more effectively manage the fleeting and persistent challenges associated with their parental school choice journey, such as the ability to play an active role at their child's school and in the home. A single parent with no nearby family or substantial social network was like a person on a long school choice journey who had to do all the driving alone.

The level of nonfinancial resources available to a family tended to be closely associated with the structure of the family unit. Certain types of families could be identified based on the combination of family structure and family resources. Our now fully developed conceptual framework, reproduced as Figure 7.1 along with the descriptions of family types, shows how family types are often associated with a focus on particular levels of student outcomes—as discussed in chapter 4—and furthermore, that the achievement of these outcomes is influenced by the intervening impacts of the program administration and the participating schools.

The OSP is an example of a relatively well-designed school choice program that targets low-income families. It was found to have empowering impacts on many of its family participants. Yet the program's ability to be fully effective in meeting the ultimate goal of improved student outcomes may have been hampered by resource limitations and the unanticipated demands associated with some families. Some participating schools, our findings indicated, were by and large unprepared to cope with the academic and other needs of their OSP students and the inability of many parents to meet school requirements for participation in their child's education. The school choice journey might have been both longer and more rewarding if the tour guide had been better resourced and better prepared for the needs of the travelers.

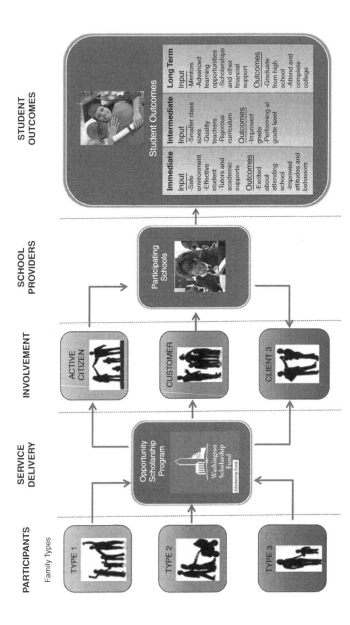

Figure 7.1 Complete Logic Model of How Family Types Influence Student Outcomes

The Political Environment

School voucher programs remain contentious in the United States. Republicans tend to support vouchers as a free-market education reform that encourages consumer choice and brings accountability to education by forcing schools to compete for resources. Republicans also support school choice as an expansion of individual liberty. Although many Democrats in urban areas support vouchers, particularly as a matter of social justice, the Democratic Party in the United States formally opposes school vouchers, preferring to target resources on government-run public schools and increasingly on public charter schools. The national teachers' unions—the largest organizational contributors to the Democratic Party in 2008—strongly oppose school vouchers as well.[26]

We learned something very important about the many people who supported and opposed the OSP. Regardless of their political philosophy and the different opinions they held about the best way to pursue education reform, in our interviews, all of the stakeholders stated earnestly that they want the best for children from low-income backgrounds. The interviews highlighted the eagerness of grassroots advocates, nonprofit leaders, policy makers, and other members of the broader District of Columbia community to improve educational opportunities for low-income students and their families. The sharp differences centered on the means by which they would get there and not the end game they all seemed to share.

The OSP was launched amid considerable debate about school reform in the United States in general and the District of Columbia in particular. Many of the stakeholders that we interviewed indicated that school vouchers magnified the policy debate around the effectiveness of traditional public, public charter, and private schools. On the one hand, some Democrats see the OSP as a temporary, localized measure to improve the academic performance of a handful of students:

> I think the Democrats that support it, see it as a sort of a temporary patch for a failing education system, and, you know, kids only get one chance to go through school. And since D.C. schools are not performing well, the idea is, well, we will offer at least a small number of the kids a chance for a better education until we can get the D.C. schools fixed.[27]

For the program administrator, the difficulties of dealing with underprepared parents, the political pressures on the program, and the basic challenges of program administration produced a sort of "perfect storm" during the school choice journey. The WSF often faced political and social pressures from families, the school community, grassroots advocates, national organizations, and policy makers, which impeded their capacity to manage the day-to-day program delivery challenges.

> There was so much political pressure when the program first started to focus on enrollment and that once it [legislation] passed there was really no time to actually sit down and plan the implementation.[28]
> I think one of the challenges of the program is the administration of the program. It's so easy since it's government money to have a bureaucracy over-bureaucratize things and want to put in rules and regulations.[29]

Moreover, some of the staff at the WSF felt that the political pressures on them to demonstrate results from the program were unfair:

> It takes three to five years to see academic performance. So, to have a program designed to determine that question that ends in five years is sort of counterintuitive.[30]

Six years after program launch, in the spring of 2010, the pressure became too much and the WSF surrendered its role as administrator of the OSP. The DC Investment Trust Corporation took over as guide for the school choice journey and appears to have implemented the newly reauthorized program more cautiously and with somewhat greater sensitivity to the political environment surrounding it.

As a final word on the political environment, we must end *The School Choice Journey* where it started—with the families that participated in the OSP and form the basis for this study. One of the ultimate signs of success is the extent to which parents and other community members are willing to express their satisfaction for a program through their participation in the political process. We assumed that, before their involvement in the OSP, most of the participating parents had not been very actively involved in the political process, and we confirmed that during the focus groups. Of the parents who participated in the focus groups during the spring of 2007, nearly 70 percent reported that they "were not politically active." During those focus groups, we attempted to assess the extent to which parents might be willing to engage the political process in support of the OSP. These parents noted that they would be very interested in helping to "save the program" if necessary. When given the option between best expressing themselves through voting, protesting, writing letters, or testifying before the city council and Congress, the vast majority of parents preferred expressing their support for the OSP via direct testimony. Many of them felt they could best convey the significance of the program and its impact on their children by personally sharing their stories.

However, during our last set of focus groups with parents during the spring of 2008, many of them did not appear to be monitoring the growing opposition to the program. From a local standpoint, for example, none of the salient political leaders who had supported the "three-sector strategy" that birthed the OSP remained in office. These individuals were central members of a very powerful coalition that formed to establish the OSP. Within two years after the program was launched, these individuals were replaced by a new group of leaders who, though never opposing the OSP publicly, did not lobby Congress to reauthorize what parents generally viewed as a successful pilot program.

Many parents believed that their overwhelming support for the program, which was best reflected by the dramatic changes they witnessed in their children's attitudes and behaviors, would be enough to convince policy makers not only to reauthorize but also to expand the program. Most of them did not understand the political controversy surrounding the issue of publicly funded private school vouchers. They did, however, recognize that the forces building in opposition to the program and the lack of strong political support for it at the local level would make reauthorization very difficult. But something had happened that made it difficult for them to meekly accept the seemingly inevitable results of the political attack on the program and return to low-performing schools (public or private) that are not in the best interest of their children—they were exposed to choice and the sense of empowerment that is often associated with it. They realized, beginning in 2009, that if they wanted to continue their school choice journey and welcome other families onboard, they would have to fight for it.

And fight for it they did. As described in chapter 6, with the support of local grassroots and national advocacy organizations like DC Parents for School Choice and the Black Alliance for Educational Options (BAEO), hundreds of parents and students of the OSP rallied to save the program. Program participants stepped forward and publicly acknowledged their participation in and support for the program, which many were reluctant to do just a few years earlier. Participants-turned-activists such as Latasha Bennett, Ronald Holassie, and Tiffany Dunston went toe-to-toe with members of Congress who opposed the program, attacking their claims and parrying their arguments in heated congressional testimony. Ironically, the OSP would not have been nearly as successful in moving participants from clients and consumers to active citizens had policy makers opposed to the program not tried to take it away from them.

This sense of empowerment engendered by the Opportunity Scholarship Program could have long-term benefits for many of the families. It appears that the OSP has raised their awareness about different school models and activated their involvement in policy matters that affect education. Having tasted the triumph of program reauthorization, the parents and students in the OSP that fought so hard to continue their school choice journey likely will bring greater confidence to future political battles to advance and defend their interests.

Recommendations for Program Improvement Based on
Lessons from the Political Environment

We offer the following suggestions to individuals and organizations that may be interested in providing educational options or supports to low-income families:

- It is important to make a distinction between "forming a coalition to establish or create a school choice program" and "building a coalition to sustain it." Most often, the individuals who help establish the program will not be among the group that attempts to sustain it. Thus, prospective program designers must develop a strategy to sustain the school choice program during the initial planning and preparation phase.
- Proponents of the program must find a way to unite the OSP families with other low-income and dissatisfied parents from other school sectors in order to advance school choice in general. In other words, the kind of "three-sector strategy" of education reform that underlay the DC School Choice Incentive Act needs to be translated into a similar "three-sector strategy" of political mobilization in favor of preserving and extending a variety of quality school choices for low-income urban families. The recent movement surrounding National School Choice Week could be a vehicle for doing so.[31]

The School Choice Journey in the District of
Columbia and Beyond

When the District of Columbia Opportunity Scholarship Program was enacted in 2004, it became just the eighth publicly funded private school choice program in the United States and only the fifth such program to be funded by a government appropriation as opposed to tax credits.[32] Only the Milwaukee Parental Choice Program (1990), Cleveland Scholarship and Tutoring Program (1995), McKay Scholarships for Students with Disabilities Program (1999), and Ohio Autism Scholarship Program (2003) preceded the OSP as school voucher programs. As of this writing,

20 states operate 36 different private school choice programs. While the families in the OSP were on their nine-year school choice journey, the country itself embarked upon a broad-based expansion of private school choice. School choice journeys are underway in states as politically and demographically disparate as Rhode Island, Alabama, Iowa, and Utah. Legislatures are seriously considering enacting new parental school choice programs in states such as Alaska, New Jersey, Arkansas, Montana, North Carolina, and Tennessee. As private school choice is extended to more families in the United States, we hope that they and their supporters are guided by the travels of the families who braved the pioneering District of Columbia Opportunity Scholarship Program. The journey may be challenging, but, with help, it can deliver many travelers to a new and more empowered destination.

Appendix I

Description of Sampling Method

We attempted to draw a participant sample that was highly represen-tative of the entire population of the OSP families. Even though our study is not a causal analysis or quantitative program evaluation, we employed various techniques commonly used in such studies to enhance the representativeness of the findings that we present here.[1] Most families participating in the OSP entered the program in two large application cohorts—Cohort 1 in 2004 and Cohort 2 in 2005.[2] They include students who, at application, were entering the elementary, middle, and high school grades.[3] About 9 percent of the OSP families claim Hispanic ethnicity.[4] To portray the lived reality of the OSP families, we would need to include representatives of all of these important clientele groups. In addition, the experience of the OSP could easily differ depending upon the language a family speaks at home or the grade level of private school in which a child is using a scholarship.[5] We therefore implemented a stratified random sampling technique, stratifying on student grade-level at application and language spoken at home, in drawing our study participants from cohorts 1 and 2.

Of necessity, we employed slightly different recruitment and selec-tion techniques for Cohorts 1 and 2. During the fall of 2004, the WSF hosted a general orientation for first-year families. The WSF allowed the research team to introduce the study and invite interested parents to complete a simple consent form that included information about the grade levels of their children participating in the OSP and the language spoken most often at home. The study was also publicized by the WSF in follow-up correspondence to parents, including many who did not attend the orientations. A total of 230 Cohort 1 families, out of about

900 families that entered the OSP in that first cohort, volunteered for the study. A total of 15 participant families were randomly selected from this pool to fill each of our four sample strata:

- Spanish-language student (in any grade),
- English-language student in elementary,
- English-language student in middle school, and
- English-language student in high school.

Our Cohort 1 participant sample therefore included 60 families.

The fall of 2005 brought a second large cohort of families into the OSP. The WSF did not hold a single orientation for these Cohort 2 families, instead relying on mailings, a high school orientation session, and a monthly series of parent empowerment meetings to help them acclimate to the program.[6] The WSF allowed representatives of the School Choice Demonstration Project research team to present at the high school orientation and the December 2005 empowerment meetings. They also again permitted us to include an insert in one of their mailings to all Cohort 2 families that described our study and invited families to participate. A total of 32 Cohort 2 families volunteered for the study at the high school and empowerment group meetings and an additional 60 families volunteered in response to the mailing. We had few volunteers to draw from within two categories of our selection stratification system: Spanish-language (any grade) and English-speaking high school students. We enrolled all 13 Cohort 2 Spanish-language family volunteers and all 7 Cohort 2 English-language high school student family volunteers into our study. We then randomly selected 15 English-language elementary student families and 15 English-language middle student families randomly from those oversubscribed categories to give us a total of 50 Cohort 2 study participants. The 110 families from Cohorts 1 and 2 thus selected to participate in the study represented approximately 180 students that received scholarships from the OSP.

We held separate focus group discussions with the middle and high school students in our participating families during years 1 and 2 of our study. Only a small number of students—18 in Cohort 1 and 17 in Cohort 2—participated in one or more of our student focus groups. Most of these teenage students were hesitant to share much information about their experiences. As a result, the student focus groups were discontinued after the second year of the study and, from that point on, our research focused exclusively on contributions from parents.

As our longitudinal study progressed, the OSP students in some of our study families dropped out of the program. By year 4, our study sample included enough parents of former scholarship users in Cohorts 1 and 2 that we organized them into their own topical focus group for the final session.

Appendix II

Copy of Focus Group Guide

2004 Fall Parent Focus Group Moderator's Guide

December 14, 2004

I.   Greetings   (5 minutes)

Good evening. My name is xxx. Thank you for coming to participate in today's focus group.

- The purpose of our group is to get your opinions about your experiences with the DC Opportunity Scholarship Program.
- Your thoughts will be useful in helping to improve the program.
- If you have participated in focus groups before, you know how the process works.
- We encourage you to express your views freely. There are no right or wrong answers.
- Let's discuss some of the ground rules before we begin. We will have an informal discussion during which I will ask some questions. We would like to know what each of you thinks.
- I will ask other staff in the room to introduce themselves:
- They are here to observe and take notes. All of your comments are confidential and will never be connected to you in any way. Only group results will be reported. To ensure that we get everything you are saying, an audiotape recording is being made of this session. The tape enables us to focus on having a free-flowing conversation with you and less on hand note taking. *WE WILL START THE TAPE RECORDER NOW.*

II.   Introductions   (5 minutes)

Ok, let's get acquainted by going around the table and introducing our-selves, giving only our first name. I will start, by saying again that my name is _____.

III.   Focus group questions   (70 minutes)

Theme 1—Exercising Choice

Question 1

What motivated you to apply for the DC Choice Scholarship Program?

> *How did you find out about the program?*
> *Before you learned about this program, what effort had you made to pursue other education options for your child(ren)?*

Question 2

What did you look for in selecting a school for your child(ren)?

> *Did you involve your child in the selection process?*
> *Who did you rely on for information about different schools?*
> *What source of information was most helpful to you in selecting the school that your child(ren) attends?*

Theme 2—Parents critique of the program and recommendations for improvement:

Question 1

What have been the most beneficial aspects of the program thus far?

> *Do you feel that your child is performing better in his/her new school?*
> *What recommendations would you make about getting the word out about this program to other parents?*

Question 2

What haven't you liked about the DC Scholarship program?

> *Have you encountered any obstacles in participating in the program?*
> *What, if any, are your concerns about enrolling your child in a non-public school?*
> *What recommendations would you make to the program administrators about the program?*

Break—10 minutes

Theme 3—Understanding parent attitudes and beliefs about their different roles:

Question 1

What role should parents have in promoting and supporting education within the home?

How involved should parents be in selecting the school(s) their child attends?

Question 2

What is the role of parents in the schools their child attends?

Theme 4—Parent support needs and advice to other parents

Question 1

What support will you need to successfully help your child(ren) adjust to his/her new school?

How satisfied are you with the amount of information that you are receiving from your child's private school?
What advice would you give parents like you who might be interested in the scholarship program?

Question 2

At this point, do you think your child will remain in his/her new school for the rest of the year?

How important is your child's experience with his/her new school to your decision to keep them in the program?
What recommendations would you make about getting the word out about this program to other parents?

IV.   Wrap-up and Closing   (10 minutes)

Now that you had a chance to hear one another's perspectives on the issue of parent support, what other comments or questions do you think we need to discuss this evening?

Did anyone have any final comments or questions?

Thank you all for coming today. We appreciate the time you took to sit down and share with us. Your opinions have been very informative.

Total Planned Time: 90 minutes

Appendix III

Key Stakeholder Personal Interview Guide

Objective

The interviews were designed to solicit multiple perspectives from local stakeholders who were very knowledgeable about the program, and who in some cases were intimately involved in some aspect of the program. Their perspectives range from individuals who staunchly opposed the program because it violated the District of Columbia Home Rule to those who have had direct contact with the participating families.

Interview Questions

The interviews were conducted in person and lasted about 30–45 minutes. All respondents were asked three basic questions:

1. What have been the strengths and limitations of the Program from your perspective?
2. What would you say to someone who might be interested in replicating the OSP in their city?
3. What do you think will be the fate of the OSP?

List of Interviewees

1. Khari Brown, Capital Partners for Education
2. Lisa Brown-Simon and other members of the Washington Scholarship Fund
3. Kaleem Caire, Next Generation Foundation, formerly with Fight for Children

4. Kevin Chavous, Democrats for Education Reform, Former District of Columbia City Council Member and Chairman of the Education Committee

5. Mary Levy, District of Columbia Parents United

6. Bruno Manno, Walton Family Foundation, formerly with the Annie E. Casey Foundation

7. Virginia Walden-Ford, District of Columbia Parents for School Choice

8. Anthony Williams, Children First, Former Mayor of the District of Columbia

Appendix IV

Polling Script

2008 Focus Group and Polling Questions

1) **What city do you currently live in?**
   - Alexandria, VA
   - Atlanta, GA
   - New York City
   - Richmond, VA
   - Washington, DC

2) **How old are you?**
   - 18–25
   - 26–30
   - 31–35
   - 36–40
   - 41–45
   - 46–50
   - 51–55
   - 56+

3) **What is your favorite form of entertainment?**
   - Listening to music
   - Movies
   - Sports
   - Exercise
   - Travel
   - Watching TV

4) **What is your relationship with the student you are representing today?**
   - Mother
   - Father

- Grand parent
- Foster parent
- Family member
- Other

5) **What is the gender of the child that you are representing?**
   - Male
   - Female

6) **What grade is your child currently attending?**
   - 3rd
   - 4th
   - 5th
   - 6th
   - 7th
   - 8th
   - 9th
   - 10th
   - 11th
   - 12th

7) **Which type of school did your child attend before the OSP?**
   - Public
   - Public charter
   - Private
   - Other

8) **How many children in your family originally received the Opportunity Scholarship?**
   - 1
   - 2
   - 3
   - 4
   - 5

9) **How many of your children are currently utilizing the Scholarship?**
   - 1
   - 2
   - 3
   - 4
   - 5
   - 0

10) **How many focus groups related to this study have you attended?**
   - 1
   - 2
   - 3
   - 4
   - 5

11) **Where did your family reside when you entered the Program?**
   - Ward 1
   - Ward 2
   - Ward 3
   - Ward 4
   - Ward 5
   - Ward 6
   - Ward 7
   - Ward 8
   - Other

12) **In which part of the city does your family currently reside?**
   - Ward 1
   - Ward 2
   - Ward 3
   - Ward 4
   - Ward 5
   - Ward 6
   - Ward 7
   - Ward 8
   - Other

13) **What is the significance or importance of the scholarship to you and your family?**
   - Educational opportunity
   - Financial help
   - Safety
   - Exposure to diversity
   - Religious exposure
   - Rigorous curriculum
   - Ample resources
   - Improved student performance
   - Higher expectations of students

14) **How do you measure or assess your child's academic improvement?**
- Changed student attitude
- Changed student behavior
- Student motivation Level
- Student grades
- Feedback from teachers
- Standardized test scores
- Improved attendance
- Other

15) **What are the best indicators of your child's academic progress?**
- Improved attitude toward school
- Improved study habits
- Completing homework on time
- Improved attendance
- Improved behavior
- Improved grades
- Improved standardized test scores
- Other

16) **In retrospect, what were the most helpful sources of information?**
- Brochures
- School fair
- School visits
- Advice from other parents
- Meeting with teachers
- Meeting administrators
- School directory
- Information sessions with the WSF
- Other

17) **What were the greatest challenges your family experienced with the Program?**
- Choosing the right school for your child
- Increasing your parental involvement
- Transportation
- Meeting the new academic standards
- Increased student work load
- Navigating financial procedures
- Adjusting to the new school student code of conduct
- Maintaining residency in the District of Columbia
- Other

18) **How welcoming were the teachers and administrators at your child's school when you first started in the Program?**
    - Not very welcoming
    - Somewhat welcoming
    - Welcoming
    - Very welcoming

19) **How welcoming were parents of other students when you first started in the program?**
    - Not very welcoming
    - Somewhat welcoming
    - Welcoming
    - Very welcoming

20) **How welcoming are the teachers and administrators now?**
    - Not very welcoming
    - Somewhat welcoming
    - Welcoming
    - Very welcoming

21) **How welcoming are parents of other students now?**
    - Not very welcoming
    - Somewhat welcoming
    - Welcoming
    - Very welcoming

22) **Has your child ever been "singled out" because they are receiving an Opportunity Scholarship?**
    - Yes
    - No
    - Don't know

23) **If so, was the situation addressed by a school administrator?**
    - Yes
    - No

24) **Based on your experience, was it necessary to make special allowances for your child?**
    - Very unnecessary
    - Somewhat unnecessary
    - Necessary
    - Somewhat necessary

25) **Has your involvement in your child's academic life increased since your child entered the program?**
   - Much more involved
   - Somewhat more involved
   - Same level of involvement
   - Less involved

26) **Do you currently volunteer your time to school activities?**
   - Yes
   - No

27) **Are you an active member of a parent organization at your child's school?**
   - Yes
   - No

28) **If you answered yes to the last question, what is your level of activity in this parent organization:**
   - Very active
   - Active
   - Somewhat active
   - Not active

29) **What were your child's greatest academic challenges before entering the OSP?**
   - Reading basic skills
   - Reading comprehension
   - Math
   - Social skills
   - Discipline
   - Behavior
   - Student attitude about learning
   - Not being challenged academically
   - Ineffective teaching

30) **What were the greatest challenges your family faced while in the Scholarship Program?**
   - Transportation
   - Not prepared for the academic challenges
   - Student was not excited about attending the school
   - Pressure from their peers in the neighborhood
   - Other

31) **What support systems are necessary for your child to succeed?**
   - Individualized attention in the classroom
   - Mentoring
   - Tutoring
   - Better communication with teachers
   - Other

32) **Who or what was your greatest source of support within the Program?**
   - Other parents
   - A parent organization
   - Teachers
   - School administrators
   - The WSF
   - Other

33) **What resources or supports would have helped you to play a more active role in your child's experiences within the OSP?**
   - Transportation assistance
   - Tutorial support
   - Family support
   - More funding
   - Support from the school
   - Support from the WSF
   - Other

34) **My family is very satisfied with the OSP.**
   - Strongly agree
   - Agree
   - Somewhat agree
   - Neutral
   - Somewhat disagree
   - Disagree
   - Strongly disagree

35) **OSP improved since your child entered the Program.**
   - Strongly agree
   - Agree
   - Somewhat agree
   - Neutral
   - Somewhat disagree
   - Disagree
   - Strongly disagree

36) **What is the primary source of your satisfaction?**
- My child's academic development
- My child's safety
- Quality of the school my children now attend
- My child's confidence level
- My child's plans for college
- Other

37) **If you were to leave the OSP, in what type of school would you most likely enroll your child?**
- Another private school in DC
- Public school in DC
- Public charter school in DC
- Private school outside of DC
- Public school outside of DC
- Public charter school outside of DC
- Other

38) **Aside from the education of your child, what is the most significant issue facing your family?**
- Housing
- Employment
- Health care
- Transportation
- Other

39) **My family's financial situation has improved since we enrolled in the OSP.**
- Strongly agree
- Agree
- Somewhat agree
- Neutral
- Somewhat disagree
- Disagree
- Strongly disagree

40) **What option is your child most likely to pursue after high school?**
- Employment
- Employment training program
- Certificate program
- Two-year college

- Four-year college
- National service
- Military
- Not sure
- Other

41) **The focus groups allowed my family to thoughtfully express our experiences with the OSP?**
- Strongly agree
- Agree
- Somewhat agree
- Neutral
- Somewhat disagree
- Disagree
- Strongly disagree

Appendix V

Overview of Distinguishing Attitudes and Behaviors

Item	Client Approach	Consumer Approach	Citizen Approach
Perspective on schools in general	Take what exists as given	Demand schools that can effectively fulfill important student and sometime family needs	Help to create schools that fulfill important needs through active civic involvement
Information about schools and school selection	Will often rely on accepting the recommendations of program staff	Gather multiple sources of information and visit a variety of schools—comparison shop	Comparison shop but also think about how the best school for one's child could, with work, become even better—see potentiality as well as actuality
Intermediary support	Heavy-handed, with lots of oversight and authority to ensure that the schools are high quality and students are appropriately placed and served	Advisory, by gathering and circulating comprehensive and accurate information about schools—like Consumer Reports or a more extensive version of My School Chooser	Minimal and arm's length. Any intermediary organization with substantial authority should either comprise or be governed by participating parents and others who support and advocate for family interest
Addressing student social and behavior development, including gender-specific and peer-related issues	May not completely understand or is unwilling to accept student's developmental challenges. Most likely will request that school authorities make special exceptions for students whose previous schools did not instill discipline	Recognizes student's social developmental challenges and will help students' transition into school and nurture positive peer relationship.	Work extensively with student and collaboratively with staff to get the student to adjust behaviors to satisfy high school expectations for discipline—take ownership of the problem
Addressing student educational challenges	Hope that the school will correct the problem eventually—view private schooling inherently as a panacea, at minimum safer	Recognizes student's developmental challenges and seeks additional services—tutoring, different teacher, etc. If not resolved, exercise exit option	Personal intervention—supplement school work with collaborative educational work with the student at home and visit school regularly to ensure student is receiving attention. If widespread at school, propose educational changes at the school

New school culture transition, specifically managing potential stigma	Quietly accepts the new school as a consequence of receiving a benefit and not an opportunity; would stay or leave regardless of fit and other reasonable factors	Object to any distinction between voucher and non-voucher students at your child's school, as all are bringing resources to the school—will threaten exit if school is not a fit	Seeks a school community and culture that the child and family can thrive, where they will be embraced warmly and will object to unfair treatment
Parental Involvement		Some involvement in monitoring the school and assisting the student with homework—protecting your investment	Active in PTO or other grassroots organization associated with the school. Community activist regarding educational improvement in general
Parental participant in school-based activities	Minimal—let the experts take care of it.	Partners with school to improve over	Is willing to volunteer or assume a leadership role
Role transition entering high school	Does not involve child in the process. In fact, the child often assumes a larger role in managing decision related to school	Recognizes that child is mature enough to be actively involved in the decision-making process and encourages child participation in the school selection	Student and parent understand the significant of high schools and use it as opportunity prompt
Measuring student progress and satisfaction	Defers to the assessments of others about their child and is not highly motivated to express satisfaction or the lack thereof	Solicits feedback from a variety of sources about their child's progress. Satisfaction stems from noticeable signs that the child is excited about learning.	Students' progress and parent satisfaction fuel parents' support of and commitment to their child's school and the program generally.
Political involvement regarding protecting program	Let other people handle it. Sanguine view that government programs never go away	Write letter or share personal story—committed to retaining your personal school choice opportunity	Participate in and organize protests focused on reauthorization and expansion of program to others—active lobbying

Notes

Introduction The School Choice Journey: School Vouchers and the Empowerment of Urban Families

1. Title III of Division C of the *Consolidated Appropriations Act*, 2004, P.L. 108–99.
2. Linda Darling-Hammond, *The Flat World and Education: How America's Commitment to Equity Will Determine Our Future* (New York: Teachers College Press, 2010), 4; Tony Wagner, *The Global Achievement Gap: Why Even Our Best Schools Don't Teach the New Survival Skills Our Children Need—and What We Can Do About It* (New York: Basic Books, 2010).
3. Thomas L. Friedman, *The World is Flat: A Brief History of the Twenty-First Century* (New York: Farrar, Straus and Giroux, 2006).
4. Frederick Hess, *The Same Thing Over and Over: How School Reformers Get Stuck in Yesterday's Ideas* (Cambridge, MA: Harvard University Press, 2010); Charles Payne, *So Much Reform, So Little Change* (Cambridge, MA: Harvard Education Publishing Group 2008); Gaston Alonso, Noel Anderson, Celina Su, and Jeanne Theoharis, *Our Schools Suck: Students Talk Back to a Segregated Nation on the Failures of Urban Education* (New York: New York University Press, 2009).
5. "Program for International Student Assessment (PISA): 2006 Results," US Department of Education, Institute of Education Sciences National Center for Education Statistics, accessed November 16, 2009, http://nces.ed.gov/surveys/pisa/pisa2006highlights.asp.
6. Ibid.
7. Jihyun Lee, Wendy S. Grigg, and Patricia L. Donahue, "The Nation's Report Card: Reading 2007," US Department of Education, Institute of Education Sciences, National Center for Education Statistics, accessed April 30, 2010, http://nces.ed.gov/pubsearch/pubsinfo.asp?pubid=2007496.
8. Jay P. Greene and Marcus A. Winters, "Leaving Boys Behind: Public High School Graduation Rates," *Manhattan Institute for Policy Research* CR no. 48 (2006), http://www.manhattan-institute.org/html/cr_48.htm.
9. Jody Heymann, *Forgotten Families: Ending the Growing Crisis Confronting Children and Working Parents in the Global Economy* (New York: Oxford University Press, 2006).
10. Charlotte Rosenzweig, "A Meta-analysis of Parenting and School Success: The Role of Parents in Promoting Students' Academic Performance"

(presentation, Annual Meeting of the American Educational Research Association, Seattle, WA, 2001).

11. Thomas Stewart, Juanita Lucas-McLean, Laura I. Jensen, Christina Fetzko, Bonnie Ho, and Sylvia Segovia, "Family Voices on Parental School Choice in Milwaukee: What Can We Learn From Low-Income Families? Milwaukee Evaluation Report 19," *School Choice Demonstration Project at University of Arkansas*, April 2010, 4, http://www.uark.edu/ua/der/SCDP/Milwaukee_Eval/Report_19.pdf.

12. Patrick J. Wolf, "School Voucher Programs: What the Research Says About Parental School Choice," *Brigham Young University Law Review*, 2008(2), 417.

13. Terry M. Moe, *Schools, Vouchers and the American Public* (Washington, DC: Brookings Institution Press, 2002).

14. *Zelman v. Simmons-Harris*, 536 U.S. 639 (2002).

15. "American Federation for Children," accessed July 1, 2011, http://www.federationforchildren.org/.

16. See for example E. Vance Randall and Bruce Cooper, "Parent Triggers, Parental Choice, and Educational Reform" (presentation, Inaugural International School Choice and Reform Academic Conference, Nova Southeastern University, Fort Lauderdale, Florida, January 14–17, 2012).

17. *Consolidated Appropriations Act, U.S. Code*, Sec 303 (2004).

18. "State and County QuickFacts," *U.S. Census Bureau*, 2010, http://quickfacts.census.gov/qfd/states/11000.html).

19. "Ward 8 Profile of Selected Demographic and Socio-Economic Characteristics, Census 2000," *District of Columbia Office of Planning/State Data Center*, http://www.dc.gov/OP/State%20Data%20Center/Tables/By%20Geography/Wards/DCOP_SDC_Profile%202000--Ward%208.pdf.; "Ward 3 Profile of Selected Demographic and Socio-Economic Characteristics, Census 2000," *District of Columbia Office of Planning/State Data Center*, http://planning.dc.gov/DC/Planning/DC+Data+and+Maps/DC+Data/Tables/Data+by+Topic/Population/Census+2000+Profile+Ward+3.

20. David Garrison, Marni Allen, Margery Turner, Jennifer Comey, Barika Williams, Elizabeth Guernsey, Mary Filardo, Nancy Huvendick, and Ping Sung. "Planning for Quality Schools: Meeting the Needs of District Families," *DC Office of the State Superintendent of Education with Brookings Urban Institute 21st Century Schools Fund*, March 2008, http://www.brookings.edu/~/media/research/files/reports/2008/4/24%20dc%20schools%20garrison/0424_dc_schools_garrison.

21. William G. Howell and Paul E. Peterson, with Patrick J. Wolf and David E. Campbell, *The Education Gap: Vouchers and Urban Schools* (Washington: Brookings Institution Press, 2002); John F. Witte, *The Market Approach to Education: An Analysis of America's First Voucher Program* (Princeton, NJ: Princeton University Press, 2000).

22. See for example Patrick Wolf, Babette Gutmann, Michael Puma, Brian Kisida, Lou Rizzo, Nada Eissa, and Matthew Carr, "Evaluation of the DC

Opportunity Scholarship Program: Final Report," *National Center for Education Evaluation and Regional Assistance, Institute of Education Sciences, US Department of Education,* 2010, http://ies.ed.gov/ncee/pubs/20104018/pdf/20104018.pdf.

23. The reports were written under the auspices of the School Choice Demonstration Project, formerly at Georgetown University and currently at the University of Arkansas. The annual reports can be accessed at http://www.uaedreform.org/evaluation-of-the-dc-opportunity-scholarship-program/.

24. Helen Ingram and Anne Schneider, "The Social Construction of Target Populations: Implication for Politics and Policy," *American Political Science Review* 87, no. 2 (June 1993): 334–47; Joe Soss, "Lessons of Welfare: Policy Design, Political Learning, and Political Action," *The American Political Science Review* 93, no. 2 (June 1999): 363–81.

25. Joe Soss, "Lessons of Welfare: Policy Design, Political Learning, and Political Action," *The American Political Science Review* 93, no. 2 (June 1999): 363–81.

26. See especially Patrick J. Wolf, Brian Kisida, Babette Gutmann, Michael Puma, Nada Eissa, and Lou Rizzo, "School Vouchers and Student Outcomes: Experimental Evidence from Washington, DC," *Journal of Policy Analysis and Management,* 32(2), April 2013: 246–70.

27. Ben Levin, *How to Change 5000 Schools: A Practical and Positive Approach for Leading Change at Every Level* (Cambridge, MA: Harvard Education Publishing Group 2008), 2.

1 What Is School Choice, and Why Did Some Parents Choose School Vouchers?

1. "Fiscal and Calendar Year 2009 TANF: Total Number of Recipients," *US Department of Health and Human Services,* accessed November 18, 2009, http://www.acf.hhs.gov/programs/ofa/data-reports/caseload/2009/2009_recipient_tan.htm.

2. For example see Joe Soss, "Lessons of Welfare: Policy Design, Political Learning, and Political Action," *The American Political Science Review* 93, no. 2 (1999): 363–81; Yeheskel Hasenfeld, "Organizational Forms as Moral Practices: The Case of Welfare Departments," *The Social Service Review* 74, 3 (2000): 329–51; Helen Ingram and Anne Schneider, "Constructing Citizenship: The Subtle Messages of Policy Design," in *Public Policy for Democracy,* eds. Helen Ingram and Steven Rathgeb Smith (Washington, DC: Brookings Institution, 1993), 68–94.

3. For example see Jeffrey Manditch Prottas, *People Processing: The Street-Level Bureaucrat in Public Service Bureaucracies* (Lexington, MA.: Lexington Books, 1979); Mary Jo Bane and David T. Ellwood D. T. *Welfare Realities: From Rhetoric to Reform* (Cambridge, MA: Harvard University Press, 1994); Joe Soss, "Lessons of Welfare: Policy Design, Political Learning, and Political Action," *The American Political Science Review* 93, no. 2 (1999): 363–81;

Yeheskel Hasenfeld, "Organizational Forms as Moral Practices: The Case of Welfare Departments," *The Social Service Review* 74, no. 3 (2000): 329–51.

4. Erik Oddvar Eriksen and Jarle Weigard, "The End of Citizenship? New Roles Challenging the Political Order," *ARENA Working Papers Series* (2009), accessed November 3, 2009, http://www.arena.uio.no/publications/wp99_26. htm; Tobias Jung, "Citizens, Co-producers, Customers, Clients, Captives: Consumerism and Public Services," *University of Edinburgh Business School* (2009), accessed November 18, 2009, http://www.tandfonline.com/doi/abs/10.1080/14719031003787940#.Uulfp7CA3cs.

5. Thomas Stewart and Patrick Wolf, "The Evolution of Parental School Choice," in *Customized Schooling: Beyond Whole-School Reform*, eds. Frederick M. Hess and Bruno V. Manno (Cambridge, MA: Harvard Education Press, 2011), 91–106; Tobias Jung, "Citizens, Co-producers, Customers, Clients, Captives: Consumerism and Public Services," *University of Edinburgh Business School* (2009), accessed November 18, 2009, http://www.tandfonline.com/doi/abs/10.1080/14719031003787940#.Uulfp7CA3cs.

6. Judith N. Shklar, *American Citizenship: The Quest for Inclusion* (Cambridge, MA.: Harvard University Press, 1998).

7. Ibid.

8. Andrea Louise Campbell, *How Policies Make Citizens: Senior Political Activism and the American Welfare State* (Princeton, NJ: Princeton University Press, 2003), 1.

9. "Income and Current Election Participation," *Comparative Study of Electoral Systems*, 2005, accessed November 18, 2009, http://www.umich.edu/~cses/resources/results/CSESresults_IncomeParticipation.htm.

10. Helen Ingram and Anne Schneider, "The Social Construction of Target Populations: Implication for Politics and Policy," *American Political Science Review* 87, no. 2 (June 1993): 334–47.

11. Theda Skocpol, *Protecting Soldiers and Mothers: The Political Origins of Social Policy in the United States* (Cambridge, MA: Harvard University Press, 1992).

12. Helen Ingram and Anne Schneider, "The Social Construction of Target Populations: Implication for Politics and Policy," *American Political Science Review* 87, no. 2 (June 1993): 334–47.

13. See for example Suzanne Mettler and Joe Soss, "The Consequences of Public Policy for Democratic Citizenship: Bridging Policy Studies and Mass Publics," *Perspectives on Politics*, 2 (2004), 55–73; Suzanne Mettler and Jeffrey M. Stonecash, "Government Program Usage and Political Voice," *Social Science Quarterly* 89, no. 2 (2008): 273–93.

14. Amber Wichowsky and Donald P. Moynihan, "Measuring How Administration Shapes Citizenship: A Policy Feedback Perspective on Performance Management," *Public Administration Review* 68, no. 5 (2008, Sept/Oct): 908–21.

15. Joe Soss, "Lessons of Welfare: Policy Design, Political Learning, and Political Action," *The American Political Science Review* 93, no. 2(1999): 363–81.

16. SSDI participant, in Joe Soss, ibid.

17. AFDC participant, in Joe Soss, ibid.

18. SSDI participant, in Joe Soss, ibid.

19. AFDC participant, in Joe Soss, ibid.

20. Aaron Skinner, "A Case Study: The Disempowering of Homeless, Adolescent, Single Mothers in a New York City Transitional Living Shelter," *Cornell University Undergraduate Research Paper,* (2006), accessed November 18, 2009, http://aap.cornell.edu/aap/crp/programs/cusp/programs/summer/upload/Undergrad_06-Skinner.pdf.

21. Comment heard in Homeless Shelter staff training workshop, from Aaron Skinner, "A Case Study: The Disempowering of Homeless, Adolescent, Single Mothers in a New York City Transitional Living Shelter," *Cornell University Undergraduate Research Paper,* (2006), accessed November 18, 2009, http://aap.cornell.edu/aap/crp/programs/cusp/programs/summer/upload/Undergrad_06-Skinner.pdf.

22. Aaron Skinner, "A Case Study: The Disempowering of Homeless, Adolescent, Single Mothers in a New York City Transitional Living Shelter," *Cornell University Undergraduate Research Paper,* (2006), accessed November 18, 2009, http://aap.cornell.edu/aap/crp/programs/cusp/programs/summer/upload/Undergrad_06-Skinner.pdf.

23. Marcia B. Cohen, "An Empowerment-oriented Framework for Practice with Homeless Mentally Ill Clients," Paper presented to the *5th National Symposium on Doctoral Research in Social Work* (1989), accessed November 18, 2009, https://kb.osu.edu/dspace/bitstream/1811/32667/1/5_Cohen_paper.pdf.

24. AFDC participant, in Joe Soss, "Lessons of Welfare: Policy Design, Political Learning, and Political Action," *The American Political Science Review* 93, no. 2(1999): 363–381.

25. Ibid.

26. Virginia Walden Ford, *Voices, Choices, and Second Chances* (Washington, DC: DC Parents for School Choice, 2005).

27. Scott Franklin Abernathy, *School Choice and the Future of American Democracy* (Ann Arbor: University of Michigan Press, 2005); Jennifer L. Hochschild and Nathan Scovronick, *The American Dream and the Public Schools* (New York, NY: Oxford University Press, 2003); Jeffrey R. Henig, *Rethinking School Choice: Limits of the Market Metaphor* (Princeton, NJ: Princeton University Press, 1994); Albert O. Hirschman, *Exit, Voice, and Loyalty* (Cambridge, MA: Harvard University Press, 1970).

28. Justice Breyer dissenting opinion in *Zelman v. Simmons-Harris,* 536 U.S. 639 (2002).

29. Mark Warren, "Democratic Theory and Self-Transformation," *American Political Science Review* 86, no. 1 (1992): 8–23.

30. Benjamin R. Barber, B. *Strong Democracy: Participatory Politics for a New Age* (Berkeley: University of California Press, 1984), 295–6.

2   The History of Vouchers and Education Reform
in Washington, DC

1. Jay P. Greene and Marcus A. Winters, "Leaving Boys Behind: Public High School Graduation Rates," *Manhattan Institute for Policy Research* CR no. 48 (2006), http://www.manhattan-institute.org/html/cr_48.htm.
2. "Urban Poverty and Slum Upgrading," *The World Bank Group*, http://go.worldbank.org/KT759KE9S0; "Urban Poverty: An Overview," *The World Bank Group*, http://go.worldbank.org/KT759KE9S0; District of Columbia Fiscal Policy Institute, "District of Columbia Poverty Demographics," March 2009, http://District of Columbiafpi.org/wp-content/uploads/2009/03/poverty1.pdf.; Community Survey 3-Year Estimate, "District of Columbia," http://factfinder.census.gov/servlet/ACSSAFFFacts?_event=Search&_lang=en&_sse=on&geo_id=04000US11&_state=04000US11.
3. C. Eugene Steuerle, Van Doorn Ooms, George Peterson, and Robert D. Reischauer (eds.) *Vouchers and the Provision of Public Services* (Washington, DC: Brookings Institution Press, 2000).
4. "The Case against Vouchers," *National Education Association*, http://www.nea.org/home/19133.htm.
5. Thomas Paine, *The Rights of Man: Answer to Mr. Burke's Attack on the French Revolution* (London: J. S. Jordan, 1791).
6. John Stuart Mill, *Utilitarianism, on Liberty, Essay on Bentham*, ed. Mary Warnock (New York: Meridian, 1962), 239.
7. Milton Friedman, "The Role of Government in Education," in *Economics and the Public Interest*, ed. Robert Solo (New Brunswick, NJ: Rutgers University Press, 1955).
8. Here we limit our consideration of voucher programs to those that involve direct government expenditure to qualified families. As of this writing, an additional 16 programs provide tax credits to corporations or individuals who contribute to private-school scholarship organizations, allowing them to issue "tax-credit scholarships" that operate like vouchers but have different funding and constitutional status. Long-running government "tuitioning" programs in Maine and Vermont pay private school tuition for students without a public school in their town but restrict the payments to secular schools and therefore are excluded from our list of private school voucher programs.
9. Specifically, the income ceiling to qualify initially for a voucher is 300 percent of the poverty level or less in Milwaukee and Racine, and 185 percent of the poverty level or less in Cleveland and the District of Columbia.
10. The means test for the new low-income voucher programs in Ohio and Wisconsin is a family income at or below 185 percent of the poverty line, which is the income ceiling for the Federal Lunch Program. Indiana's means test is a family income below 150 percent of the Federal Lunch Program eligibility ceiling for a partial-tuition voucher and 100 percent of the Federal Lunch Program for a full-tuition voucher, while the income ceiling for Louisiana's program is 250 percent of the poverty line. The higher-income

eligibility ceilings for the Indiana program means that a family of four earning as much as $63,964 per year qualifies for a partial-tuition voucher while that same family earning less than $42,643 qualifies for a full-tuition voucher. A family of four in Louisiana is income-eligible for full-tuition voucher if they earn less than $57,625 annually. Thus, the new statewide means-tested programs in Indiana and Louisiana are open to a good proportion of what we would consider to be the middle class as well as all low-income families.

11. A pioneering voucher program in Arizona was restricted to students in foster care that otherwise would have to change public schools whenever they were placed with a new family. Arizona's foster care voucher program was declared unconstitutional by the Arizona Supreme Court but has been reconstituted as the Empowerment Savings Account (ESA) program where government funds are provided to families to spend as they choose on education-related services, including college tuition, to avoid constitutional concerns.

12. Thomas D. Snyder, Alexandra G. Tan, and Charlene M. Hoffman, "Digest of Education Statistics 2005," *National Center for Education Statistics*: NCES 2006–030, July 2006, http://files.eric.ed.gov/fulltext/ED492945.pdf.

13. John F. Witte, *The Market Approach to Education: Evidence from America's First Voucher Program* (Princeton, NJ: Princeton University Press, 2000), 58–9.

14. David J. Fleming, Joshua M. Cowen, John F. Witte, and Patrick J. Wolf, "Similar Students, Different Choices: Who Uses a School Voucher in an Otherwise Similar Population of Students?" *Education and Urban Society* (in press).

15. Harry Brighouse, *School Choice and Social Justice* (New York: Oxford University Press, 2000); Joseph P. Viteritti, *Choosing Equality: School Choice, the Constitution, and Civil Society* (Washington, DC: Brookings Institution Press, 1999).

16. Carolyn Sattin-Bajaj, *Unaccompanied Minors: Immigrant Youth, School Choice, and the Pursuit of Equity* (Harvard Education Press, in press).

17. For summaries see for example Greg Forster, *A Win-Win Solution: The Empirical Evidence on School Choice* (Indianapolis, IN: Friedman Foundation, 2013); Jay P. Greene, *Education Myths: What Special-Interest Groups Want You to Believe About Our Schools and Why It Isn't So* (Lanham, MD: Rowman & Littlefield Publishers, 2005); Frederick Hess, *Revolution at the Margins* (Washington, DC: Brookings Institution Press, 2002).

18. Patrick J. Wolf, "School Voucher Programs: What the Research Says About Parental School Choice," *Brigham Young University Law Review* (2008): 2.

19. Brian P. Gill, P. Michael Timpane, Karen E. Ross, and Dominic J. Brewer, *Rhetoric Versus Reality: What We Know and What We Need to Know About Vouchers and Charter Schools* (Santa Monica, CA: Rand Education, 2001), 128–9.

20. John F. Witte, *The Market Approach to Education: An Analysis of America's First Voucher Program* (Princeton, NJ: Princeton University Press, 2000), 118.

21. Jay P. Greene, William G. Howell, and Paul E. Peterson, "Lessons from the Cleveland Scholarship Program," in *Learning from School Choice*, eds. Paul

E. Peterson and Bryan C. Hassel (Washington, DC: Brookings Institution Press, 1998), 370.

22. Jay P. Greene and Greg Forster, "Vouchers for Special Education Students: An Evaluation of Florida's McKay Scholarship Program," *Manhattan Institute for Policy Research, Civic Report* 38 (June 2003).

23. Paul E. Peterson and David E. Campbell, "An Evaluation of the Children's Scholarship Fund," *Program on Education Policy and Governance at Harvard University*, PEPG/01–03 (May 2001), p. 2.

24. James S. Coleman and Thomas Hoffer, *Public and Private High Schools: The Impact of Communities* (New York, NY: Basic Books, 1987); Derek Neal, "The Effects of Catholic Secondary Schooling on Educational Achievement," *Journal of Labor Economics* 15 (1997): 98–123.

25. Joshua M. Cowen, David J. Fleming, John F. Witte, Patrick J. Wolf, and Brian Kisida, "School Vouchers and Student Attainment: Evidence from a State-Mandated Study of Milwaukee's Parental Choice Program," *Policy Studies Journal*, 41, no. 1 (Winter 2013): 147–67.

26. William G. Howell and Paul E. Peterson, with Patrick J. Wolf and David E. Campbell, *The Education Gap: Vouchers and Urban Schools* (Washington, DC: Brookings Institution Press, 2002).

27. John Barnard, Constantine E. Frangakis, Jennifer L. Hill, and Donald B. Rubin, "Principal Stratification Approach to Broken Randomized Experiments: A Case Study of School Choice Vouchers in New York City," *Journal of the American Statistical Association* 98, no. 462 (June 2003): 299–323.

28. Alan B. Krueger and Pei Zhu, "Another Look at the New York City School Voucher Experiment," *American Behavioral Scientist* 47, (2004): 658–98.

29. John F. Witte, *The Market Approach to Education: An Analysis of America's First Voucher Program* (Princeton, NJ: Princeton University Press, 2000); Jay P. Greene, Paul E. Peterson, and Jiangtao Du, "Effectiveness of School Choice: The Milwaukee Experiment," *Education and Urban Society* 31 (January 1999): 190–213; Cecelia E. Rouse, "Private School Vouchers and Student Achievement: An Evaluation of the Milwaukee Parental Choice Program," *The Quarterly Journal of Economics* 113, no. 2 (May 1998): 553–602.

30. John F. Witte, Deven Carlson, Joshua M. Cowen, David J. Fleming, and Patrick J. Wolf, "The MPCP Longitudinal Educational Growth Study Final Year Report," *School Choice Demonstration Project at University of Arkansas*, 2012, http://www.uark.edu/ua/der/SCDP/Milwaukee_Eval/Report_29.pdf.

31. Kim K. Metcalf, Stephen D. West, Natalie A. Legan, Kelli M. Paul, and William J. Boone, "Evaluation of the Cleveland Scholarship and Tutoring Program, Summary Report 1998–2002," *Indiana University School of Education*, 2003; Jay P. Greene, William G. Howell, and Paul E. Peterson, "Lessons from the Cleveland Scholarship Program," in *Learning from School Choice*, eds. Paul E. Peterson and Bryan C. Hassel (Washington, DC: Brookings Institution Press, 1998).

32. Jay P. Greene, "Vouchers in Charlotte," *Education Matters,* 1, no. 2(2001): 55–60; David N. Figlio. "Evaluation of the Florida Tax Credit Scholarship Program: Participation, Compliance and Test Scores in 2009–10," Report to the Florida Department of Education, August 2011.

33. Joshua M. Cowen, David J. Fleming, John F. Witte, and Patrick J. Wolf, "Going Public: Who Leaves a Large, Longstanding, and Widely Available Urban Voucher Program?" *American Educational Research Journal* 49, no. 2 (2012): 231–56.

34. William G. Howell and Paul E. Peterson, with Patrick J. Wolf and David E. Campbell, *The Education Gap: Vouchers and Urban Schools,* Revised Edition (Washington, DC: Brookings Institution Press, 2006), 66–7.; John F. Witte, *The Market Approach to Education: An Analysis of America's First Voucher Program* (Princeton, NJ: Princeton University Press, 2000), 147–48.

35. Bryan C. Hassel, *The Charter School Challenge: Avoiding the Pitfalls, Fulfilling the Promise* (Washington, DC: Brookings Institution Press, May 1999).

36. Patrick J. Wolf and Daniel S. Hoople, "Looking Inside the Black Box: What Schooling Factors Explain Voucher Gains in Washington, DC," *Peabody Journal of Education* 81, (2006): 7–26.

37. William G. Howell et al., *The Education Gap: Vouchers and Urban Schools,* Revised Edition (Washington, DC: Brookings Institution Press, 2006): 158–66.

38. Casey J. Lartique Jr., "The Need for Educational Freedom in the Nation's Capital," *CATO Institute,* Policy Analysis No. 461, December 10, 2002.

39. Jay P. Greene and Marcus A. Winters, "Leaving Boys Behind: Public High School Graduation Rates," *Manhattan Institute for Policy Research,* CR no. 48 (April 2006), http://www.manhattan-institute.org/html/cr_48.htm.

40. Valerie Strauss and Sari Horwitz, "Students Caught in a Cycle of Classroom Failures," *Washington Post,* February 20, 1997, A01.

41. Casey J. Lartique Jr., "The Need for Educational Freedom in the Nation's Capital," *CATO Institute,* Policy Analysis No. 461, December 10, 2002, p. 9.

42. Title III of Division C of the *Consolidated Appropriations Act,* 2004, P. L. 108–99.

43. Ibid., Section 303.

44. In 2006, Congress amended the law so that, once in the program, families could earn up to 300 percent of the poverty level and still retain their scholarships.

45. A handful of private schools in the District of Columbia exclusively serve students with severe disabilities, usually under contract with the DCPS. The overall set of 104 private schools in the District of Columbia also includes some highly specialized schools such as a ballet school.

46. Patrick Wolf et al., "Evaluation of the District of Columbia Opportunity Scholarship Program: Impacts After One Year," *US Department of Education* (Washington, DC: US Government Printing Office, 2007), p. 17.

47. Wolf et al., "Evaluation of the District of Columbia Opportunity Scholarship Program," p. 15.

48. Wolf et al., "Evaluation of the District of Columbia Opportunity Scholarship Program," p. 8.

49. Patrick Wolf et al., "Evaluation of the District of Columbia Opportunity Scholarship Program: First-Year Report on Participation," US Department of Education, National Center for Education Evaluation and Regional Assistance (Washington, DC: US Government Printing Office), 35.

50. Patrick Wolf et al., "Evaluation of the District of Columbia Opportunity Scholarship Program: Second-Year Report on Participation," US Department of Education, Institute of Education Sciences (Washington, DC: US Government Printing Office, 2006), 11.

51. Patrick Wolf et al., "Evaluation of the District of Columbia Opportunity Scholarship Program: Impacts After One Year," *US Department of Education* (Washington, DC: US Government Printing Office, 2007); Patrick Wolf et al., "Evaluation of the District of Columbia Opportunity Scholarship Program: Impacts After Two Years," US Department of Education, Institute of Education Sciences (Washington, DC: US Government Printing Office, 2008); Patrick Wolf et al., "Evaluation of the District of Columbia Opportunity Scholarship Program: Impacts After Three Years," US Department of Education, Institute of Education Sciences (Washington, DC: US Government Printing Office, 2009). Patrick Wolf et al., "Impact Evaluation of the District of Columbia Opportunity Scholarship Program: Final Report," US Department of Education, Institute of Education Sciences (Washington, DC: US Government Printing Office, 2010); Patrick J. Wolf, Brian Kisida, Babette Gutmann, Michael Puma, Nada Eissa, and Lou Rizzo, "School Vouchers and Student Outcomes: Experimental Evidence from Washington, DC," *Journal of Policy Analysis and Management* 32, no. 2 (April 2013): 246–70.

52. See Perry Bacon Jr., "House bill draws criticism from GOP," *The Washington Post*, February 26, 2009, sec. A06. Sam Dillon, "Democrats Limit Future Financing for Washington Voucher Program," *New York Times*, February 28, 2009, sec. A11. "Presumed Dead: Politics Is Driving the Destruction of the District's School Voucher Program," *The Washington Post,* April 11, 2009, sec. A12.

53. "The Value of Education Choices: Saving the D.C. Opportunity Scholarship Program," Hearing before the US Senate Committee on Homeland Security and Governmental Affairs, February 16, 2011, http://hsgac.senate.gov/public/index.cfm?FuseAction=Hearings.Hearing&Hearing_id=f200a5b4-c1b6-41-c7-a3c1-fa6d242535ef; "The DC Opportunity Scholarship Program: Keeping the Door Open," Hearing before the US House Committee on Oversight and Reform, Subcommittee on Health Care, DC, Census, and the National Archives, March 1, 2011, http://oversight.house.gov/index.php?option=com_content&view=article&id=1149:3-1-11-qthe-dc-opportunity-scholarship-program-keeping-the-door-openq&catid=35:subcommittee-on-health-care-and-dc-

54. Trip Gabriel, "Budget Deal Fuels Revival of School Vouchers," *New York Times*, April 14, 2011.

55. The legislative changes include a higher maximum voucher value of $8,000 for elementary and middle school students and $12,000 for high school students, an increased annual appropriation of $20 million, and the launch of a new rigorous program evaluation.

56. Lindsey Burke, "Obama Budget Ends Funding for D.C. School Choice Program," *The Foundry*, April 12, 2013, accessed April 24, 2013, http://blog.heritage.org/2013/04/12/obama-budget-ends-funding-for-d-c-school-choice-program/

57. Clark Moustakas, *Phenomenological Research Methods* (Thousand Oaks, CA: Sage, 1994).

58. Caroline Dyer, "Researching and Implementation of Educational Policy: A Backward Mapping Approach," *Comparative Education* 35, no. 1 (1999): 45–61; David L. Morgan, *Focus Group as Qualitative Research*, Second Edition (London: Sage, 1997); David W. Stewart and Prem N. Shamdasani, *Focus Groups: Theory and Practice* (London: Sage, 1992).

59. Gary King, Robert O. Keohane, and Sidney Verba, *Designing Social Inquiry: Scientific Inference in Qualitative Research* (Princeton, NJ: Princeton University Press, 1994).

3 What Were Families Looking for in the Voucher Program?

1. For example, based on calculations of statistics on the Milwaukee Public Schools (MPS) website and in annual school choice reports the oldest and largest urban private school choice program in the United States, the Milwaukee Parental Choice Program enrolled about 20 percent of eligible students. Patrick J. Wolf, "The Comprehensive Longitudinal Evaluation of the Milwaukee Parental Choice Program: Summary of Third Year Reports," (University of Arkansas, SCDP Milwaukee Evaluation Report #14, April 2010), http://www.uark.edu/ua/der/SCDP/Milwaukee_Eval/Report_14.pdf; "District Fact Sheet," *Milwaukee Public Schools*, http://mpsportal.milwaukee.k12.wi.us/portal/server.pt?open=512&objID=367&mode=2&in_hI_userid=2&cached=true.

2. Parent of High School Student, Focus Group, Spring 2005.

3. Valerie Martinez, Kenneth Godwin, and Frank R. Kemerer, "Public School Choice in San Antonio: Who Chooses and with What Effects?" in *Who Chooses? Who Loses? Culture, Institutions, and the Unequal Effects of School Choice*, eds. Bruce Fuller and Richard F. Elmore (New York: Teachers College Press, 1996), 54; Laura S. Hamilton and Kacey Guin, "Understanding How Families Choose Schools," in *Getting Choice Right: Ensuring Equity and Efficiency in Education Policy*, eds. Julian R. Betts and Tom Loveless (Washington, DC: Brookings Institution Press, 2005), 42.

4. Milton Friedman, "The Role of Government in Education," in *Economics and the Public Interest*, ed. Robert A. Solo (Piscataway, NJ: Rutgers University Press, 1955).

5. Bruce Fuller, Richard Elmore, and Gary Orfield, "Policy Making in the Dark: Illuminating the School Choice Debate," in *Who Chooses? Who Loses? Culture, Institutions and the Unequal Effects of School Choice,* eds. Bruce Fuller and Richard Elmore (New York: Teachers College Press, 1996), 9.

6. Jeffrey R. Henig, *Rethinking School Choice: Limits of the Market Metaphor* (Princeton, NJ: Princeton University Press, 1994), 206.

7. James Kelly III and Benjamin Scafidi, *More Than Scores: An Analysis of Why and How Parents Choose Private Schools* (Indianapolis, IN: Friedman Foundation, 2013), 6.

8. Amy Stuart Wells, "African American Students' View of School Choice," in *Who Chooses? Who Loses? Culture, Institutions, and the Unequal Effects of School Choice,* eds. Bruce Fuller and Richard Elmore (New York: Teachers College Press, 1996), 43, 45; Wolf et al., "Evaluation of the DC Opportunity Scholarship Program: Impacts After One Year," (Washington, DC: Government Printing Office, 2007) C-5; William G. Howell and Paul E. Peterson, with Patrick J. Wolf and David E. Campbell, *The Education Gap: Vouchers and Urban Schools* (Washington: Brookings Institution Press, 2002), 110–12.

9. Cassandra M. D. Hart, "Contexts Matter: Selection in Means-Tested School Voucher Programs," *Educational Evaluation and Policy Analysis,* accessed January 24, 2014, http://epa.sagepub.com/content/early/2013/10/17/0162373 713506039

10. Spanish-speaking Parent, Focus Group, Spring 2005.

11. Parent of High School Student, Focus Group, Fall 2004.

12. Parent of Elementary School Student, Focus Group, Spring 2005.

13. Middle School Student, Focus Group, Spring 2005.

14. Parent of Elementary School Student, Focus Group, Fall 2004.

15. Parents of Hispanic Student, Focus Group, Spring 2005.

16. Parent of High School Student, Focus Group, Fall 2004.

17. Parent of Middle School Student, Focus Group, Spring 2005.

18. Parent Interview, July 2008.

19. Stewart et al., "An Example of a Successful Chooser," in "Family Reflections on the District of Columbia Opportunity Scholarship Program: Final Support Report," *University of Arkansas: School Choice Demonstration Project,* January 2009, 12.

20. High School Student, Focus Group, Spring 2005.

21. Wolf et al., "Evaluation of the DC Opportunity Scholarship Program: Impacts After One Year," (Washington, DC: US Government Printing Office, 2007), Figure 2–2, p. 16, http://ies.ed.gov/ncee/pubs/20074009/.

22. Washington Scholarship Fund, *Opportunity Scholarship Program: School Directory 2004–05,* Washington, DC, 2004.

23. Wolf et al., "Evaluation of the DC OSP," Table 2–7, p. 21.

24. Wolf et al., "Evaluation of the DC OSP," Table 2–7, p. 21.

25. Bruce Fuller, Richard F. Elmore, and Gary Orfield, "Policy Making in the Dark: Illuminating the School Choice Debate," in *Who Chooses? Who Loses?*

Culture, Institutions, and the Unequal Effects of School Choice, eds. Bruce Fuller and Richard F. Elmore (New York: Teachers College Press, 1996), 3.

26. Dara Zeehandelaar and Amber Winkler, *What Parents Want: Education Preferences and Trade-Offs,* (Washington, DC: Thomas B. Fordham Institute, August 2013), Table 2b.

27. Ibid., 28–35.

28. James P. Kelly, III, and Benjamin Scafidi, "More Than Scores: An Analysis of Why and How Parents Choose Private Schools" (Indianapolis, IN: Friedman Foundation for Educational Choice, 2013), 11.

29. Paul Teske, Jody Fitzpatrick, and Gabriel Kaplan, "Opening Doors: How Low-Income Parents Search for the Right School," (Seattle, WA: Center on Reinventing Public Education, 2007), accessed January 6, 2014, http://files. eric.ed.gov/fulltext/ED495279.pdf

30. Jennifer L. Steele, Georges Vernez, Michael A. Gottfried, and Michael Schwam-Baird, "The Transformation of a School System: Principal, Teacher, and Parent Perceptions of Charter and Traditional Schools in Post-Katrina New Orleans" (Washington, DC: RAND Education, 2011), Table 6.4, p. 57.

31. Patrick J. Wolf and Thomas Stewart, *Understanding School Shopping in Detroit* (Detroit, MI: Michigan Future, 2012), p. 6, accessed January 6, 2014, http://www.uark.edu/ua/der/SCDP/Detroit/Detroit_Shoppers_Report-Final.pdf

32. Patrick J. Wolf, "Comment on Joseph Viteritti's 'School Choice: How an Abstract Idea Became a Political Reality,'" in *Brookings Papers on Education Policy,* ed. Diane Ravitch (Washington, DC: Brookings Institution Press, 2005), 167.

33. Laura S. Hamilton and Kacey Guin, "Understanding How Families Choose Schools," in *Getting Choice Right: Ensuring Equity and Efficiency in Education Policy,* eds. Julian R. Betts and Tom Loveless (Washington: Brookings, 2005), 44.

34. Ibid., 49.

35. Mark Schneider, Paul Teske, and Melissa Marschall, *Choosing Schools: Consumer Choice and the Quality of American Schools* (Princeton, NJ: Princeton University Press, 2000), 107.

36. Patrick Wolf et al., "Evaluation of the DC Opportunity Scholarship Program: Impacts After One Year" (Washington, DC: US Government Printing Office, 2007), C-7; Patrick J. Wolf, Paul E. Peterson, and Martin R. West, "Results of a School Voucher Experiment: The Case of Washington, D.C., After Two Years," Harvard University Program on Education Policy and Governance, PEPG/01–05 (Cambridge, MA, August 2001), Table 3.

37. Abraham Maslow, "A Theory of Human Motivation," *Psychological Review* 50 (July 1943): 370–96.

38. Parent of Middle School Student, Focus Group, Spring 2006.

39. Parent of High School Student, Focus Group, Spring 2006.

40. Parent of Elementary School Student, Focus Group, Spring 2006.

41. Parent of Elementary School Student, Focus Group, Spring 2006.

42. Hispanic Parent, Focus Group, Spring 2007.

43. Parent of Elementary School Student, Focus Group, Spring 2008.

44. Parent of Middle School Student, Focus Group, Spring 2006.

45. Parent of Elementary School Student, Focus Group, Spring 2006.

46. Parent of a Cohort 1 Middle School Student, Focus Group, Spring 2004.

47. Parent of Elementary School Student, Focus Group, Fall 2004.

48. Parent of Middle School Student, Focus Group, Spring 2006.

49. Parent of Middle School Student, Focus Group, Spring 2006.

50. Parent of Elementary School Student, Focus Group, Spring 2007.

51. Parent of Elementary School Student, Focus Group, Spring 2007.

52. Parent of High School Student, Focus Group, Spring 2006.

53. Parent of High School Student, Focus Group, Spring 2007.

54. Laura S. Hamilton and Kacey Guin, "Understanding How Families Choose Schools," in *Getting Choice Right: Ensuring Equity and Efficiency in Education Policy*, eds. Julian R. Betts and Tom Loveless (Washington, DC: Brookings Institution Press, 2005), 46.

55. Information asymmetry occurs when one party to a transaction, either the buyer or the seller, has significantly better information than the other regarding the quality of the product and the true cost of producing it. For background on the theory of information asymmetry, see William A. Niskanen, Jr., *Bureaucracy and Representative Government* (Chicago: Aldine-Atherton, 1971); Armen A. Alchian and Harold Demsetz, "Production, Information Costs, and Economic Organization," *American Economic Review* 62 (1972): 777–95; Terry M. Moe, "The New Economics of Organization," *American Journal of Political Science* 28 (1984): 739–77.

56. Jeffrey R. Henig, *Rethinking School Choice* (Princeton, NJ: Princeton University Press, 1994), 210.

57. Laura Hamilton with Kacey Guin, "The Demand Side of School Choice: Understanding How Families Choose Schools," in *School Choice: Doing It the Right Way Makes a Difference*, National Working Commission on Choice in K–12 Education (Washington, DC: Brookings Institution Press, 2003), 10.

58. Amy Stuart Wells, "African-American Students' View of School Choice," in *Who Chooses? Who Loses? Culture, Institutions, and the Unequal Effects of School Choice*, eds. Bruce Fuller and Richard Elmore (New York: Teachers College Press, 1996), 36.

59. Brian Kisida and Patrick J. Wolf, "School Governance and Information: Does Choice Lead to Better-Informed Parents?" *American Politics Research* 38 no. 5 (2010): 783–805.

60. Parent of High School Student, Focus Group, Spring 2005.

61. Parent of High School Student, Focus Group, Spring 2005.

62. This development was a major theme of our second qualitative report on the program. See Stephen Q. Cornman, Patrick J. Wolf, and Thomas Stewart, "New Education Consumers: Parent and Student Voices on the Second Year of the D.C. Opportunity Scholarship Program," Report of the School Choice Demonstration Project, Georgetown University, Washington, DC,

May 2007, SCDP 07–01, http://www.uaedreform.org/SCDP/DC_Research/PSV2.pdf.

63. Spanish-speaking Parents, Focus Group, Spring 2005.
64. Parent of Middle School Student, Focus Group, Spring 2006.
65. Parent of High School Student, Focus Group, Spring 2006.
66. Parent of Elementary School Student, Focus Group, Spring 2007.
67. Parent of Hispanic Student, Focus Group, Spring 2007.
68. Parent Interview, Focus Group, Spring 2008.
69. Parent of Elementary School Student, Focus Group, Spring 2005.
70. Interview with WSF staff members, Spring 2007.
71. Parent of High School Student, Focus Group, Fall 2004.
72. Parent of High School Student, Focus Group, Fall 2004.
73. Parent of Elementary School Student, Focus Group, Spring 2006.
74. Robert D. Putnam, "Bowling Alone: America's Declining Social Capital," *Journal of Democracy* 6, no. 1 (January 1995): 65–78.

4 What Major Challenges Did Families Experience Using Private School Vouchers?

1. Howell, W. and Peterson, P. *The Education Gap: Vouchers and Urban Schools* (Washington, DC, Brookings Institution Press, 2002), 94–102.
2. A total of 2,881 students initially used Opportunity Scholarships offered to them from 2004 through 2008. Across those years between 53 and 65 percent of the OSP students enrolled in Catholic schools, and the Center City Consortium Schools included 12 of the 23 Archdiocesan Catholic schools participating in the program. Assuming that an average of 60 percent of the OSP students attended Catholic schools, and 52 percent of those attending Catholic schools enrolled specifically in Consortium schools, the CCCS is estimated to have enrolled about 900 different OSP students from 2004 through 2008. Calculations derived from Patrick Wolf, Babette Gutmann, Michael Puma, Lou Rizzo, Nada O. Eissa, and Marsha Silverberg, "Evaluation of the DC Opportunity Scholarship Program: Impacts After One Year," US Department of Education, Institute of Education Sciences, National Center for Education Evaluation and Regional Assistance, Washington, DC: US Government Printing Office, 2007, 16, 20; Patrick Wolf, Babette Gutmann, Michael Puma, Brian Kisida, Lou Rizzo, and Nada O. Eissa, "Evaluation of the DC Opportunity Scholarship Program: Impacts After Two Years," US Department of Education, Institute of Education Sciences, National Center for Education Evaluation and Regional Assistance, Washington, DC: US Government Printing Office, NCEE 2008–4023, June 2008, 15; Patrick Wolf, Babette Gutmann, Michael Puma, Brian Kisida, Lou Rizzo, and Nada O. Eissa, "Evaluation of the DC Opportunity Scholarship Program: Impacts After Three Years," US Department of Education, Institute of Education Sciences, National Center for Education Evaluation and Regional Assistance, Washington, DC: US Government Printing Office, NCEE 2009–4050, March 2009; xix,16.

3. Theola Labbe, "D.C. Catholic Schools Follow National Trend," *Washington Post*, April 11, 2008, http://www.washingtonpost.com/wp-dyn/content/article/2008/04/10/AR2008041003780.html.

4. Please note that only 15 percent of parents participating in the focus group reported that their child had attended private schools prior to the OSP.

5. See for example Joshua M. Cowen, David J. Fleming, John F. Witte, and Patrick J. Wolf, "Going Public: Who Leaves a Large, Longstanding, and Widely Available Urban Voucher Program?" *American Educational Research Journal* 49, no. 2 (Spring 2012): 231–56; Russell W. Rumberger, "Student Mobility and Academic Achievement," *ERIC Digest*, EDO-PS-02-1, (June 2002); Eric A. Hanushek, John F. Kain, and Steven G. Rivkin, "Disruption Versus Tiebout Improvement: The Costs and Benefits of Switching Schools," *Journal of Public Economics* 88, (2004): 1721–46.

6. Patrick J. Wolf and Daniel S. Hoople, "Looking Inside the Black Box: What Schooling Factors Explain Voucher Gains in Washington, DC," *Peabody Journal of Education* 81, (2006): 7–26.

7. Ibid.

8. For examples, see William G. Howell and Paul E. Peterson, *The Education Gap: Vouchers and Urban Schools.* (Washington, DC: Brookings Institution Press, 2006); Anthony S. Bryk, Valerie E. Lee, and Peter Blakeley, *Catholic Schools and the Common Good* (Cambridge, MA: Harvard University Press, 1993).

9. Mark Schneider, Paul Teske, and Melissa Marschall, *Choosing Schools: Consumer Choice and the Quality of American School* (Princeton, NJ: Princeton University Press, 2000), 12.

10. John E. Brandl, *Money and Good Intentions are Not Enough: Or Why a Liberal Democrat Thinks States Need Both Competition and Community* (Washington, DC: Brookings Institution Press, 1998).

11. George A. Akerlof and Rachel E. Kranton, "Identity and Schooling: Some Lessons for the Economics of Education," *Journal of Economic Literature* 40, no. 4 (2002): 1167–201.

12. Samuel Bowles and Herbert Gintis, "The Moral Economy of Communities: Structured Populations and the Evolution of Pro-social Norms," *Evolution and Human Behavior* 19, (1998): 3–25.

13. Amy Stuart Wells, "African-American Students' View of School Choice," in *Who Chooses? Who Loses? Culture, Institutions and the Unequal Effects of School Choice*, eds. Bruce Fuller and Richard F. Elmore (New York: Teachers College Press, 1996), 37.

14. Amy Stuart Wells, "African-American Students' View of School Choice," in *Who Chooses? Who Loses?: Culture, Institutions and the Unequal Effects of School Choice*, eds. Bruce Fuller and Richard F. Elmore (New York: Teachers College Press, 1996), 26.

15. Amy Stuart Wells, "African-American Students' View of School Choice," in *Who Chooses? Who Loses?: Culture, Institutions and the Unequal Effects of School Choice*, eds. Bruce Fuller and Richard F. Elmore (New York: Teachers College Press, 1996), 32.

16. Patrick J. Wolf, William G. Howell, and Paul E. Peterson, "School Choice in Washington, DC: An Evaluation after One Year," Program on Education Policy and Governance, PEPG 00–08, (Cambridge, MA: Harvard University, 2000); Eric A. Hanushek and Steven G. Rivkin, "Does Public School Competition Affect Teacher Quality?" in *The Economics of School Choice*, ed. Caroline Minter Hoxby, (Chicago: University of Chicago Press, 2003), 23–7; Fred M. Neumann, BetsAnn Smith, Elaine Allensworth, and Anthony S. Bryk, "School Instructional Program Coherence: Benefits and Challenges," *Consortium on Chicago School Research*, January 2001.

17. Parent of Middle School Student, Focus Group, Spring 2005.

18. Parent of Middle School Student, Focus Group, Spring 2006.

19. Thomas Stewart, Patrick Wolf, and Stephen Cornman, "Parent and Student Voices on the First Year of the Opportunity Scholarship Program," *Georgetown University Public Policy Institute: School Choice Demonstration Project*, 2005, 33–6.

20. Parent of Hispanic Student, Focus Group, Spring 2005.

21. Parent of High School Student, Focus Group, Spring 2006.

22. Parent of High School Student, Focus Group, Spring 2005.

23. Parent of High School Student, Focus Group, Winter 2004.

24. Parent of High School Student, Focus Group, Spring 2005.

25. Parent of High School Student, Focus Group, Spring 2005.

26. Parent of High School Student, Focus Group, Spring 2005.

27. Parent of Elementary School Student, Focus Group, Spring 2006.

28. Parent of Middle School Student, Focus Group, Spring 2005.

29. Parent of Elementary School Student, Focus Group, Spring 2006.

30. Parent of Middle School Student, Focus Group, Spring 2006.

31. A Utah voucher law that was repealed in a referendum had an innovative design of providing government support to all families on a sliding scale based on family income. Such an arrangement would avoid the "ineligibility cliff" that so many OSP families feared falling off of merely by earning a few extra dollars.

32. As part of this arrangement, only new high school students entering the OSP were eligible to receive the services offered by CPE. In an attempt to compare and contrast the experiences of first- and second-year high school students based on whether they received or did not receive these comprehensive support services, we invited several second-year high school families to participate in this study.

33. Parent of High School Student, Focus Group, Spring 2006.

34. Parent of High School Student, Focus Group, Spring 2007.

35. Parent of Elementary School Student, Focus Group, Spring 2007.

36. Spanish-speaking Parent Focus Group, Spring 2005.

37. Parent of Elementary School Student, Focus Group, Spring 2007.

38. Thomas Stewart, Patrick J. Wolf, Stephen Cornman, and Kenann McKenzie-Thompson, "Satisfied, Optimistic, yet Concerned: Parent Voices on the Third Year of the DC Opportunity Scholarship Program," Georgetown University Public Policy Institute: School Choice Demonstration Project, 2007, 29.

39. Patrick J. Wolf, Babette Gutmann, Michael Puma, Lou Rizzo, Nada Eissa, and Marsha Silverberg, "Evaluation of the DC Opportunity Scholarship Program: Impacts after One Year," US Department of Education, Institute of Education Sciences, (Washington, DC: US Government Printing Office, 2007), 17.

40. Parent of Elementary School Student, Focus Group, Spring 2007.

41. Parent of Middle School Student, Focus Group, Spring 2008.

42. The WSF noted during the interview that providing families with subway passes was an easy way for families to access transportation without having to pay anything out of pocket. The WSF also felt that the availability of free lunches was extremely important for the OSP families because most of them were eligible for and received free and reduced school meals prior to joining the OSP.

43. Only two parents participating in the focus groups noted that they had attended the Parent Empowerment group meetings.

44. Parent of High School Student, Focus Group, Spring 2006.

45. Thomas Stewart, Patrick J. Wolf, Stephen Q. Cornman, and Kenann McKenzie-Thompson, and Jonathan Butcher, "Family reflections on the District of Columbia Opportunity Scholarship Program," *University of Arkansas: School Choice Demonstration Project,* 2009, 50.

46. David P. Baker and David L. Stevenson, "Mother's Strategies for Children's School Achievement: Managing the Transition to High School," *Sociology of Education* 59. no. 3 (1986): 156–66; "Easing the Transition to High School: Research and Best Practices Designed to Support High School Learning," *National High School Center* (Washington, DC: American Institutes for Research), accessed July 10, 2013, http://www.betterhighschools.org/docs/NHSC_TransitionsReport.pdf.

47. Megan Cottrell, "The Trouble with TANF: Why Welfare Just Doesn't Work," *True/Slant,* accessed August 20, 2009, http://www.chicagonow.com/blogs/one-story-up/2009/08/the-trouble-with-tanf.html.

48. Steven G. Anderson, Anthony P. Halter, and Brian M. Gryzlak. "Difficulties after Leaving TANF: Inner-city Women Talk about Reasons for Returning to Welfare," *Social Work,* 49, no. 2 (2004, April): 185–94.

5   How Do Families Measure Student Progress, Satisfaction, and Success?

1. Christopher Lubienski and Sarah T. Lubienski, "Charter, Private, Public Schools and Academic Achievement: New Evidence from NAEP Mathematics Data," *Columbia University: National Center for the Study of Privatization in Education* (2006), http://www.ncspe.org/publications_files/OP111.pdf.

2. See especially Harry P. Hatry, *Performance Measurement: Getting Results,* Second edition (Washington, DC: Urban Institute Press, 2006).

3. For examples see William G. Howell, Patrick J. Wolf, David E. Campbell, and Paul E. Peterson, "School Vouchers and Academic Performance: Results from

Three Randomized Field Trials," *Journal of Policy Analysis and Management* 21 (April 2002): 191–217; John F. Witte, *The Market Approach to Education: An Analysis of America's First Voucher Program* (Princeton, NJ: Princeton University Press, 2000); Eric Hanushek, John Kain, Steven Rivkin, and Gregory Branch, "Charter School Quality and Parental Decision Making with School Choice," *Journal of Public Economics* 91, nos 5–6 (June 2007): 823–48; "Multiple Choice: Charter School Performance in 16 States," *Center for Research on Education Outcomes* (Stanford, CA: CREDO); Caroline M. Hoxby, Sonali Murarka, and Jenny Kang, "How New York City's Charter Schools Affect Achievement," *New York City Charter Schools Evaluation Project,* September 2009, http://users.nber.org/~schools/charterschoolseval/how_NYC_charter_schools_affect_achievement_sept2009.pdf.

4. Thomas Stewart et al., "Family Reflections on the DC Opportunity Scholarship Program," *University of Arkansas: School Choice Demonstration Project,* Fourth-Year Report (2009): 28–9.

5. George A. Akerlof and Rachel E. Kranton, "Identity and Schooling: Some Lessons for the Economics of Education," *Journal of Economic Literature* 40 (2002): 1167–201; Samuel Bowles and Herbert Gintis, "The Moral Economy of Communities: Structured Populations and the Evolution of Pro-social Norms," *Evolution and Human Behavior* 19 (January 1998): 3–25.

6. Parent of High School Student, Focus Group, Spring 2006.

7. Parent of Middle School Student, Focus Group, Spring 2006.

8. Parent of Elementary School Student, Focus Group, Spring 2006.

9. Parent of Elementary School Student, Focus Group, Spring 2007.

10. Parent of Elementary School Student, Focus Group, Spring 2007.

11. Parent of Middle School Student, Focus Group, Spring 2007.

12. Parent of Hispanic Middle School Student, Cohort 2, Spring 2008.

13. James P. Kelly, III, and Benjamin Scafidi, "More Than Scores: An Analysis of Why and How Parents Choose Private Schools" (Indianapolis, IN: Friedman Foundation, 2013).

14. For a review, see Brian P. Gill, P. Michael Timpane, Karen E. Ross, and Dominic J. Brewer, *Rhetoric Versus Reality: What We Know and What We Need to Know About Vouchers and Charter Schools,* (Santa Monica, CA: RAND Education, 2001), 128–34.

15. Julie Trivitt and Patrick J. Wolf, "School Choice and the Branding of Catholic Schools," *Education Finance and Policy* 6, no. 2 (Spring 2011): 202–45.

16. Parent of Elementary School Student, Interview, Fall 2005

17. Thomas Stewart, Juanita Lucas-McLean, Laura I. Jensen, Christina Fetzko, Bonnie Ho, and Sylvia Segovia, "Family Voices on Parental School Choice in Milwaukee: What Can We Learn from Low-income Families?" *School Choice Demonstration Project at University of Arkansas,* SCDP Milwaukee Evaluation Report #19, April 2010, 5–6, http://www.uark.edu/ua/der/SCDP/Milwaukee_Eval/Report_19.pdf.

18. Joshua M. Cowen, David J. Fleming, John F. Witte, and Patrick J. Wolf, "Going Public: Who Leaves a Large, Longstanding, and Widely Available

Urban Voucher Program?" *American Educational Research Journal* 49, no. 2 (Spring 2012): 231–56.

19. Thomas Stewart and Patrick J. Wolf, "Parent and Student Experiences with Choice in Milwaukee, Wisconsin," *School Choice Demonstration Project at University of Arkansas*, March 2009, Milwaukee Evaluation Report #13, 24, http://www.uaedreform.org/downloads/2009/03/report-13-parent-and-student-experiences-with-choice-in-milwaukee-wisconsin.pdf.

20. Greg Forster and Christian D'Andrea, "An Empirical Evaluation of the Florida Tax Credit Scholarship Program," *The Friedman Foundation for Educational Choice* (August 2009), http://www.friedmanfoundation.org/downloadFile.do?id=383.

21. Parent of Elementary School Student, Focus Group, Spring 2005.

22. Parent of High School Student, Focus Group, Spring 2005.

23. Parent of Middle School Student, Focus Group, Spring 2005.

24. Parent of Elementary School Student, Focus Group, Spring 2006.

25. Parent of Middle School Student, Focus Group, Spring 2004.

26. Parent Interview, Spring 2005.

27. Parent of High School Student, Focus Group, Spring 2005.

28. Middle School Parent Interview, Fall 2006.

29. Parents of Elementary School Students, Focus Group, Spring 2007.

30. Parent Interview, Spring 2008.

31. Parent of Elementary School Student, Focus Group, Spring 2007.

32. Parent of Middle School Student, Focus Group, Spring 2005.

33. Parent Interview, Spring 2008.

34. Parent of Elementary School Student, Focus Group, Spring 2006.

35. Parent of Elementary School Student, Focus Group, Spring 2006.

36. Parent Interview, Spring 2008.

37. Parent of Middle School Student, Focus Group, Spring 2007.

38. Parent of High School Student, Focus Group, Spring 2005.

39. Parent of Middle School Student, Focus Group, Spring 2006.

40. Parent of High School Student, Focus Group, Spring 2006.

41. Parent of Elementary School Student, Focus Group, Spring 2005.

42. Parent of Middle School Student, Focus Group, Spring 2007.

43. Parent of High School Student, Focus Group, 2007.

44. Parent of High School Student, Focus Group, Spring 2006.

45. Parent of Elementary School Students, Focus Group, Spring 2007.

46. Parent of Middle School Student, Focus Group, Spring 2007.

47. Parent of Hispanic Student, Focus Group, Spring 2006.

48. Thomas Stewart, Patrick J. Wolf, and Stephen Q. Cornman, "Parent and Student Voices on the First Year of the D.C. Opportunity Scholarship Program," *School Choice Demonstration Project at Georgetown University*, SCDP 05–01, October 2005, vi, http://files.eric.ed.gov/fulltext/ED508628.pdf.

49. Parent of High School Student, Focus Group, Spring 2006.

50. For example, see Greg Forster and Christian D'Andrea, "An Empirical Evaluation of the Florida Tax Credit Scholarship Program," *The Friedman*

Foundation for Educational Choice (2009), http://www.friedmanfoundation. org/downloadFile.do?id=383; Thomas Stewart and Patrick J. Wolf, "Parent and Student Experiences with Choice in Milwaukee," *University of Arkansas: School Choice Demonstration Project* Report #13 (2009), http://www.uark. edu/ua/der/SCDP/Milwaukee_Eval/Report_13.pdf.

51. For example: Joe Soss, "Lessons of Welfare: Policy Design, Political Learning, and Political Action," *The American Political Science Review* 93, no. 2 (June 1999): 363–81; Helen Ingram and Anne L. Schneider, "The Social Construction of Target Populations: Implication for Politics and Policy," *The American Political Science Review* 87, no. 2 (1993): 334–47.

52. Mark Schneider, Paul Teske, and Melissa Marschall, *Choosing Schools: Consumer Choice and the Quality of American Schools* (Princeton, NJ: Princeton University Press, 2000), 107.

6 School Vouchers and the Empowerment of Urban Families

1. See especially Alexis de Tocqueville, *Democracy in America* (New York: Doubleday, 1969); Alistair MacIntyre, *After Virtue: A Study in Moral Theory* (South Bend, IN: University of Notre Dame Press, 1984); Anthony S. Bryk, Valerie E. Lee, and Peter B. Holland, *Catholic Schools and the Common Good* (Cambridge, MA: Harvard University Press, 1993); John E. Brandl, *Money and Good Intentions Are Not Enough* (Washington: Brookings Institution Press, 1998); George A. Akerlof and Rachel E. Kranton, "Identity and Schooling: Some Lessons for the Economics of Education," *Journal of Economic Literature* 40 (2002): 1167–201.

2. Michael Birnbaum, "Families, Activists Rally to Restore 216 Rescinded Tuition Vouchers," *Washington Post*, August 21, 2009, B03.

3. "The DC Opportunity Scholarship Program: Preserving School Choice for All," Hearing of the United States Senate Committee on Homeland Security and Government Affairs, May 13, 2009.

4. *Let Me Rise: The Fight for School Choice in the Nation's Capital*, narrated by Juan Williams, Heritage Foundation, Washington, DC, 2010.

5. Elmer Eric Schaatsneider, *The Semi-Sovereign People* (New York: Holt, Rinehart and Winston, 1967); Frances Fox Piven and Richard A. Cloward, *Poor People's Movements* (New York: Vintage Books, 1979); James S. Coleman, Thomas Hoffer, and Sally Kilgore, *High School Achievement: Public, Catholic, and Private Schools Compared* (New York: Basic Books, 1982); Richard G. Niemi and Jane Junn, *Civic Education* (New Haven, CT: Yale University Press, 1998); Robert D. Putnam, *Bowling Alone: The Collapse and Revival of American Community* (New York: Simon & Schuster, 2000).

6. Thomas Stewart, "Urban Poverty and Prisons: The Political Socialization of Inner City Males," PhD Dissertation: Harvard University (1994); Peter Bachrach and Morton S. Baratz, *Power and Poverty: Theory and Practice* (New York: Oxford University Press, 1970).

7. Frances Fox Piven and Richard A. Cloward, *Poor People's Movements: Why They Succeed, How They Fail* (New York: Vintage Press, 1979); David Greenstone and Paul E. Peterson, *Race and Authority in Urban Politics: Community Relations and the War on Poverty* (Chicago: University of Chicago Press, 1976); Peter Bachrach, *The Theory of Democratic Elitism* (Boston: Little, Brown, 1967).

8. Parent of Elementary School Student, Cohort 1, Spring 2007.

9. David C. Berliner and Bruce J. Biddle, *The Manufactured Crisis: Myths, Fraud, and the Attack on America's Public Schools* (Reading, MA: Addison-Wesley, 1995), 173–80.

10. Charles Leslie Glenn Jr., *The Myth of the Common School* (Amherst: University of Massachusetts Press, 1987); Jay P. Greene, *Education Myths* (Lanham, MD: Rowman & Littlefield, 2005), Chapter 17.

11. Terry M. Moe, *Schools, Vouchers, and the American Public* (Washington, DC: Brookings Institution Press, 2001).

12. Paul DiPerna, "Schooling in America Survey: What Do Mothers Say about K-12 Education?" Polling Paper No. 15, Friedman Foundation for Educational Choice, May 8, 2013, accessed January 24, 2014, http://www.edchoice.org/CMSModules/EdChoice/FileLibrary/1000/Schooling-in-America-Survey.pdf.

13. Terry M. Moe, "Cooking the Questions?" *Education Next* 2, no. 1 (Spring 2002): 71–77.

14. Terry M. Moe, *Schools, Vouchers, and the American Public* (Washington, DC: Brookings Institution Press, 2001); Paul DiPerna, "Schooling in America Survey: What Do Mothers Say about K-12 Education?" Polling Paper No. 15, Friedman Foundation for Educational Choice, May 8, 2013, accessed January 24, 2014, http://www.edchoice.org/CMSModules/EdChoice/FileLibrary/1000/Schooling-in-America-Survey.pdf.

15. Dick M. Carpenter II, "School Choice Signals: Research Review and Survey Experiments," Friedman Foundation for Educational Choice, January 7, 2014, accessed January 24, 2014, http://www.edchoice.org/CMSModules/EdChoice/FileLibrary/1035/SCHOOL-CHOICE-SIGNALS-Research-Review-and-Survey-Experiments.pdf.

16. See for example Terry M. Moe, *Special Interest: Teachers Unions and America's Public Schools* (Washington, DC: Brookings Institution Press, 2011); Michael Birnbaum, "Families, Activists Rally to Restore 216 Rescinded Tuition Vouchers," *Washington Post*, August 21, 2009, B03; "The Case Against Vouchers," *National Education Association*, accessed July 13, 2014, http://www.nea.org/home/19133.htm.

17. Terry M. Moe, *Special Interest: Teachers Unions and America's Public Schools* (Washington, DC: Brookings Institution Press, 2011), 282–87; Deborah Simmons, "School Vouchers at Risk: Low-income D.C. Students May Lose Out," *Washington Times*, November 30, 2009, A17.

18. Perry Bacon Jr., "House Bill Draws Criticism from GOP," *Washington Post*, February 26, 2009, A06; Natalie Lester, "D.C. Parents to Push Congress to Keep Vouchers," *Washington Times*, February 27, 2009, A01; Sam Dillon,

"Democrats Limit Future Financing for Washington Voucher Program," *New York Times*, February 28, 2009, A11; George F. Will, "Obama's Budget Follies," *Washington Post*, April 23, 2009.

19. "Obama's School Choice: Democrats Want to Kill Vouchers for 1,700 Kids," unsigned editorial, *Wall Street Journal*, February 25, 2009, A12; "Voucher Subterfuge: Hoping No One Notices, Congressional Democrats Step Between 1,800 D.C. Children and a Good Education," *Washington Post,* February 25, 2009, A18.

20. See for example "Lieberman, Collins Urge Education Secretary to Reverse," Capitol Hill Press Release, April 21, 2009; Greg Toppo, "More Black Lawmakers Open to School Vouchers," *USA Today*, May 12, 2009; Deborah Simmons, "Voucher Proponents Rally Against Ending; Rescinding Scholarship a 'Slap in the Face,'" *Washington Times*, August 19, 2009, A15.

21. Greg Pierce, "Civil Rights Issue," *Washington Times*, May 6, 2009, A06.

22. Joseph Lawler, "No One Vouching for Them," *American Spectator Online*, May 7, 2009, accessed July 13, 2013, http://www.lexisnexis.com/lnacui2api/api/version1/getDocCui?oc=00240&hl=t&hns=t&hnsd=f&perma=true&lni=7VN1-CPM1-2RG6-P0MC&hv=t&csi=143292&hgn=t&secondRedirectIndicator=true

23. "A Reprieve on Vouchers: President Obama Shows Some Wisdom and Compassion Toward D.C. Schoolchildren. Will Congress Help?" Unsigned editorial, *Washington Post*, May 7, 2009, A22.

24. Bill Turque and Shailagh Murray, "Obama Offers D.C. Voucher Compromise," *Washington Post,* May 7, 2009, B01; Jason L. Riley, "A President and His Priorities," *Wall Street Journal*, May 8, 2009.

25. Patrick Wolf, Babette Gutmann, Michael Puma, Brian Kisida, Lou Rizzo, and Nada O. Eissa, "Evaluation of the DC Opportunity Scholarship Program: Impacts After Three Years," US Department of Education, Institute of Education Sciences, National Center for Education Evaluation and Regional Assistance, Washington, DC: US Government Printing Office, NCEE 2009–4050, March 2009, http://ies.ed.gov/ncee/pubs/20094050/.

26. US Senate Committee on Homeland Security and Governmental Affairs, "The D.C. Opportunity Scholarship Program: Preserving School Choice for All," hearing agenda, May 13, 2009, accessed July 15, 2013, http://www.hsgac.senate.gov/hearings/the-dc-opportunity-scholarship-program-preserving-school-choice-for-all.

27. "Parents Fight to Keep Children Out of D.C. Public Schools," ABC News 7—WJLA, May 13, 2009; Bill Turque, "With Critics Quiet, Hearing Praises D.C. School Voucher Program," *Washington Post*, May 14, 2009, A1; "Beach Reading for Mr. Obama," unsigned editorial, *Washington Post*, August 28, 2009.

28. Bill Turque, "With Critics Quiet, Hearing Praises D.C. School Voucher Program," *Washington Post*, May 14, 2009, A1.

29. Michael Neibauer, "Bill Introduced to Save D.C. School Vouchers," *Washington Examiner*, May 23, 2009.

30. "Children First: A DC Scholarship Program Has Bipartisan Backing," *Washington Post*, unsigned editorial, August 3, 2009.

31. Michael Birnbaum, "Families, Activists Rally to Restore 216 Rescinded Tuition Vouchers," *Washington Post*, August 21, 2009, B03.

32. Michael Birnbaum, "Hundreds of Voucher Pupils Unaccounted For," *Washington Post*, September 17, 2009; Mark Segraves, "Congress Grills Director of School Voucher Program," WTOP News, September 16, 2009, accessed September 17, 2009, http://www.wtop.com/?nid=25&sid=1764154.

33. "Washington Scholarship Fund Shows 100% of Federal Funds Accounted For, In Response to Senator Durbin's Request," Press Release, Washington Scholarship Fund, September 22, 2009; Michael Birnbaum, "More Oversight Urged for Voucher Schools," *Washington Post*, September 30, 2009.

34. Mary Bruce, "Bipartisan Supporters Call on Congress to Reauthorize D.C. Voucher Program," *ABC News*, September 30, 2009; Brian O'Connell, "Free to Choose," *American Spectator*, October 1, 2009; Sheryl Blunt, "Not Free to Choose: D.C. Students and Parents Rally for School-Choice," *Weekly Standard*, October 7, 2009.

35. Sheryl Blunt, "Not Free to Choose: D.C. Students and Parents Rally for School-Choice," *Weekly Standard*, October 7, 2009.

36. Robert Tomsho, "D.C. School Vouchers Have a Brighter Future Outlook in Congress," *Wall Street Journal*, October 19, 2009; Deborah Simmons, "School Vouchers at Risk: Low-income D.C. Students May Lose Out," *Washington Times*, November 30, 2009; "Save the Vouchers: A Worthy D.C. Program Deserves Congress's Support," unsigned editorial, *Washington Post*, November 22, 2009.

37. Michael Birnbaum, "Limits Are Likely on DC School Vouchers," *Washington Post*, December 10, 2009.

38. Seth Stern, "Ideological Battle Spells Trouble for Vouchers," *Congressional Quarterly Weekly*, January 18, 2010, 166.

39. "Step Up for DC Vouchers," unsigned editorial, *Washington Post*, March 23, 2010, A18.

40. Patrick Wolf, Babette Gutmann, Michael Puma, Brian Kisida, Lou Rizzo, Nada Eissa, and Matthew Carr, "Evaluation of the DC Opportunity Scholarship Program: Final Report," *National Center for Education Evaluation and Regional Assistance, Institute of Education Sciences, US Department of Education*, 2010, xv.

41. Ibid.

42. Debra Viadero, "DC Voucher Program Boosts Grad Rates But Not Test Scores," *Education Week*, June 23, 2010; Mike DeBonis, "DC School Vouchers—The Last Word?" *Washington Post*, June 23, 2010; "DC's Successful Voucher Program Deserves a Second Life," unsigned editorial, *Washington Post*, June 23, 2010, A16.

43. Barbara Hollingsworth, "Boehner Revives D.C. Voucher Program," *Washington Examiner*, January 26, 2011.

44. Emily Belz, "Speaker John Boehner and Sen. Joe Lieberman Introduce Bill to Reopen a School Voucher Program That Democrats Shut Down," *World Magazine*, January 27, 2011; "The Value of Education Choices: Saving the D.C. Opportunity Scholarship Program," Hearing of the US Senate Committee on Homeland Security and Governmental Affairs, February 16, 2011; "The DC Opportunity Scholarship Program: Keeping the Door Open," Hearing of the US House Committee on Oversight and Reform, Subcommittee on Health Care, DC, Census, and the National Archives, March 1, 2011.

45. Jamison Beuerman, "Congress Poised to Reauthorize Wildly Successful DC Voucher Program," *Pelican Post*, April 1, 2011.

46. Trip Gabriel, "Budget Deal Fuels Revival of School Vouchers," *New York Times*, April 14, 2011; Paul E. Peterson, "DC Children Can Thank Boehner and Randomized Trials," *Education Next Blog*, April 10, 2011.

47. Adeshina Emmanuel, "Much-Debated Scholarship Program for D.C. Students is Renewed," *The Caucus: The Politics and Government Blog of The Times*, June 18, 2012.

48. DC Investment Trust Corporation, "DC Opportunity Scholarship Program," accessed on July 17, 2013 from http://www.dcscholarships.org/.

49. "The D.C. Voucher Example: Mr. President, How About That 97% Graduation Rate?" unsigned editorial, *Wall Street Journal*, July 12, 2013.

50. For a compelling discussion of the politics of school choice see Joseph P. Viteritti, "School Choice: How an Abstract Idea Became a Political Reality," in *Brookings Papers on Education Policy*, ed. Diane Ravitch (Washington, DC: Brookings Institution Press, 2005).

7   What Lessons Were Learned That May Help Future Travelers?

1. This phrase was made famous by Charles M. Tibout, "A Pure Theory of Local Expenditures," *Journal of Political Economy* 64, no. 5 (October 1956): 416–24.

2. See Appendix III for a complete list of the individuals who were interviewed.

3. See, for example, Morris P. Fiorina, *Retrospective Voting in American National Elections* (New Haven: Yale University Press, 1981).

4. See Appendix V for a detailed overview of distinguishing attitudes and behaviors associated with each family type.

5. Harry Brighouse, *School Choice and Social Justice* (New York: Oxford University Press, 2000); Joseph P. Viteritti, *Choosing Equality: School Choice, the Constitution, and Civil Society* (Washington, DC: Brookings Institution Press, 1999); Thomas Stewart, Juanita Lucas-McLean, Laura I. Jensen, Christina Fetzko, Bonnie Ho, and Sylvia Segovia, "Family Voices on Parental School Choice in Milwaukee: What Can We Learn from Low-income Families?" *School Choice Demonstration Project at University of Arkansas*, SCDP Milwaukee Evaluation Report #19, April 2010, 5–6, http://www.uark.edu/ua/der/SCDP/Milwaukee_Eval/Report_19.pdf.

6. Patrick Wolf, Babette Gutmann, Michael Puma, and Marsha Silverberg, "Evaluation of the DC Opportunity Scholarship Program: Second Year Report on Participation," US Department of Education, Institute of Education Sciences (Washington, DC: US Government Printing Office).

7. Interview with Representatives of the WSF, Fall 2007.

8. This statement is supported in large part based on our recent research in Milwaukee. The Milwaukee Parental School Choice Program does not have a program administrator, nor is there an entity primarily responsible for providing families with technical and other support. In fact, it appears that means-tested publicly funded vouchers become a reflection of the political compromise that is struck between the opponents and proponents of the program.

9. Interview with representative of the WSF, Fall 2007.

10. Interview with representative of the WSF, Fall 2007.

11. Interview with representative of the WSF, Fall 2007.

12. Interview with representative of the WSF, Fall 2006.

13. Interview with representative of the WSF, Fall 2007.

14. This is true at the high school level, but the southeast and northeast parts of the city have several private elementary schools close to where OSP families are concentrated.

15. Interview with representative of the WSF, Fall 2007.

16. Interview with representative of the WSF, Fall 2006.

17. Interview with school representative, Spring 2008.

18. Interview with school representative, Spring 2008.

19. Interview with school representative, Spring 2008.

20. Interview with school representative, Spring 2008.

21. Interview with school representative, Spring 2008.

22. Interview with school representative, Spring 2008.

23. Interview with school representative, Spring 2008.

24. Interview with school representative, Spring 2008.

25. In a separate study, we visited a private high school in the Milwaukee Parental Choice Program that provides this type of intensive summer preparation for incoming ninth-graders.

26. "The Case Against Vouchers," *National Education Association*, accessed January 7, 2010, http://www.nea.org/home/19133.htm; "Obama's School Choice: Democrats Want to Kill Vouchers for 1,700 Kids," unsigned editorial, *Wall Street Journal*, February 25, 2009, A12; Robert Maranto, "Congressional Democrats' War on Science," *Front Page Magazine*, accessed April 4, 2009, from http://frontpagemagazine.com.

27. Interview with community leader, Fall 2008.

28. Interview with representative from the WSF, Fall 2006.

29. Interview with community leaders, Fall 2008.

30. Interview with community leaders, Fall 2008.

31. See National School Choice Week accessed on July 18, 2013, at: http://www.schoolchoiceweek.com/

32. *School Choice Now: The Year of School Choice*, School Choice Yearbook 2011–12 (Washington, DC: Alliance for School Choice, January 2012).

Appendix I   Description of Sampling Method

1. We acknowledge having been significantly influenced by the efforts of Gary King, Robert O. Keohane, and Sidney Verba in this regard. In their book, *Designing Social Inquiry: Scientific Inference in Qualitative Research* (Princeton, NJ: Princeton University Press), they argue that qualitative researchers can and should enhance the internal and external validity of their studies by employing scientific strategies of case selection and sampling that are commonly employed in quantitative analysis.

2. Patrick J. Wolf, Babette Gutmann, Michael Puma, Brian Kisida, Lou Rizzo, and Nada O. Eissa, *Evaluation of the DC Opportunity Scholarship Program: Impacts After Two Years*, US Department of Education, Institute for Education Sciences, National Center for Education Evaluation and Regional Assistance (Washington, DC: US Government Printing Office), NCEE 2008–4023, June 12, 2008, Table 1, p. xv.

3. Patrick J. Wolf, Babette Gutmann, Michael Puma, and Marsha Silverberg, "Evaluation of the DC Opportunity Scholarship Program: Second Year Report on Participation," US Department of Education, Institute for Education Sciences, National Center for Education Evaluation and Regional Assistance (Washington, DC: US Government Printing Office, 2006), Table 3–4, p. 14, http://ies.ed.gov/ncee/pubs/20064003/

4. Ibid., estimated from Tables 3–5, 18.

5. Separating participants by the language they spoke at home was also logistically important, as it permitted us to conduct focus groups and interviews in the native language of all participants.

6. The high school orientations were run by Capital Partners in Education, an organization in the District that has for decades provided privately funded scholarships for low-income students to attend participating private schools and that was a partner with the WSF in securing the contract of implementation of the OSP.

Works Cited

"A Reprieve on Vouchers: President Obama Shows Some Wisdom and Compassion toward D.C. Schoolchildren. Will Congress Help?" (May 7, 2009). Unsigned editorial, *Washington Post*, A22.

Abernathy, S. F. (2005) *School Choice and the Future of American Democracy* (Ann Arbor: University of Michigan Press).

Akerlof, G. A. & Kranton, R. E (2002) "Identity and Schooling: Some Lessons for the Economics of Education," *Journal of Economic Literature*, 40(4), 1167–201.

Alchian, A. A. & Demsetz, H. (1972) "Production, Information Costs, and Economic Organization," *American Economic Review*, 62.

Alonso, G., Anderson, N.,S., Su, C., & Theoharis, J. (2009) *Our Schools Suck: Students Talk Back to a Segregated Nation on the Failures of Urban Education* (New York: New York University Press).

American Federation for Children (2011) http://www.federationforchildren.org/ (home page), date accessed July 1, 2011.

Anderson, S. G., Halter, A. P., & Gryzlak, B. M. (April, 2004) "Difficulties After Leaving TANF: Inner-City Women Talk about Reasons for Returning to Welfare," *Social Work*, 49(2), 185–94.

Bachrach, P. (1967) *The Theory of Democratic Elitism* (Boston: Little, Brown and Company).

Bachrach, P. & Baratz, M. S. (1970) *Power and Poverty: Theory and Practice* (New York: Oxford University Press).

Bacon, Jr., P. (February 26, 2009) "House Bill Draws Criticism from GOP," *Washington Post*, sec. A06.

Bane, M. J., & Ellwood, D. T. (1994) *Welfare Realities: From Rhetoric to Reform* (Cambridge, MA: Harvard University Press).

Baker, D. P. & Stevenson, D. L. (1986) "Mother's Strategies for Children's School Achievement: Managing the Transition to High School," *Sociology of Education*, 59(3), 156–66.

Barber, B. (1984) *Strong Democracy: Participatory Politics for a New Age* (Berkeley: University of California Press).

Barnard, J., Frangakis, C. E., Hill, J. L., & Rubin, D. B. (June, 2003) "Principal Stratification Approach to Broken Randomized Experiments: A Case Study of School Choice Vouchers in New York City," *Journal of the American Statistical Association*, 98(462), 299–323.

"Beach Reading for Mr. Obama" (August 28, 2009). Unsigned editorial, *Washington Post.*

Belz, E. (January 27, 2011) 'Speaker John Boehner and Sen. Joe Lieberman Introduce Bill to Reopen a School Voucher Program That Democrats Shut Down," *World Magazine.*

Berliner, D. C. and Biddle, B. J. (1995) *The Manufactured Crisis: Myths, Fraud, and the Attack on America's Public Schools* (Reading, MA: Addison-Wesley).

Beuerman, J. (April 1, 2011) "Congress Poised to Reauthorize Wildly Successful DC Voucher Program," *Pelican Post.*

Birnbaum, M. (August 21, 2009) "Families, Activists Rally to Restore 216 Rescinded Tuition Vouchers," *Washington Post,* B03.

Birnbaum, M. (September 17, 2009) "Hundreds of Voucher Pupils Unaccounted For," *Washington Post.*

Birnbaum, M. (September 30, 2009) "More Oversight Urged for Voucher Schools," *Washington Post.*

Birnbaum, M. (December 10, 2009) "Limits Are Likely on DC School Vouchers," *Washington Post.*

Bloom, H. S. (1984) "Accounting for No-Shows in Experimental Evaluation Designs," *Evaluation Review,* 8(2), 225–46.

Blunt, S. (October 7, 2009) "Not Free to Choose: D.C. Students and Parents Rally for School-Choice," *Weekly Standard.*

Bowles, S. & Gintis, H. (1998). "The Moral Economy of Communities: Structured Populations and the Evolution of Pro-Social Norms," *Evolution and Human Behavior,* 19, 3–25.

Brandl, J. E. (1998). *Money and Good Intentions are Not Enough: Or Why a Liberal Democrat Thinks States Need Both Competition and Community* (Washington, DC: Brookings Institution Press).

Brighouse, H. (2000). *School Choice and Social Justice* (New York: Oxford University Press).

Bruce, M. (September 30, 2009) "Bipartisan Supporters Call on Congress to Reauthorize D.C. Voucher Program," *ABC News.*

Bryk, A., Holland, P. B., & Lee, V. (1993) *Catholic Schools and the Common Good* (Cambridge, MA: Harvard University Press.)

Burke, L. (April 12, 2013) "Obama Budget Ends Funding for D.C. School Choice Program," *The Foundry,* http://blog.heritage.org/2013/04/12/obama-budget-ends-funding-for-d-c-school-choice-program/, date accessed April 24, 2013.

Campbell, A. L. (2003) *How Policies Make Citizens: Senior Political Activism and the American Welfare State,* (Princeton, NJ: Princeton University Press).

Carpenter II, D. M. (January, 2014) *School Choice Signals: Research Review and Survey Experiments,* Friedman Foundation for Educational Choice, http://www.edchoice.org/CMSModules/EdChoice/FileLibrary/1035/SCHOOL-CHOICE-SIGNALS-Research-Review-and-Survey-Experiments.pdf, date accessed January 24, 2014.

"Children First: A DC Scholarship Program Has Bipartisan Backing" (August 3, 2009). Unsigned editorial, *Washington Post*.

Cohen, M. (1989). *An Empowerment Oriented Framework for Practice with Homeless Mentally Ill Clients*. Paper presented to the 5th National Symposium on Doctoral Research in Social Work, https://kb.osu.edu/dspace/bit-stream/1811/32667/1/5_Cohen_paper.pdf, date accessed November 18, 2009.

Coleman, J. S., Hoffer, T., & Kilgore, S. (1982) *High School Achievement: Public, Catholic, and Private Schools Compared* (New York: Basic Books).

Coleman, J. S. & Hoffer, T. (1987) *Public and Private High Schools: The Impact of Communities* (New York: Basic Books).

Comparative Study of Electoral Systems (2005) *Income and Current Election Participation,* http://www.umich.edu/~cses/resources/results/CSESresults_IncomeParticipation.htm, date accessed November 18, 2009.

Consolidated Appropriations Act (2004) U.S. Code, P.L. 108–99.

Cornman, S. Q., Stewart, T., & Wolf, P. J. (May, 2007) *The Evolution of School Choice Consumers: Parent and Student Voices on the Second Year of the D.C. Opportunity Scholarship Program*, University of Arkansas School Choice Demonstration Project, accessed at http://hpi.georgetown.edu/scdp/files/PSV2.pdf.

Cottrell, M. (August 20, 2009). The Trouble with TANF: Why Welfare Just Doesn't Work [Blog Post], *Chicago Now*, http://www.chicagonow.com/blogs/one-story-up/2009/08/the-trouble-with-tanf.html.

Cowen, J. M., Fleming, D. J., Witte, J. F., & Wolf, P. J. (2012) "Going Public: Who Leaves a Large, Longstanding, and Widely Available Urban Voucher Program?" *American Educational Research Journal*, 49(2), 231–56.

Cowen, J. M., Fleming, D. J., Witte, J. F., Wolf, P. J., & Kisida, B. (2013) "School Vouchers and Student Attainment: Evidence from a State-Mandated Study of Milwaukee's Parental Choice Program," *Policy Studies Journal*, 41(1), 147–67.

Darling-Hammond, L. (2010) *The Flat World and Education: How America's Commitment to Equity Will Determine Our Future* (New York: Teachers College Press).

DC Investment Trust Corporation, "DC Opportunity Scholarship Program," http://www.dcscholarships.org/date accessed July 17, 2013.

"DC's Successful Voucher Program Deserves a Second Life," (June 23, 2010). Unsigned editorial, *Washington Post*, A16.

de Tocqueville, A. (1969) *Democracy in America* (New York: Doubleday).

DeBonis, M. (June 23, 2010) "DC School Vouchers—The Last Word?" *Washington Post*.

Dillon, S. (February 28, 2009) "Democrats Limit Future Financing for Washington Voucher Program," *The New York Times*, sec. A11.

DiPerna, P. (May 8, 2013) *Schooling in America Survey*, Polling Paper No. 15, Friedman Foundation for Educational Choice, http://www.edchoice.org/CMSModules/EdChoice/FileLibrary/1000/Schooling-in-America-Survey.pdf, date accessed on January 24, 2014.

District of Columbia Office of Planning (2002) *Profile of Selected Demographic and Socioeconomic Characteristics, 2000 Census for Wards 3 and 8* (Washington, DC).

District of Columbia School Choice Incentive Act of 2003, Title III of Division C of the *Consolidated Appropriations Act*, 2004, Pub. L. 108–99.

Dyer, C. (1999) "Researching and Implementation of Educational Policy: A Backward Mapping Approach," *Comparative Education* 35(1), 45–61.

Emmanuel, A. (June 18, 2012) "Much-Debated Scholarship Program for D.C. Students is Renewed," *The Caucus: The Politics and Government Blog of the Times*.

Eriksen, E. O. & Weigard, J. (2009) "The End of Citizenship? New Roles Challenging the Political Order," ARENA Working Papers Series, http://www.arena.uio.no/publications/wp99_26.htm, date accessed November 3, 2009.

Figlio, D. N. (August, 2011) *Evaluation of the Florida Tax Credit Scholarship Program: Participation, Compliance and Test Scores in 2009–10,*" Report to the Florida Department of Education.

Fiorina, M. P. (1981) *Retrospective Voting in American National Elections* (New Haven: Yale University Press).

Fleming, D. J., Cowen, J. M., Witte, J. F., & Wolf, P. J. (in press) "Similar Students, Different Choices: Who Uses a School Voucher in an Otherwise Similar Population of Students?" *Education and Urban Society*.

Ford, V. W. (2005) *Voices, Choices, and Second Chances* (Washington, DC: DC Parents for School Choice).

Forster, G. & D'Andrea, C. (August, 2009) "An Empirical Evaluation of the Florida Tax Credit Scholarship Program," *The Friedman Foundation for Educational Choice*, http://www.friedmanfoundation.org/downloadFile.do?id=383.

Forster, G. (2013) *A Win-Win Solution: The Empirical Evidence on School Choice* (Indianapolis, IN: Friedman Foundation).

Friedman, M. (1955) "The Role of Government in Education" in R. Solo (ed.) *Economics and the Public Interest* (New Brunswick, NJ: Rutgers University Press, 1955).

Friedman, T. L. (2006) *The World is Flat: A Brief History of the Twenty-First Century* (New York: Farrar, Straus and Giroux).

Fuller, B., Elmore, R., & Orfield, G. (1996) "Policy Making in the Dark: Illuminating the School Choice Debate," in B. Fuller and R. Elmore (eds.) *Who Chooses? Who Loses? Culture, Institutions and the Unequal Effects of School Choice* (New York: Teachers College Press).

Gabriel, T. (April 14, 2011) "Budget Deal Fuels Revival of School Vouchers," *The New York Times*.

Gill, B. P., Timpane, P. M., Ross, K. E., & Brewer, D. J. (2001) *Rhetoric Versus Reality: What We Know and What We Need to Know about Vouchers and Charter Schools* (Santa Monica, CA: Rand Education).

Glenn, C. L. Jr. (1987) *The Myth of the Common School* (Amherst, MA: University of Massachusetts Press).

Greene, J. P. (2005) *Education Myths* (Lanham, MD: Rowman & Littlefield).

Greene, J. P., Howell, W. G., & Peterson, P. E. (1998) "Lessons from the Cleveland Scholarship Program" in P. E. Peterson and B. C. Hassel (eds.) *Learning from School Choice* (Washington, DC: Brookings Institution Press).

Greene, J. P., Peterson, P. E., & Du, J. (1999) "Effectiveness of School Choice: The Milwaukee Experiment," *Education and Urban Society*, 31, 190–213.

Greene, J. P (2001) "Vouchers in Charlotte," *Education Matters*, 1(2), 55–60.

Greene, J. P. & Forster, G. (June, 2003) "Vouchers for Special Education Students: An Evaluation of Florida's McKay Scholarship Program," *Manhattan Institute for Policy Research, Civic Report* 38.

Greene, J. P. (2005) *Education Myths: What Special-Interest Groups Want You to Believe About Our Schools and Why it Isn't So* (Lanham, MD: Rowman & Littlefield Publishers).

Greene, J. P. & Winters, M. A. (June, 2006) "Leaving Boys Behind: Public High School Graduation Rates," *Manhattan Institute for Policy Research*, Civic Report No. 48.

Greenstone, D. & Peterson, P. E. (1976) *Race and Authority in Urban Politics: Community Relations and the War on Poverty* (Chicago: University of Chicago Press).

Hamilton, L. & Guin, K. (2003) "The Demand Side of School Choice: Understanding How Families Choose Schools," in *School Choice: Doing It the Right Way Makes a Difference,* National Working Commission on Choice in K–12 Education (Washington, DC: Brookings Institution Press).

Hamilton, L. S. & Guin, K. (2005) "Understanding How Families Choose Schools," in J. R. Betts and T. Loveless (eds.) *Getting Choice Right: Ensuring Equity and Efficiency in Education Policy* (Washington, DC: Brookings Institution Press).

Hanushek, E. A. & Rivkin, S. G. (2003) "Does Public School Competition Affect Teacher Quality?" In C. M. Hoxby (ed.) *The Economics of School Choice* (Chicago: University of Chicago Press).

Hanushek, E. A., Kain, J. F., & Rivkin, S. G. (2004) "Disruption Versus Tiebout Improvement: The Costs and Benefits of Switching Schools," *Journal of Public Economics*, 88(2004): 1721–46.

Hanushek, E., Kain, J., Rivkin, S., & Branch, G. (2006) "Charter School Quality and Parental Decision Making with School Choice," *Journal of Public Economics*, 91(5–6): 823–48.

Hart, C. (2013) "Contexts Matter: Selection in Means-Tested School Voucher Programs," *Educational Evaluation and Policy Analysis*, 36(2), 186–206.

Hasenfeld, Y. (2000) "Organizational Forms as Moral Practices: The Case of Welfare Departments," *The Social Service Review*, 74(3), 329–51.

Hassel, B. C. (May, 1999) *The Charter School Challenge: Avoiding the Pitfalls, Fulfilling the Promise* (Washington, DC: Brookings Institution Press).

Hatry, H. P. (2006) *Performance Measurement: Getting Results*, Second edition (Washington, DC: Urban Institute Press).

Henig, J. R. (1994) *Rethinking School Choice: Limits of the Market Metaphor* (Princeton, NJ: Princeton University Press).

Hess, F. (2002) *Revolution at the Margins* (Washington, DC: Brookings Institution Press).

Hess, F. (2010) *The Same Thing Over and Over: How School Reformers Get Stuck in Yesterday's Ideas* (Cambridge, MA: Harvard University Press).

Heymann, J. (2006) *Forgotten Families: Ending the Growing Crisis Confronting Children and Working Parents in the Global Economy* (New York: Oxford University Press).

Hirschman, A. O. (1970) *Exit, Voice, and Loyalty* (Cambridge, MA: Harvard University Press.)

Hochschild, J. & Scovronick, N. (2003) *The American Dream and the Public Schools* (New York: Oxford University Press).

Hollingsworth, B. (January 26, 2011) "Boehner Revives D.C. Voucher Program," *Washington Examiner.*

Howell, W. G. & Peterson, P. E., with Wolf, P. J. & Campbell, D. E. (2000) *The Education Gap: Vouchers and Urban Schools* (Washington, DC: Brookings Institution Press).

Howell, W. G., Wolf, P. J., Campbell, D. E., & Peterson, P. E. (April, 2002) "School Vouchers and Academic Performance: Results from Three Randomized Field Trials," *Journal of Policy Analysis and Management*, 21, 191–217.

Howell, W. G. & Peterson, P. E., with Wolf, P. J. & Campbell, D. E. (2006) *The Education Gap: Vouchers and Urban Schools*, Revised Edition (Washington, DC: Brookings Institution Press).

Hoxby, C. M., Murarka, S., & Kang, J. (September, 2009) "How New York City's Charter Schools Affect Achievement" (Cambridge, MA: New York City Charter Schools Evaluation Project).

Ingram, H. M. & Schneider, A. L. (1993) "Constructing Citizenship: The Subtle Messages of Policy Design" in H. Ingram & S. R. Smith (eds.) *Public Policy for Democracy* (Washington, DC: Brookings Institution Press), pp. 68–94.

Jung, T. & Osborne, S. P. (2009) "Citizens, Co-producers, Customers, Clients, Captives: Consumerism and Public Services," Briefing Paper, University of Edinburgh Business School., http://www.scothub.org/publications/consumerismbriefingpaper.pdf, date accessed November 18, 2009.

Kelly III, J. & Scafidi, B. (2013) *More Than Scores: An Analysis of Why and How Parents Choose Private Schools* (Indianapolis, IN: Friedman Foundation).

King, G., Keohane, R.O., & Verba, S. (1994) *Designing Social Inquiry: Scientific Inference in Qualitative Research* (Princeton, NJ: Princeton University Press).

Kisida, B. & Wolf, P.J. (2010) "School Governance and Information: Does Choice Lead to Better-Informed Parents?" *American Politics Research*, 38(5), 783–805.

Krueger, A. B. & Zhu, P. (2003) "Another Look at the New York City School Voucher Experiment," *American Behavioral Scientist,* 47(2004), 658–98.

Labbe, T. (April 11, 2008) "D.C. Catholic Schools Follow National Trend," *Washington Post*, http://www.washingtonpost.com/wp-dyn/content/article/2008/04/10/AR2008041003780.html.

Lartique Jr., C. J. (December 10, 2002) *The Need for Educational Freedom in the Nation's Capital*, CATO Institute, Policy Analysis No. 461.

Lawler, J. (May 7, 2009) "No One Vouching for Them," *American Spectator Online*, http://www.lexisnexis.com/lnacui2api/api/version1/getDocCui?oc=0 0240&hl=t&hns=t&hnsd=f&perma=true&lni=7VN1-CPM1-2RG6-P0MC& hv=t&csi=143292&hgn=t&secondRedirectIndicator=true, date accessed July 13, 2013.

Lee, J., Grigg, W. S., & Donahue, P. L. (2007) *The Nation's Report Card: Reading 2007*, US Department of Education, Institute of Education Sciences, National Center for Education Statistics (Washington, DC), http://nces.ed.gov/pub-search/pubsinfo.asp?pubid=2007496, date accessed April 30, 2010.

Lester, N. (February 27, 2009) "D.C. Parents to Push Congress to Keep Vouchers," *Washington Times*, A01. *Let Me Rise: The Fight for School Choice in the Nation's Capital* [film] (2010) narrated by Juan Williams, Heritage Foundation, Washington, DC.

Levin, B. (2008) *How to Change 5000 Schools: A Practical and Positive Approach for Leading Change at Every Level* (Cambridge, MA: Harvard Education Publishing Group).

"Lieberman, Collins Urge Education Secretary to Reverse" (April 21, 2009) Capitol Hill Press Release.

Lubienski, C. & Lubienski, S. T. (2006) "Charter, Private, Public Schools and Academic Achievement: New Evidence from NAEP Mathematics Data," Columbia University: National Center for the Study of Privatization in Education.

MacIntyre, A. (1984) *After Virtue: A Study in Moral Theory* (South Bend, IN: University of Notre Dame Press).

Maranto, R. (April 4, 2009) "Congressional Democrats' War on Science," *Front Page Magazine*, http://archive.frontpagemag.com/readArticle.aspx?ARTID=34800.

Martinez, V. Godwin, K., & Kemerer, F. R. (1996) "Public School Choice in San Antonio: Who Chooses and with What Effects?" in B. Fuller and R. F. Elmore (eds.) *Who Chooses? Who Loses? Culture, Institutions, and the Unequal Effects of School Choice* (New York: Teachers College Press).

Maslow, A. (July, 1943) "A Theory of Human Motivation," *Psychological Review*, 50, 370–96.

Meeting the Needs of District Families (March 2008) Planning for Quality Schools (DC Office of the State Superintendent of Education with Brookings Urban Institute 21st Century Schools Fund, Washington, DC).

Metcalf, K. K., West, S. D., Legan, N. A., Paul, K. M., & Boone, W. J. (2003) Evaluation of the Cleveland Scholarship and Tutoring Program, Summary Report 1998–2002. Bloomington, IN: Indiana University School of Education.

Mettler, S. & Soss, J. (2004) "The Consequences of Public Policy for Democratic Citizenship: Bridging Policy Studies and Mass Publics," *Perspectives on Politics*, 2, 55–73.

Mettler, S. & Stonecash, J. M. (2008) "Government Program Usage and Political Voice," *Social Science Quarterly*, 89(2), 273–93.

Mill, J. S. (1962) *Utilitarianism, on Liberty, Essay on Bentham*, in M. Warnock (ed.) (New York: Meridian).

Milwaukee Public Schools (2010) District Fact Sheet, http://mpsportal.milwaukee.k12.wi.us/portal/server.pt?open=512&objID=367&mode=2&in_hI_userid=2&cached=true.

Moe, T. M. (1984) "The New Economics of Organization," *American Journal of Political Science*, 28(4), 739–77.

Moe, T. M. (2002) *Schools, Vouchers and the American Public* (Washington, DC: Brookings Institution Press).

Moe, T. M. (2002) "Cooking the Questions?" *Education Next*, 2(1), 70–77.

Moe, T. M. (2011) *Special Interest: Teachers Unions and the c America's Public Schools* (Washington, DC: Brookings Institution Press).

Morgan, D. L. (1997) *Focus Group as Qualitative Research*, Second Edition (London: Sage).

Moustakas, C. (1994) *Phenomenological Research Methods* (Thousand Oaks, CA: Sage).

Multiple Choice: Charter School Performance in 16 States (2009, June) Center for Research on Education Outcomes (CREDO), Stanford, CA: CREDO.

National Center for Education Statistics (2006) US Dept. of Education/Institute for Education Sciences, Publication No. NCES 2006–030. Digest Of Education Statistics TBL. 50.

National Education Association (2014) *The Case Against Vouchers*, http://www.nea.org/home/19133.htm.

National High School Center (n.d.) "Easing the Transition to High School: Research and Best Practices Designed to Support High School Learning," American Institutes for Research, Washington, DC, http://www.betterhighschools.org/docs/NHSC_TransitionsReport.pdf, date accessed July 10, 2013.

National School Choice Week, http://www.schoolchoiceweek.com/ (home page), date accessed July 18, 2013.

Neal, D. (1997) "The Effects of Catholic Secondary Schooling on Educational Achievement," *Journal of Labor Economics*, 15, 98–123.

Neibauer, M. (May 23, 2009) "Bill Introduced to Save D.C. School Vouchers," *Washington Examiner.*

Neumann, F. M., Smith, B., Allensworth, E., & Bryk, A. S. (2001) *School Instructional Program Coherence: Benefits and Challenges* (Chicago: Consortium on Chicago School Research).

Niemi, R. G. & Junn, J. (1998) *Civic Education* (New Haven, CT: Yale University Press).

Niskanen, Jr., W. A. (1971) *Bureaucracy and Representative Government* (Chicago: Aldine-Atherton).

"Obama's School Choice: Democrats Want to Kill Vouchers for 1,700 Kids," (February 25, 2009). Unsigned editorial, *Wall Street Journal*, A12.

O'Connell, B. (October 1, 2009) "Free to Choose," *American Spectator.*

Paine, T. (1791) *The Rights of Man: Answer to Mr. Burke's Attack on the French Revolution* (London, England: J. S. Jordan).

"Parents Fight to Keep Children Out of D.C. Public Schools" (May 13, 2009) ABC News 7—WJLA.

Payne, C. (2008) *So Much Reform, So Little Change* (Cambridge, MA: Harvard Education Publishing Group).

Peterson, P. E. & Campbell, D. E. (May, 2001) "An Evaluation of the Children's Scholarship Fund", Program on Education Policy and Governance. Harvard University, Cambridge, MA, PEPG/01–03.

Peterson, P. E. (April 10, 2011) "DC Children Can Thank Boehner and Randomized Trials," *Education Next Blog.*

Pierce, G. (May 6, 2009) "Civil Rights Issue," *Washington Times*, A06.

Piven, F. F. & Cloward, R. A. (1979) *Poor People's Movements* (New York: Vintage Books).

"Presumed Dead: Politics Is Driving the Destruction of the District's School Voucher Program" (April 11, 2009), *The Washington Post*, sec. A12.

Prottas, J. M. (1979) *People Processing.* (Lexington, MA: Heath).

Putnam, R. D. (January, 1995) "Bowling Alone: America's Declining Social Capital," *Journal of Democracy*, 65–78.

Randall, E. V. & Cooper, B. (January, 2012) "'Parent Triggers,' Parental Choice, and Educational Reform." Paper presented at the Inaugural International School Choice and Reform Academic Conference, Nova Southeastern University, Fort Lauderdale, FL.

Riley, J. L. (May 8, 2009) "A President and His Priorities," *The Wall Street Journal.*

Rosenzweig, C. (April, 2001) *A Meta-analysis of Parenting and School Success: The Role of Parents in Promoting Students' Academic Performance.* Paper presented at the annual meeting of the American Educational Research Association, Seattle, WA.

Rouse, C. E. (1998) "Private School Vouchers and Student Achievement: An Evaluation of the Milwaukee Parental Choice Program," *The Quarterly Journal of Economics,* 113(2), 553–602.

Rumberger, R. W. (June, 2002) "Student Mobility and Academic Achievement," *ERIC Digest*, EDO-PS-02-1.

"Save the Vouchers: A Worthy D.C. Program Deserves Congress's Support" (November 22, 2009). Unsigned editorial, *Washington Post.*

Sattin-Bajaj, C. (in press) *Unaccompanied Minors: Immigrant Youth, School Choice, and the Pursuit of Equity* (Cambridge, MA: Harvard Education Press).

Schaatsneider, E. E. (1967) *The Semi-Sovereign People* (New York: Holt, Rinehart and Winston, 1967).

Schneider, A. L. & Ingram, H. M. (June, 1993) "Social Construction of Target Populations: Implications for Politics and Policy," *The American Political Science Review*, 87(2), 334–47.

Schneider, M., Teske, P., & Marschall, M. (2000) *Choosing Schools: Consumer Choice and the Quality of American Schools* (Princeton, NJ: Princeton University Press).

School Choice Now: The Year of School Choice (January, 2012) School Choice Yearbook 2011–12 (Washington, DC: Alliance for School Choice).

Segraves, M. (September 16, 2009) "Congress Grills Director of School Voucher Program," WTOP News, www.wtop.com/?nid=25&sid=1764154, date accessed September 17, 2009.

Shamdasani, D. W. & P. N. (1992) *Focus Groups: Theory and Practice* (London: Sage).

Shklar, J. N. (1998) *American Citizenship: The Quest for Inclusion* (Cambridge, MA: Harvard University Press).

Simmons, D. (August 19, 2009) "Voucher Proponents Rally Against Ending; Rescinding Scholarship a 'Slap in the Face,'" *Washington Times*, A15.

Simmons, D. (November 30, 2009) "School Vouchers at Risk: Low-Income D.C. Students May Lose Out," *Washington Times*, A17.

Skinner, A. (2006). "A Case Study: The Disempowering of Homeless, Adolescent, Single Mothers in a New York City Transitional Living Shelter," Cornell University Undergraduate Research Paper, http://aap.cornell.edu/aap/crp/programs/cusp/programs/summer/upload/Undergrad_06-Skinner.pdf, date accessed November 18, 2009.

Skocpol, T. (1992). *Protecting Soldiers and Mothers: The Political Origins of Social Policy in the United States* (Cambridge, MA: Harvard University Press).

Soss, J. (June, 1999) "Lessons of Welfare: Policy Design, Political Learning, and Political Action," *The American Political Science Review*, 93(2), 363–81.

Steele, J. L., Vernez, G. Gottfried, M. A., & Schwam-Baird, M. (2011) *The Transformation of a School System: Principal, Teacher, and Parent Perceptions of Charter and Traditional Schools in Post-Katrina New Orleans* (Washington, DC: RAND Education).

"Step Up for DC Vouchers" (March 23, 2010). Unsigned editorial, *Washington Post*, A18.

Stern, S. (January 18, 2010) "Ideological Battle Spells Trouble for Vouchers," *Congressional Quarterly Weekly*, p. 166.

Steuerle, C. E., Ooms, V. D., Peterson, G., & Reischauer, R. D. (eds.) (2000) *Vouchers and the Provision of Public Services* (Washington, DC: Brookings Institution Press).

Stewart, T. (1994) Urban Poverty and Prisons: The Political Socialization of Inner City Males (PhD Dissertation: Harvard University).

Stewart, T., Wolf, P. J., & Cornman, S. Q. (October, 2005) "Parent and Student Voices on the First Year of the DC Opportunity Scholarship Program," University of Arkansas School Choice Demonstration Project, accessed at http://www.uaedreform.org/wp-content/uploads/PSV1.pdf.

Stewart, T., Wolf, P. J., Cornman, S. Q., & McKenzie-Thompson, K. (December, 2007) *Satisfied, Optimistic, Yet Concerned: Parent Voices on the Third Year of the DC Opportunity Scholarship Program,* University of Arkansas School Choice Demonstration Project, accessed at http://www.uacdreform.org/wp-content/uploads/PSV3.pdf.

Stewart, T., Wolf, P. J. Cornman, S. Q., McKenzie-Thompson, K., & Butcher, J. (January, 2009) *Family Reflections on the District of Columbia Opportunity Scholarship Program, Final Summary Report*, University of Arkansas School

Choice Demonstration Project, accessed at http://www.uaedreform.org/wp-content/uploads/2009/01/Family_Reflections_DCOSP_2009_Final.pdf.

Stewart, T. & Wolf, P. J. (March, 2009) Parent and Student Experiences with Choice in Milwaukee, Wisconsin, Report of the School Choice Demonstration Project, University of Arkansas, Fayetteville, AR, Milwaukee Evaluation Report #13, http://www.uark.edu/ua/der/SCDP/Milwaukee_Eval/Report_13.pdf.

Stewart, T., Lucas-McLean, J., Jensen, L. I., Fetzko, C., Ho, B., & Segovia, S. (April, 2010) Family Voices on Parental School Choice in Milwaukee: What Can We Learn From Low-income Families?, Milwaukee Evaluation Report 19, School Choice Demonstration Project, University of Arkansas, Fayetteville, AR, p. 4, accessed at http://www.uark.edu/ua/der/SCDP/Milwaukee_Eval/Report_19.pdf.

Stewart, T. & Wolf, P. J. (2011) "The Evolution of Parental School Choice," in F. M. Hess & B. Manno (eds.), Customized Schooling (Cambridge, MA: Harvard Education Press), pp. 91–106.

Strauss, V. & Horwitz, S. (February 20, 1997) "Students Caught in a Cycle of Classroom Failures," Washington Post, p. A01.

Teske, P., Fitzpatrick, J., & Kaplan, G. (2007) "Opening Doors: How Low-Income Parents Search for the Right School" (Seattle, WA: Center on Reinventing Public Education), http://files.eric.ed.gov/fulltext/ED495279.pdf, date accessed January 6, 2014.

"The DC Opportunity Scholarship Program: Keeping the Door Open" (March 1, 2011) Hearing before the US House Committee on Oversight and Reform, Subcommittee on Health Care, DC, Census, and the National Archives, http://oversight.house.gov/index.php?option=com_content&view=article&id=1149:3-1-11-qthe- dc-opportunity-scholarship-program-keeping-the-door-openq&catid=35:subcommittee-on-health-care-and-dc-.

"The DC Opportunity Scholarship Program: Preserving School Choice for All," (May 13, 2009) Hearing of the United States Senate Committee on Homeland Security and Government Affairs, http://www.hsgac.senate.gov/hearings/the-dc-opportunity-scholarship-program-preserving-school-choice-for-all.

"The D.C. Voucher Example: Mr. President, How About That 97% Graduation Rate?" (July 12, 2013). Unsigned editorial, Wall Street Journal.

"The Value of Education Choices: Saving the D.C. Opportunity Scholarship Program" (February 16, 2011) Hearing before the US Senate Committee on Homeland Security and Governmental Affairs, http://hsgac.senate.gov/public/index.cfm?FuseAction=Hearings.Hearing&Hearing_id=f200a5b4-c1b6-41c7-a3c1-fa6d242535ef.

Thomas B. Fordham Institute (August, 2013) What Parents Want: Education Preferences and Trade-Offs, Washington, DC.

Tibout, C. M. (October, 1956) "A Pure Theory of Local Expenditures," Journal of Political Economy, 64(5), 416–24.

Tomsho, R. (October 19, 2009) "D.C. School Vouchers Have a Brighter Future Outlook in Congress," Wall Street Journal.

Toppo, G. (May 12, 2009) "More Black Lawmakers Open to School Vouchers," *USA Today.*

Trivitt, J. & Wolf, P.J. (2011) "School Choice and the Branding of Catholic Schools," *Education Finance and Policy,* 6(2), 202–45.

Turque, B. & Murray, S. (May 7, 2009) "Obama Offers D.C. Voucher Compromise," *Washington Post,* B01.

Turque, B. (May 14, 2009) "With Critics Quiet, Hearing Praises D.C. School Voucher Program," *Washington Post,* A1.

US Census Bureau (2005–2007) *Urban Poverty: An Overview,* http://web.world-bank.org/WBSITE/EXTERNAL/TOPICS/EXTURBANDEVELOPMENT/E XTURBANPOVERTY/0,,contentMDK:20227679~menuPK:473804~pagePK: 148956~piPK:216618~theSitePK:341325,00.html.

US Census Bureau (2010) *State and County QuickFacts for Washington, DC, 2010,* http://quickfacts.census.gov/qfd/states/11000.html.

US Census Bureau (2014) *American FactFinder: Washington, DC,* http://fact-finder2.census.gov/faces/nav/jsf/pages/community_facts.xhtml.

US Department of Education, Institute of Education Sciences National Center for Education Statistics, *Program for International Student Assessment (PISA): 2006 Results* (Washington, DC), http://nces.ed.gov/surveys/pisa/pisa-2006highlights.asp, date accessed November 16, 2009.

US Department of Health and Human Services (2009). *TANF: Total Number of Recipients,* http://www.acf.hhs.gov/programs/ofa/data-reports/casel-oad/2009/2009_recipient_tan.htm, date accessed November 18, 2009.

Viadero, D. (June 23, 2010) "DC Voucher Program Boosts Grad Rates But Not Test Scores," *Education Week.*

Viteritti, J. P. (1999) *Choosing Equality: School Choice, the Constitution, and Civil Society* (Washington, DC: Brookings Institution Press).

Viteritti, J. P. (2005) "School Choice: How an Abstract Idea Became a Political Reality," in D. Ravitch (ed.) *Brookings Papers on Education Policy* (Washington, DC: Brookings Institution Press).

"Voucher Subterfuge: Hoping No One Notices, Congressional Democrats Step between 1,800 D.C. Children and a Good Education," (2009, February 25) *Washington Post,* A18.

Wagner, T. (2010) *The Global Achievement Gap: Why Even Our Best Schools Don't Teach the New Survival Skills Our Children Need—and What We Can Do About It* (New York: Basic Books).

Warren, M. (1992) "Democratic Theory and Self-Transformation," *American Political Science Review,* 86(1).

Washington Scholarship Fund (2004) *Opportunity Scholarship Program: School Directory 2004–05,* Washington, DC.

"Washington Scholarship Fund Shows 100% of Federal Funds Accounted for, in Response to Senator Durbin's Request," (September 22, 2009) Press Release, Washington Scholarship Fund.

Wells, A. S. (1996) "African American Students' View of School Choice" in B. Fuller and R. Elmore (eds.) *Who Chooses? Who Loses? Culture, Institutions, and the Unequal Effects of School Choice* (New York: Teachers College Press).

Wichowsky, A. & Moynihan, D. P. (Sept./Oct., 2008) "Measuring how Administration shapes Citizenship: A Policy Feedback Perspective on Performance Management," *Public Administration Review,* 68(5), 908–21.

Will, G. F. (April 23, 2009) "Obama's Budget Follies," *The Washington Post.*

Witte, J. F. (2000) *The Market Approach to Education: An Analysis of America's First Voucher Program* (Princeton, NJ: Princeton University Press).

Witte, J. F., Carlson, D., Cowen, J. M., Fleming, D. J., & Wolf, P. J. (2012) *The MPCP Longitudinal Educational Growth Study Final Year Report*, School Choice Demonstration Project, University of Arkansas, Fayetteville, AR, http://www.uark.edu/ua/der/SCDP/Milwaukee_Eval/Report_29.pdf.

Wolf, P. J. (2005) "Comment on Joseph Viteritti's 'School Choice: How an Abstract Idea Became a Political Reality," in D. Ravitch (ed.) *Brookings Papers on Education Policy* (Washington, DC: Brookings Institution Press).

Wolf, P. J. (2008) "School Voucher Programs: What the Research Says about Parental School Choice," *Brigham Young University Law Review,* 2.

Wolf, P. J. (April, 2010) "The Comprehensive Longitudinal Evaluation of the Milwaukee Parental Choice Program: Summary of Third Year Reports," (University of Arkansas, SCDP Milwaukee Evaluation Report #14), http://www.uark.edu/ua/der/SCDP/Milwaukee_Eval/Report_14.pdf.

Wolf, P. J., Howell, W. G., & Peterson, P. E. (2000) "School Choice in Washington, DC: An Evaluation after One Year," Program on Education Policy and Governance, PEPG 00–08, Harvard University, Cambridge, MA.

Wolf, P. J. and Hoople, D. S. (2006) "Looking Inside the Black Box: What Schooling Factors Explain Voucher Gains in Washington, DC," *Peabody Journal of Education,* 81(2006), 7–26.

Wolf, P. J., Gutmann, B., Eissa, N., Puma, M., & Silverberg, M. (2005) "Evaluation of the DC Opportunity Scholarship Program: First Year Report on Participation," US Department of Education, Institute of Education Sciences (Washington, DC: US Government Printing Office).

Wolf, P. J., Gutmann, B., Puma, M., & Silverberg, M. (2006) "Evaluation of the DC Opportunity Scholarship Program: Second Year Report on Participation," US Department of Education, Institute of Education Sciences (Washington, DC: US Government Printing Office).

Wolf, P. J., Gutmann, B., Puma, M., Rizzo, L., Eissa, N., & Silverberg, M. (2007) "Evaluation of the District of Columbia Opportunity Scholarship Program: Impacts After One Year," US Department of Education, Institute of Education Sciences (Washington, DC: US Government Printing Office).

Wolf, P. J., Gutmann, B., Puma, M., Kisida, B., Rizzo, L., Eissa, N., & Silverberg, M. (2008) "Evaluation of the District of Columbia Opportunity Scholarship Program: Impacts After Two Years," US Department of Education, Institute of Education Sciences (Washington, DC: US Government Printing Office).

Wolf, P. J., Gutmann, B., Puma, M., Kisida, B., Rizzo, L., Eissa, N., & Silverberg, M. (2009) "Evaluation of the District of Columbia Opportunity Scholarship

Program: Impacts after Three Years," US Department of Education, Institute of Education Sciences (Washington, DC: US Government Printing Office).

Wolf, P. J., Gutmann, B., Puma, M., Kisida, B., Rizzo, L. Eissa, N., & Carr, M. (2010) "Evaluation of the DC Opportunity Scholarship Program: Final Report," NCEE 2010–4018 (Washington, D.C.: National Center for Education Evaluation and Regional Assistance, Institute of Education Sciences, US Department of Education, accessed at http://ies.ed.gov/ncee/pubs/20104018/pdf/20104018.pdf).

Wolf, P. J. Peterson, P. E., & West, M. R. (August, 2001) "Results of a School Voucher Experiment: The Case of Washington, D.C., After Two Years," *Harvard University Program on Education Policy and Governance*, PEPG/01–05 (Cambridge, MA).

Wolf, P. J. & Stewart, T. (2012) "Understanding School Shopping in Detroit" (Detroit, MI: Michigan Future, Inc.), http://www.uark.edu/ua/der/SCDP/Detroit/Detroit_Shoppers_Report-Final.pdf, date accessed 6 January 2014.

Wolf, P. J., Kisida, B., Gutmann, B., Puma, M., Eissa, N., & Rizzo, L. (April, 2013) "School Vouchers and Student Outcomes: Experimental Evidence from Washington, D.C.," *Journal of Policy Analysis and Management*, 32(2), 246–70.

Zelman v. Simmons-Harris (2002) 536 U.S. 639.

Index

Printed in the United States of America